FOREVER ENGLAND

Forever England

The Life of Rupert Brooke

MIKE READ

MAINSTREAM
PUBLISHING

EDINBURGH AND LONDON

For Dr Peter Miller and Prue Miller
Two spirited friends who have also
trodden the Brooke path

Copyright © Mike Read, 1997

First published in Great Britain in 1997 by
MAINSTREAM PUBLISHING COMPANY (EDINBURGH) LTD
7 Albany Street
Edinburgh EH1 3UG

This edition 2000

ISBN 1 84018 301 2

A catalogue record for this book is available from the British Library

Typeset in Berkeley and Ellington
Printed and bound in Great Britain by Butler and Tanner Ltd, Frome

CONTENTS

ACKNOWLEDGEMENTS

Iam very grateful to the following people whom I met while putting this book together. Without their interest, help and enthusiasm, the whole escapade would have been less fun and less fruitful. In no particular order they are: Alison Jenkins; Peter Ward; Winifred Kinsman; Edith Hoare; Dr Peter Miller; Prue Miller; Pippa Harris; the Finlinsons; the staff at Sidmouth Museum; Robin Callan; Tom Hinton; the staff at the Orchard Tea Rooms Grantchester; David Sykes; Tony Johnson; the staff at Beaulieu Heritage; Mrs C.A. Dineen; Roy Jackman; Sye Atkinson; Lt. Col. Tony Claydon and Mrs Claydon; Jack Palmer; K.A. Hook; the Provost, Scholars and Domus Bursar, King's College, Cambridge; Sebastian Doggart; the Rev. Noel Sandford; Leslie Bearman; Lord and Lady Archer; Sebastian Carter; Clive at the *Queen Adelaide* Croydon; Mr Chaffey; Roy and Mary Webber; the Curator of The Museum at Blandford; the staff at Beadales School; Rusty Maclean at the Temple Reading Room, Rugby School; Bob Drennan, Director of Drama, Rugby School; Brian Walton, Housemaster of School Field Rugby; Barbara Davis; the Dymock Poet's Society; Linda Hart; the staff at the *Black Bear*, Wareham; Sandra Carlisle; Mike Gibbons at Kilmartin; Bill and Jan Rademaker; Tim and Catie Jenkins; Mark Keen; Dai Michael at Coleg Harlech; Tony and Judith Newbery; Mark Ramage; Jeff Cooper; Gillian Patterson; Earl Schenk; Nick and Nancy Redgers; Lord Hastings; Selina Hastings; Lady Moorea Black; the staff at the University of Texas at Austin; Bob Withers, British Consul for French Polynesia; Miss J.A.L. Nunn; Ian Cornfield, Director of Research, the Fabian Society; the staff at Bournemouth Reference Library; Mrs Hart; Elaine and Roy Timperly; Peter Greenslade; Peter Mitchell; Roger Westwood; Sue Willer; the staff at the *Pink & Lily*; the staff at the *Green Dragon*, Market Lavington; the staff at the *Crown Inn*, Everleigh; Mr and Mrs Tony Eley at Gatton Gate House; E.N. Willmore; Vivienne King; Karen Berkley; Peter Hook; the staff at the *Mermaid Inn*, Rye; Tim Cribb; Theo Peacey; Nick Peacey; Richard Havers; Anne and Jeremy Powell, Palladour Books; Julian Rota, Bertram Rota; the John Ireland Trust; Jon Stallworthy; Andrew Motion; The Brooke Trustees; Messrs Faber and Faber; the staff at the National Library of Australia; Jerry and Delphine Isaaman. I offer my sincere apologies for any omissions.

PREFACE

The human race chooses its own icons. Which members will be put on a pedestal is decided by popular opinion alone. The status cannot be bought, nor decided upon by governing bodies.

James Dean made a handful of films, where others have made dozens, yet he remains the cult figure of films. Marilyn Monroe could never be considered a great actress, yet her name is still on everyone's lips over 30 years after her death. Many artists from the rock and roll era are no longer with us, but as an influential icon, John Lennon still stands head and shoulders above the others. Oscar Wilde wrote only a few plays, one novel and some poetry, before being carted unceremoniously off to jail, and yet people still argue over a century later as to the colour of the grapes that Lord Alfred Douglas insisted Oscar buy him.

So what are the ingredients? A tragic death – a young death, vulnerability, rebelliousness, an enigmatic persona, an unfulfilled life, an undefinable charisma, and identification with a large enough group of people who regard their icon as a touchstone. Invariably and somewhat implausibly, the powerful feeling for these people fails to diminish with time, each generation keeping the flame alive and maintaining the spirit of the person they cherish.

Rupert Brooke had only one small book of poems published in his lifetime and yet his image and everything he was meant to have stood for, is as alive in the late 1990s as it was in the Edwardian and Georgian periods. In spite of suffering periods of bubble-bursting iconoclasm, the 'Young Apollo' of World War I will not lie down.

Many poets have lived a full, rich, long life, with their output spanning 40, 50, 60 years or more, yet Brooke's name shines more brightly and his image looms larger than most.

Following his death in 1915 at the age of 27 on the way to Gallipoli, his Commander-in-Chief, General Sir Ian Hamilton, reflected on why Brooke seemed special:

Is it because he was a hero? – There were thousands.
Is it because he looked a hero? – There were few.

7

Is it because he had genius? – There were others.
But Rupert Brooke held all three gifts of the gods in his hand . . .

So who was Rupert Brooke and why does his likeness and poetry still affect millions, almost 85 years after his death? This was the quest I set myself when I decided that I would track down and experience at first hand, the places that influenced this extraordinary young man to write his poetry and letters, and the areas that he loved. My travels took me to the banks of the Teign, Eden, Beaulieu, Ouse and Granta rivers, to Dartmoor, the depths of the New Forest, the very tip of the Lizard, and the hills of Surrey. My wanderings also took in the picturesque villages of Penshurst, East Knoyle, Market Lavington and Bucklers Hard, and the seaside towns of Eastbourne, Hastings, Bournemouth, Sidmouth and Clevedon. I journeyed south to Rye on the East Sussex coast, north to Moffat in Scotland, east to Cley-next-to-the-Sea and west to Cornwall and the Welsh coast. The dozens of other places visited included Rugby, Brooke's birthplace and home, and Cambridge, where he attended King's College.

Everywhere, I met with interest, information and a fascination for a man that all but three had never met, and those only as young children. Many people were eager to know more about his life, and were surprised at his links with certain areas of the country.

Living in a media-conscious age, we have become used to people claiming relationships with the rich and famous who are no longer with us, although the phenomenon is clearly not new. I talked to many women who knew someone who had been engaged to, or had a serious affair with Brooke. When both parties are dead, it's foolish to speculate, so I've let them lie, until any details arise which might in future substantiate the claims.

For several days in the summer of 1994 I stayed in Brooke's old room at the Orchard, Grantchester, and without wishing to appear mawkish, or appeal to the cloyingly sentimental, one feels that the spirit of Brooke and his friends might just be here. 'Here', being the small corner of England that encompasses the Orchard, the Old Vicarage and the stretch of the Granta that runs past them.

CHAPTER I

Laughter and the Love of Friends

Rupert Brooke's parents, William Parker Brooke and Ruth Mary Brooke (née Cotterill), first came to Rugby School in January 1880, two weeks after their wedding, when his father took up the post of tutor for the School House. Their home was 5 Hillmorton Road – a two-storeyed red-brick villa with twin gables and bay windows, where Mrs Brooke gave birth to their first son Richard, the year after they took up residence. Their second child, a girl, died in infancy, and Mrs Brooke gave birth to Rupert on 3 August 1887; his second Christian name, Chawner, was taken from a seventeenth-century parliamentarian ancestor. A third son, Alfred, was born in 1891. The following year a vacancy occurred at the school for housemaster of School Field. Parker Brooke secured the position and with it a substantial

Rupert Chawner Brooke – 1888

9

With book in hand, Brooke as Portia in Hillbrow School's Merchant of Venice –
December 1899. His friend Owen O'Malley is on his left

The programme for Hillbrow's Christmas show – 1899

new home – a large and late Victorian house that adjoined the school.

Rugby School was founded in the mid-sixteenth century by Lawrence Sheriffe, a member of the Livery of the Grocers' Company, who had been born early in the reign of Henry VIII. During a serious illness, Sheriffe made a will that included provision for a scheme to found a school at Rugby, beginning with a schoolhouse. Subsequently he added a codicil that was to make the fortune of Rugby School. A previous legacy of £100 was revoked and in its stead the school was bequeathed one-third of a 24-acre field then 'near London', now the Lambs Conduit Street and Great Ormond Street area of the capital. The parcel of land yielded £8 a year in 1597 and £5,700 a year by 1900.

Rupert was tutored at home by a governess, Miss Tottenham, until the summer of 1897, when he began school at nearby Hillbrow as a day boy. There he befriended James Strachey, whose elder brother Lytton was to become an eminent writer and member of the Bloomsbury Group, and cousin of Duncan Grant, who was to become a well-known painter.

The school was only a hundred yards or so along the road from Rupert's home at School Field. His elder brother, Richard, saw him across what was then Watergate Road (now Barby Road), a main thoroughfare into Rugby from Coventry, among other places. From the top of the hill, the school looked out towards the village of Barby.

Hillbrow was built by William Butterfield, the Gothic Revival architect, in the 1860s as a private residence, before becoming a prep school. Later, during the 1930s, it was bought by Rugby School, and a sizeable portion of it was demolished, leaving the end of the house nearest the road as a separate building. A purpose-built boarding house was completed by 1941, next to the remaining portion of the original house, and the whole was named Kilbracken after Lord Kilbracken, the chairman of the governors (who had been Prime Minister William Gladstone's private secretary). The boarding house that already bore his name, previously sited at 1 Hillmorton Road, moved lock, stock and barrel to the new position.

In 1893, the Brookes went to St Ives in Cornwall for their summer holidays, where they met up with the English critic Sir Leslie Stephen and his family, who had taken Talland House, high above the bay, every year since 1882. The younger children, including Richard, Rupert and the two Stephen girls – who would one day find fame and be better known by their married names, Virginia Woolf and Vanessa Bell – played cricket together on a small pitch in the grounds of the house. The ball would invariably be covered with a layer of luminous paint, in order for play to continue as dusk fell. Virginia was a formidable bowler – better, apparently, than most boys of her age. In 1891, at the age of nine, Virginia had started her own domestic periodical, *Hyde Park Gate News*, at the family's London home, as a vehicle for her early writings. It may well have inspired Rupert, five years her junior, to start his own newspaper at Rugby School some while later. In 1894, the Stephens decided to quit Talland House following the building of a new hotel in its gardens, which obstructed the sea view. There were no more visits to Talland House for Rupert, and his family spent the following year's holiday at Brighton, where he bumped into his friend from prep school, James Strachey, and met his older brother Lytton for the first time.

That Christmas, Hillbrow staged a show comprising nine items. These included The Peace Egg; A Christmas Mumming Play, in which Rupert's schoolfriend W.H.G. Saunt, who would go on to Rugby with him, played the Fool; a scene from Shakespeare's *Richard III*; *the Tyger*, by William Blake; H.W. Longfellow's *Hiawatha's Chickens*; Act IV, scene one, from Shakespeare's *The Merchant of Venice*, in which Brooke played Portia, and another friend, Owen O'Malley, played Shylock. O'Malley's nickname was 'Bug', while Brooke was called 'Oyster', because of his reticence in allowing his fellows to have access to his thoughts and dreams. A letter from 'Ye Oyster' to 'Ye Bug' in the early summer of 1901 is the earliest existing piece of correspondence from Brooke. In it he bemoans the fact that he has played only '4 games of cricket this century'.

In December 1900 Brooke won the first form prize, for which his reward was a copy of naturalist Charles Waterton's *Wanderings in South America*, which had been published three years earlier. The headmistress at Hillbrow

Hillbrow prep school cricket XI with fathers. Brooke is in the centre of the middle row with his father on his left

in Brooke's day was Mrs Eden, who James Strachey remembered as 'an embittered martinet who intimidated her husband and the form assistant masters quite as much as the boys'. Her husband, the easy-going Tommy, was clearly more popular with the boys, although he was moved to comment on Rupert's attempt at Greek: 'He is inclined to throw caution to the wind.' James Strachey also recalled being sent back to the changing-room with Rupert to comb their hair properly, and being told 'You look like a couple of girls!'

In September 1901, Michaelmas Term, Rupert was transferred to his father's house at Rugby School, School Field. The houses were known by the name of the housemaster – Collins's, Stallard's, Mitchell's, Brooke's, etc., with the exception of School House and Town House. Now Brooke showed his prowess for sport, which had begun to display itself during his time at Hillbrow. School records show him taking five wickets for Brooke's against School House on 6 and 7 June 1904, hitting a three not out and 18 with the bat; and later that month, scoring 13 against Stallard's. Leading lights for Brooke's at cricket were J.E. Gordon and Perth-born twins David and William Burt-Marshall, both of whom would be wounded during the First World War, William dying of his wounds while in enemy hands. In *The Meteor*, the school magazine since 1867, an article called 'Characters of the XI 1906, described Rupert as: 'A slow bowler who at times kept a good length and puzzled the batsmen. A safe catch.'

The panoramic view from the drawing-room at School Field took in most

An extract from the house cricket score book June 1904, showing Brooke to have taken five wickets and 21 runs with the bat in the two innings match

Brooke on the tennis lawn at School Field displaying the bow legs that temporarily earned him the nickname 'Bowles'

of New Bigside, a splendid cricket pitch, which was, and still is, a cricket lover's dream setting. Cricketing heroes of the day were W.G. Grace, who was still playing first-class cricket, and C.B. Fry, the great sporting all-rounder and former captain of the Rugby School Cricket XI, and Pelham 'Plum' Warner, of Middlesex and England. Doubtless rugby's cricketing schoolboys were delighted in the recent elevation of their county team, Warwickshire, to first-class status.

Rupert also played for the house XV at Rugby football, the game invented at Rugby School in 1823. Prior to that, soccer players were allowed to catch the ball and drop-kick it, but not to run with it in their hands. M.H. Bloxham, who entered the school in 1813, noted that during the second half of a match being played on Bigside in 1823, pupil William Webb Ellis '. . . for the first time disregarded this rule, and on catching the ball, instead of retiring backwards [to take his kick] rushed forwards with the ball in his hands, towards the opposite goal . . .' This move was adopted as part of the game between 1830 and 1840, legalised at Rugby School in the 1841–42 season, and eventually became adopted everywhere when the rules to Rugby football were drawn up in 1846. For many years after this a ball that was on the ground had to be played with the feet, and it was still admissible to pick up the ball only when it was bouncing. The origins of Rugby football are undoubtedly much earlier than 1823, a variation of it having been played as 'Harpastum' by the Romans during their occupation of Britain. Various match reports refer to Rupert's ability: '. . . before half-time both Brooke and Fargus

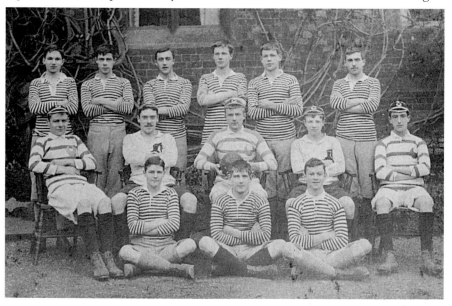

The house rugger team 1904. Brooke is third from right back row – his friend Hugh Russell-Smith is on his left

crossed the line . . .'; '. . . from an opening by the halves Brooke scored far out . . .' Again the Burt-Marshall twins and J.E. Gordon were key players.

As well as being skilled at cricket and rugby, Rupert was also a competent athlete, excelling in the steeplechase, for which he won a silver cup. But he was never very robust, the slightest ailment laying him low; he often had to miss sporting fixtures and events through illness. He was so bad over Christmas 1904 that the family doctor recommended removing him to a warmer country for a period of recuperation. He was sent to stay with Dr and Mrs Gibbons, who were friends of the Brookes, at the Villa Molfino, Rapallo, near Genoa, close to the Ligunian Sea and 100 miles east along the coast from Monaco. Accompanied by his younger brother Alfred, he spent two months in the sunshine, building up his strength, and writing poems intended for the school magazine, *The Phoenix*, a literary supplement to *The Meteor*, which Rupert and another boy had been given permission to found and edit.

The Path of Dreams

Go, heart, and pluck beside the Path of Dreams,
Where moans the wind along the shadowy streams,
        Sad Garlands wreathed of the red mournful Roses
                And Lilies o' moonbeams.

Strange blossoms faint upon that odorous air,
Vision, and wistful Memory; and there
        Love twofold with the purple bloom of Triumph
                And the wan leaf of Despair.

Go, heart; go quickly; pluck and weave thereof
Dim garlands, scattering pallid dew above,
        And far across the sighing tides of darkness
                Lay them beside my Love.

The Return

Long had I dwelt in dreams and loneliness
Until thy sad voice sighed through the dusk to me,
Hinting of joy, of better things to be,
Laughter and light beyond my dim distress.
Then I arose. Amid the fevered press
Of hot-eyed men, across the desolate sea,

Hoping a dreamer's hope I sought for thee.
Wisdom at last I found, and weariness.

Now, I was foolish, weak; I shall return
Back to the Night and Silence that I love,
Back to my dreams. It may be even yet
The old fires on the old grey altars burn,
The old gods throng their shadowy haunted grove,
Where I can sleep, and rest me, and – forget.

He also wrote a third entitled 'Afterwards'.

Afterwards

O brother, dost thou know what this thing means, to dread
The cold inevitable dawn, the sickly light,
The hours' slow passage marked by tolling bells, that smite
Madness and swift blind pangs within the aching head?

Knowst thou this too, brother, when the day is fled
How to the sleepless eyes the strange fears of the Night
Come mocking, and the bitter thoughts of old delight
Mix with the unforgiving faces of the Dead?

Ah, if thou know'st this sorrow, thou art even as I;
As one who has long outlived his jot, and would forget;
Who nurses in his festered soul a slave's dull hate
For this interminable Hell of Life; and yet
Shrinketh from ending it, in fear of what may wait
Behind the pitiless Silence of Eternity.

Rupert had also been planning to work on 'The Bastille', the title that had been laid down for the 1905 school poetry prize, but in a letter to author St John Lucas, a homosexual aesthete some nine years his senior, who had become his literary mentor during 1904, confessed that he was ill-prepared: 'I might find something out about the Bastille: for I have come away without looking it up; and my knowledge of it is a little vague at present. I have only a suspicion that it was a prison, and fell in the French Revolution.' He also admitted to Lucas his ignorance of Italian history and art. At his mentor's request, he sent him some more poems, two of which he'd written at the Villa Molfino. He would often write with the purpose of trying to impress him with his literary style.

In January

What shall I tell thee of?
Of the new sad memories one name can move?
Of the Heaven that Love brings? or of the Hell
That followeth such Love?
Of these shall I tell?

I have not forgotten yet
The mist that shrouded all things, cold and wet;
The dripping bough; the sad smell of the rotten
Leaves. How should I forget?
– Has thou forgotten?

Dost thou remember now
How our eyes met; and all things changed; and how
A glorious light thrilled all that dim December;
And a bird sang on the bough?
Dost thou remember?

The second comprised five verses that as yet had no title.

(Nameless at present)

Lo! in the end the pure clean-hearted innocent throng
Will climb the spacious star-lit road and enter Heaven;
And I shall watch far off and desolate there, among
Those that have dared the sins that cannot be forgiven.

With bitter hearts and silent lips we shall line the way,
Foul with the mire we chose and hopeless to forget,
Envying them who never learnt to hate the Day,
Nor knew the strange wrong loves we knew, nor found regret.

Yet shall I stand, defiant, glorying in my sin,
Though conquered, still unconquerable; – only this,
What if my sullen gaze should see one entering in,
– One with the sorrowful lips I once had died to kiss

One with the fluttering eyelids and grey wistful eyes
The long chin dying in the neck's pale loveliness,

17

The low voice heavy with a thousand nameless sighs,
And delicate pleading mouth that droops in weariness?

Ah! my strong pride, as once my heart, will break and die,
Hungrily I shall watch till that sad face be gone
Then turn me, knowing at last my black foul misery,
And face the dreary night, remembering, alone.

During his stay in Italy, Brooke journeyed to Pisa and Florence, where he stayed with two of his cousins, Margaret and Reeve, enjoying both the noisy spectacle of a street carnival and the awe-inspiring magnificence of the galleries. He read Oscar Wilde's *De Profundis*, which Lucas had sent him, as requested; and he corresponded with, amongst others, his schoolfriend Geoffrey Keynes, to whom in a letter from the Villa dated 12 March 1905, he talked of the next school term: '. . . we shall pull the world to pieces again. You may think me impatient. But you see that is a thing one can only do while one is young, I take it. I have made an epigram on it. Before the age of 25 you pull the World to pieces: after 25 the World pulls you to pieces. And we are getting on for 18, you know!' Alfred left Rapallo first in order to get back to Rugby in time to start school, Rupert following in mid-March.

In March, before a planned holiday with his mother at Hastings, he went to stay with his two aunts in Bournemouth. Less than a century before, the area had been nothing but a desolate and remote stretch of heathland, with not one house, other than a few fishing huts standing within three miles of what was to become the centre of the town – in the words of Thomas Hardy, 'not a sod having been turned there since the time of the Caesars'. Rupert Brooke's grandfather, the Reverend Richard England Brooke, Rector of Bath, retired to Bournemouth in 1895, by which time there were some 60,000 inhabitants – an unrivalled growth rate for a British seaside resort. He took a house called Grantchester Dene at 41 Littledown Road, where he lived with his two unmarried daughters, Harriet Elizabeth (Lizzie) and Frances May (Fanny), until his death on 27 March 1900, after which the two sisters kept the house on. Rupert had first come to stay regularly at Grantchester Dene as a boy, during the 1890s. It was here in 1896 that Rupert first discovered the poems of Robert Browning, which were to kindle his interest in the crafting of words.

From Grantchester Dene he wrote to Geoffrey Keynes, mockingly chastising him for some near-the-knuckle schoolboy remark that Keynes had written on the envelope of a letter to Rupert:

For other matters – I only admire your device for proving so unconventional, but really you know! This is to say I am staying with two faded but religious aunts. They happened to be in when the post

18

came and one of them, chancing on your letter, received quite a severe shock . . . it's not as if she were young either . . . you really must be careful! . . . I haven't as you may surmise much to do here. However, it is I think, less like hell than Italy is. Hell is a place where there are no English books!

He moved on to Southsea, some 40 or so miles east, where he wrote to local Rugby dramatist and contributor to *Punch*, Arthur Eckersley, 'The sun is about to undergo a partial eclipse on Wednesday, which appeals to my symbolic soul so much that I am thinking of writing a sonnet about it!' He continued, 'Fired by your example, I have begun a school novel,' of which the letter includes a sample. Never completed, in fact barely started, it concluded: 'silence is older and more terrible than speech. Man speaks. God is silent. Sooner or later we shall all yield to silence . . .'

From Southsea Rupert joined his mother at the Palace Hotel in Hastings. The advent of the railways had afforded thousands of people the opportunity to get away from the industrial atmosphere of the towns and cities and Hastings was an increasingly popular seaside resort. Some came to take the air, others came to live, resulting in its population rising from 3,175 in 1801 to almost 70,000 at the time of the Brookes' stay more than 100 years later. The Palace Hotel was an imposing building just east of the pier, which had been constructed in two stages during the 1880s and 1890s, the façade displaying all the wrought-iron intricacy and architectural opulence of the late Victorian period. Rupert had sent his mother a note prior to his arrival, describing his hirsute appearance: 'I haven't had my hair cut since the end of February, and it's simply grand now!' The assumed impending maternal wrath caused him to add, 'But I shall have it cut today. I daren't face you as I am.' During his stay at the Palace he read works by the English writer Walter Pater who published *Marius the Epicurean* in 1885 and *Imaginary Portrait* in 1887. Rupert also attempted to work on his projected poem, 'The Bastille'. He recounted his lack of motivation in a letter to St John Lucas: '. . . so far without producing a line. It is a most distressing task to have to write about a subject which neither interests nor inspires you. It lies heavily upon one like a nightmare.'

From the Palace Hotel Brooke also wrote to Geoffrey Keynes on 14 April, complaining in mock horror and drama:

The only tolerable things in Hastings are dinners at this Hotel. They are noble. I had some soup tonight that was tremulous with the tenseness of suppressed passion, and the entrées were odorous with the pale mystery of starlight . . . I write after dinner, by the way. The real reason of this absurd epistle is this – I wish to warn you. Be prepared. It is this . . . I am writing a Book. There will only be one copy. It will be inscribed in crimson ink on green paper. It will consist of thirteen small poems; each as beautiful, as perfect, as meaningless as a rose petal, or a dew drop. (These are not written however.) When the book is prepared I shall read it once a day for seven days. Then I shall burn the book: and die.

On 15 April Rupert returned to Rugby to the upper bench of the sixth form. He was still slaving away on 'The Bastille', and continuing to complain to Lucas about his lack of inspiration. He sent him 12 lines of other spontaneous verse: '. . . I *have* evolved twelve lines, which I enclose; but they are, I know, of a sort it is merely ridiculous for me to write.'

Only the slow rain falling
Sobs through the silence of this bitter place.
(*And in my heart returns one pale lost face*
And the old voice calling, calling, . . .)

Only the grey dawn breaking
Makes visible the long despair of rain.
(*And from weariness of sleep I turn again*
To the weariness of waking, . . .)

Only the dark wave crying
Mocks ever the loneliness of hearts that yearn.
(*Till from the weariness of Life at last I turn*
To the wariness of dying. . . .)

His entry for the previous year's poetry prize, 'The Pyramids', had received a special runner-up award; now in 1905, not withstanding his tardiness in completing 'The Bastille', he took the first prize, winning poetry books by Christina Rossetti and Browning. Mrs Brooke had both poems privately bound at Overs, a leading Rugby printer, little realising that later in the century these early verses of her schoolboy son would be so sought after that they would eventually fetch many thousands of pounds a copy.

Rupert's world was mainly confined to Rugby and almost entirely male-dominated. The exception, apart from his mother and the two aunts, was his cousin, Erica Cotterill, who lived with her parents, her mother's brother Clement and Maud his wife, at Coombe Field, Harrison Road, in Godalming, Surrey. Uncle Clem was a teacher, writer and socialist campaigner. Rupert and Erica corresponded regularly on a range of topics that invariably included their views on books and plays. He had written to her from Rugby School in

The Brooke family on the steps of School Field (standing): *Miss Tottenham (Governess at School Field), Mrs Clement Cotterill, Mr W.P. Brooke (Rupert's father), Mr Clement Cotterill (Mrs W.P. Brooke's brother), Charles Hoare (Rupert's cousin); (sitting middle row): Mrs W.P. Brooke (Rupert's mother), Miss Cissie Hoare (Rupert's cousin), Granny Cotterill (Mrs W.P. Brooke's mother), Miss Erica Cotterill (Rupert's cousin), Mrs Lucy Hoare (Mrs W.P. Brooke's sister); (sitting front row): Richard Brooke (Rupert's brother), Rupert Brooke, Alfred Brooke (Rupert's brother), Harry Hoare (Rupert's cousin)*

May 1904, affecting a self-effacing and world-weary attitude to his prize-winning poem 'The Pyramids': 'It's no use asking *me* about that poem, I have nothing to do with it . . . As a matter of fact I've disowned it long ago. It was a failure – nay more, it was a tragedy.' He also told her that he felt George Bernard Shaw's *Candida* to be the greatest play in the world. Brooke would soon share Shaw's political convictions and be heavily influenced by a book left by his bedside at Coombe Field.

21

In addition to Keynes, another school contemporary with whom he was to remain friends throughout his life was Hugh Russell-Smith. Writing later about their schooldays in an obituary for Brooke for the school magazine *The Meteor*, in 1915, he said:

> Rupert had an extraordinary vitality at school and afterwards, and it was a vitality that showed itself in a glorious enthusiasm and an almost boisterous sense of fun – qualities that are only too rare in combination . . . I see Rupert singing at the very top of his voice, with a glorious disregard for tune, the evening hymn we used to have so often at Bigside Prayers . . . I see him tearing across the grass so as not to be late for Chapel. I generally think of him with a book.

Geoffrey Keynes observed, 'Rupert, though a few months younger than I, was much wiser and more clever and he soon became the friend to whom I turned with complete confidence and admiration. I was at first unaware of the physical beauty for which he afterwards became so famous. He seemed somewhat overgrown, with cropped hair and rather bowed legs, which earned him the nickname "Bowles" among his friends.' Speaking of himself, Brooke and Russell-Smith, Keynes also reflected, 'We made up a cheerful trio, Brooke providing most of the entertainment with a flow of hilarious nonsense. Thus we climbed up the school in parallel until we found ourselves working in the same form, known as the Twenty, under a great classical scholar, Robert Whitelaw [Brooke's godfather]. Brooke was at the top of the form and I was stationed firmly at the bottom.'

Hugh Russell-Smith spent his summers at Watersgreen House, Watersgreen, Brockenhurst, in the New Forest, Hampshire, with his parents, younger brother Denham and sister Elsie, and Brooke was a frequent visitor. He wrote to Hugh in September 1905, 'I may see the fair Geoffrey before he has the happiness to be with you all at B'hurst . . . I shall probably disguise myself as Pimpo and visit you at B'hurst again . . .' It was to prove one of the many parts of England with which he would fall in love and become a regular visitor. William Gilpin, in his book *Remarks on Forest Scenery* wrote in 1791 that, 'Brockenhurst is a pleasant forest-village, lying in a bottom, adorned with lawns, groves and rivulets, and surrounded on the higher ground by vast woods. From the churchyard an expanded view opens over the whole.' It was little changed by Edwardian times.

At the beginning of the Michaelmas term, Rupert wrote from 'an abyss of loneliness and dreariness' to Lucas, complaining of an 'excess of Classics' and of being 'rather weary of football and work'. He enclosed a new poem, 'Vanitas', and posted him another a little later: 'I send you a sonnet I have just made; which seems to me to have some nice lines but to be quite incomplete as a whole.'

The Dawn

When on my night of life the Dawn shall break,
Scatt'ring the mists of dreams, the old sad gloom,
Before the terrible sunrise of the Tomb;
Shall I forget the dull memorial ache?
Shall not my tired heart, as a child, awake,
Filling the morn with music? nor retain
Aught of the sad notes of my former strain
But through that splendid day spring rise, and make
Beauty more beautiful, the dawn more fair?
Only – I fear me that I may not find
That brave smile that once lit my sunless air,
The bright swift eyes with purety there-behind,
Nor see the pale cloud of her tossing hair
Laugh and leap out along the desolate wind!

In between school, work and poetry, he borrowed an edition of Sir Thomas Malory's *Morte D'Arthur* with Aubrey Beardsley illustrations from the school's Temple reading room, edited a Liberal election paper, 'The Rugby Elector', and played numerous football matches. On the back flyleaf on his copy of the *Carmina* of Horace, which he was translating, he scribbled a few lines on Rugby football.

Our captain's a Scotsman, what more need
  we say,
And the foe sometimes collar him once, but
  no more;
If you wish the best forward in Rugby to pace
He is fat and short-sighted and honest of face.
Neither Watson nor Beck could stand up
  before Peter,
Then our Kaffir no half could be pluckier or
  neater.

Brooke also jotted down an alternative phrase to 'what more need we say': 'loves a good fray'.

As no Scotsman captained the School XV at this time, it seems likely that in this poem Brooke was referring to the School Field XV, whose captain was the Scottish half-back William Burt-Marshall. The Watson and Beck mentioned were Charles Challinor Watson, who went on to captain the School XV, and Charles Arthur Beck, a South African, from the Cape of Good

Hope, both from other houses. Although there was no mention of him by name in the poem, Brooke played alongside Ronald William Poulton, who went on to play rugby for England from 1909 to 1914. The school rugby report recorded that the 11st. 2lbs centre three-quarter R.C. Brooke 'tackles too high'.

His looks were beginning to create a stir:

> A purple and terrific scandal has arisen around me . . . it began by Dean catching me one day & informing me that 'a gentleman' in another house had been trying to buy a photo of me . . . I secretly made enquiries and found it was one I knew of old – one with the form of a Greek God, the face of Hyacinthus, the mouth of Antinous, eyes like a sunset, a smile like dawn . . . it appears that the madman worships me at a pale distance . . .

Towards the end of March, Rupert, Hugh Russell-Smith and another schoolfriend developed an eye condition called opthalmia, which put paid to reading and writing for a couple of weeks. To save the strain on their eyes, they were read to, being treated to a new book by Hilaire Belloc. Geoffrey Keynes remembers it as being *Hills and the Sea*; as that particular book was not published until October of that year it is more likely that the book was *Esto Perpetua*. Brooke was disappointed in it: '. . . it is not Belloc. I still miss that grave and fantastic irresponsibility; it is a clever book which might have been written by any of several men; I wanted one that only one could have written.' Rupert's eyes had still not healed enough for him to accompany his cousin Erica to see the play *Hippolytus*, so he resorted to developing the flirtation with his admirer at Rugby. 'How much I am in earnest – or how

School Field, Rugby. Rupert's bedroom window is on the far right at the top

much he is – I can't really say. But it is spring.' The relationship appeared to be carried out solely by letter. 'I usually address him as Hyacinth, Apollo, or Antinous, and end with a quotation from Swinburne or Catallus. I bring in odorous & jewelled phrases "The Greek Gods lived that you might be likened to them: the world was created that you might be made of gold and ivory" . . . it is all rather sweet and rather unusual; and he really looks very nice.'

Notwithstanding this schoolboy nonsense, Brooke also had a very masculine side, throwing himself enthusiastically into the discipline of the school cadet corps, where he rose swiftly to colour sergeant before being promoted to second lieutenant.

During the April school break, the Brookes repaired to Venice for a short holiday, following which Rupert went to spend a few days with his older brother Richard, who was now working for a firm in Southsea, Hampshire.

On 10 May 1906 Rupert wrote from School Field to Geoffrey Keynes, who had left Rugby the previous year:

> The Summer Term has dawned. It is my last and I weep. The same fantastic things happen, there is that strange throng of young beings, unconscious of all their youth & wonder. Another Spring dies odorously in Summer . . . but I am quite happy. To be here is wonderful and suffices. I live in a mist of golden dreams. Afterwards life will come, cold and terrible. At present I am a child.

His overwhelming sadness at the realisation that these were his final days as a pupil at School Field came pouring out in words, powerfully demonstrating his feelings in the closing lines of a letter to Keynes dated 22 June: 'That gay witch, the Summer, who charmed me three weeks ago! I have looked into her face and seen behind the rouge and the smile, the old, mocking visage of a harlot.'

During the height of his final golden summer at School Field Rupert was moved to write a poem that was eventually published as 'English Minnesong' in *The Westminster Gazette* on 16 February 1907 and later as 'The Beginning' in *Poems 1911*.

The Beginning

Some day I shall rise and leave my friends
And seek you again through the world's far ends,
You whom I found so fair,
(Touch of your hands and smell of your hair!),
My only God in the days that were.

25

My eager feet will find you again,
Though the ugly years and the mark of pain
Have changed you wholly; for I shall know
(How could I forget having loved you so?),
In the sad half-light of evening,
The face that was all my sunrising.
So then at the ends of the earth I'll stand
And hold you fiercely by either hand,
And seeing your age and ashen hair
I'll curse the thing that once you were,
Because it is changed and pale and old
(Lips that were scarlet, hair that was gold!),
And I loved you before you were old and wise,
When the flame of youth was strong in your eyes,
– And my heart is sick with memories.

Rupert was never again to find the security afforded him by Rugby School, except perhaps many years later as an officer in the Royal Naval Battalion, when once again he belonged to a unit of young men with whom he had a unique bond and sense of purpose. Brooke was moulded by the school made great by its former headmaster Thomas Arnold. Thomas Hughes, the author of *Tom Brown's Schooldays*, who had been a pupil there some years before Brooke, noted: '. . . the mark by which you may know them is, their genial and hearty freshness and youthfulness of character.' So enamoured was Hughes of Arnold's 'New Jerusalem' that in 1880 he founded the township of Rugby in Morgan County, Tennessee.

Two months before he was to go up to King's College, Cambridge, Rupert was drawn back to the Russell-Smith household in the New Forest. His obvious enjoyment of staying at Watersgreen House was displayed in a thank-you letter to Mrs Russell-Smith in August 1906:

Dear Mrs Russell-Smith

I can truthfully say that I never enjoyed a visit more in my life (with the possible exception of one to my aunt when I was nine, and discovered there for the first time Browning's poems). I never was in a home where everyone was so affectionate to one another and the world at large. It made me very envious. I now understand the secret of Hugh and Denham's unfailing cheerfulness during the term – a constant enigma. I was vastly sorry to go; I should like to have stayed five months. As it was, I was almost sociable for ten days – a rare thing for me. Many thanks for tolerating me so long. I shall soon write to one of the boys. I loved it all – even the excessive physical exercise in a way, – and especially one of the hammocks – the one further from the house. Please give my love to it – a delightful hammock!

In October, with his new life at Cambridge about to begin, Rupert was again at Bournemouth, from where he wrote to Geoffrey Keynes, '. . . I have been in this quiet place of invalids and gentlemanly sunsets for about a hundred years, ever since yesterday week.' St John Lucas was also treated to vivid descriptions from Brooke's over-imaginative scribblings during the same visit:

> Your eyeless letter found me in this strange place, which is full of moaning pines and impressionist but quite gentlemanly sunsets. With other decrepit and grey-haired invalids I drift wanly along the cliffs . . . Meanwhile I linger here and read Sordello and Beaudelaire alternately and the weather is very fine . . . I am very busy with an enormous romance of which I have written five chapters. It is really a mediaeval paraphrase of the Marble Sphinx.

It is clear that Brooke was apprehensive about leaving Rugby for Cambridge, covering his fears with an assumed equanimity! 'I have seen everything there is to see and my eyes are tired.'

CHAPTER II

King's Herald

Before October 1906 was out, Brooke was living away from home for the first time as an undergraduate of King's College, at Cambridge University. The King's College of St Nicholas in Cambridge was established by Henry VI in 1440, the monarch giving thanks 'to the honour of Almighty God, in whose hand are the hearts of Kings; of the most blessed and immaculate Virgin Mary Mother of Christ, and also of the glorious Confessor and Bishop Nicholas, Patron of my intended college, on whose festival we first saw the light'. In imitation of William Wykeham (founder of Winchester College and New College, Oxford), the King immediately closely connected his college with the King's College of Blessed Mary of Eton beside Windsor. The King's chapel is a breathtakingly unique piece of architecture, surrounded by later work from eminent architects such as William Wilkins, Sir Gilbert Scott and Sir George Boldy. Until 1857, just half a century too early for Rupert, King's College students had the right to claim degrees without examination. He became one of some 50 freshmen to join the 100 or so established King's men, and was allotted Room 14 (actually two rooms) at the top of staircase A, in Fellows' Buildings, almost in the far corner of the front court – rooms that had been occupied by the artist Aubrey Beardsley some 17 years before. Rupert had once written to his cousin Erica, while still at school, suggesting that she acquired and absorb 'one third of Swinburne, all Oscar Wilde, and the drawings of Beardsley'.

Brooke had won a scholarship to King's, where his uncle Alan Brooke was Dean of the college, as his father had done before him. As with Rupert's schooldays under his father, no favours were asked for, nor expected, except that an arrangement was reached that he would call on his uncle for tea on Saturday afternoons. At an initial, more formal meeting with the Dean he met and became friendly with Hugh Dalton, later to become Chancellor of the

The view from Brooke's study at King's Cambridge, looking over front court to the chapel

Exchequer under Prime Minister Clement Attlee in the mid-1940s. Discovering that they had much in common, Brooke and Dalton, the son of a canon of Windsor, agreed to form a society where they could discuss such mutual interests as poetry, politics and any other subjects that took their fancy, deciding on the name 'Carbonari' (the charcoal burners) after the nineteenth-century Italian revolutionaries.

Brooke also fraternised with old Rugbeians who had gone up to Cambridge, Hugh Russell-Smith, Geoffrey Keynes and Andrew Gow, and found (as he had in St John Lucas at Rugby) another literary mentor, in the 42-year-old university librarian Charles Sayle, known as 'Aunt Snayle'. Brooke was later to write in his diary on 22 February 1908: 'I do not know

Jacques Raverat

in what language to moderate my appreciation of this great man . . . great in his ideals, great in his imagination, great in his charm . . .'

Other Cambridge men with whom Rupert became close friends were Justin Brooke, who had come up to Emmanuel in 1904 and was a leading light in the university's dramatic circle, and Jacques Raverat, a Frenchman from Prunoy who had arrived at Cambridge from university at the Sorbonne, Paris, having previously been at Bedales School with Justin. Raverat had this to say of Rupert: '. . . the forehead was very high and very pure, the chin and lips admirably moulded; the eyes were small, grey-blue and already veiled, mysterious and secret. His hair was too long, the colour of tarnished gold and parted in the middle; it kept falling in his face and he threw it back with a movement of his head . . .'

The cast of Eumenides *with Brooke as Herald* (far right)

30

During his first year at King's, Rupert took time to glance over his shoulder at the past: 'I have been happier at Rugby than I can find words to say. As I looked back at five years I seemed to see almost every hour golden and radiant, and always increasing in beauty as I grew more conscious and I could not and cannot hope for, as even quite imagine, such happiness elsewhere.' The man later to become another literary mentor, Edward Marsh, a high-ranking civil servant and former Cambridge graduate who was to fly the flag for Brooke's poetry and would bring him together with many other leading poets, was to say of Brooke's time at School Field, 'He loved the house and garden, especially his own particular long grass-path, where he used to walk up and down reading.' Brooke showed misgivings about leaving Rugby for King's: 'I shall live in Cambridge very silently, in a dark corner of a great room . . . I shall never speak, but I shall read all day and night – philosophy or science – nothing beautiful any more . . .'

Once at Cambridge, he soon began to orchestrate a suitable image. To Keynes he confided: 'I shall be rather witty and rather clever and I shall spend my time pretending to admire what I think is humorous or impressive in me to admire. Even more than yourself I attempt to be "all things to all men", rather cultured among the cultured, faintly athletic among athletes, a little blasphemous among blasphemers, slightly insincere to myself . . .'

Although Rupert made no great claims to be an actor, his looks and charisma drew him to the attention of the university dramatic societies. Via Justin Brooke, and fourth-year King's man A.F. Scholfield, Rupert landed the non-speaking role of the Herald in *Eumenides*, which was being produced by the Greek play committee. It was in this production that he first made an impression on Eddie Marsh, who was in the audience. Following his triumph in *Eumenides*, Brooke became a college pin-up. Winston Churchill's cousin Sir Shane Leslie later wrote in an article for *Tatler* about him:

> . . . he suffered unusually from love-hysteria due in turn to several maidens who could be called advanced rather than advancing . . . Cambridge ladies were already reasonably advanced, chiefly because of the unchivalrous rags that broke out among the undergraduates at any sign of giving them degrees after they had endured the toil of examinations! The type of ladies whom advanced on clever men were just as clever themselves, and as advanced religiously. These seemed to fall about Brooke or rather he fell about their feet . . .

This side of him was shielded from his mother, to whom he wrote from King's of other matters: 'I am going to see the South Africans, if they play, tomorrow. As it has been raining for a week they will probably have a wet ball and be handicapped considerably, but I suppose we shan't beat them. I have an atrocious but cheap seat right behind the goal-posts . . .' This was the Springboks' first ever visit to the British Isles, rugby having been introduced there just 30 years earlier. He also informed her about his new neighbour Oscar Browning, the historian and fellow of King's already in his seventieth year, who had rooms just opposite Rupert's: 'I went to lunch with the "OB" on Sunday. He was rather quaint to watch but I did not much like him. He was so very egotistical, and a little dull . . .' If James Strachey had similar views, they didn't appear to deter him from being sexually submissive to Browning, who would have sexual intercourse with him, accompanied by a string quartet of elderly ladies, secreted behind a curtain!

In January 1907, Rupert was ill in bed at Rugby with a bout of influenza which had hit the family; his mother and elder brother Richard were also down with it. He described his ailments in letters to Geoffrey Keynes and Erica Cotterill, writing to the latter enclosing a new poem that he had just written: 'To make up for all this bosh, I shall copy out for you the wonderfullest sonnet of the century. But if you show it to respectable people they'll kill you.' Some four and a half years after his original handwritten verses were secretly read by Erica, they were published in *Poems 1911* as 'The Vision of Archangels' and would sit on the bookshelves of the 'respectable people' he once feared might blanche at them.

The Vision of Archangels

Slowly up silent peaks, the white edge of the world,
Trod four archangels, clear against the unheeding sky,
Bearing, with quiet even steps, and great wings furled,
A little dingy coffin; where a child must lie,
It was so tiny. (Yet you fancied, God could never
Have bidden a child turn from the spring and the
    sunlight,
And shut him in that lonely shell, to drop for ever
Into the emptiness and silence, into the night . . .)

They then from the sheer summit cast, and watch it fall,
Through unknown glooms, that frail black coffin –
    and therein
God's little pitiful Body lying, worn and thin,
And curled up like some crumpled, lonely flower-petal –
Till it was no more visible; then turned again
With sorrowful quiet faces downward to the plain.

On Sunday, 13 January, Richard died of pneumonia, with his father Parker Brooke by his side. The family was devastated and Rupert was feeling '. . . terribly despondent and sad . . . there is an instinct to hide in sorrow, and at Cambridge where I know nowhere properly I can be alone'. He also felt that his father was 'tired and broken by it'. He offered to stay at School Field for a while, but his parents felt they could cope. Rupert went back to Cambridge and very gradually life began to return to normal.

As Brooke became increasingly involved with student life, he began to contribute poems and reviews to *The Cambridge Review*, as well as playing Stingo in the Amateur Dramatic Club's (ADC) production of Oliver Goldsmith's sentimental comedy, *She Stoops to Conquer*. His first poem to be printed while at King's was 'The Call', in February 1907.

The Call

Out of the nothingness of sleep,
The slow dreams of Eternity,
There was a thunder on the deep:
I came, because you called me.

I broke the Night's primeval bars,
I dared the old abysmal curse,
And flashed through ranks of frightened stars
Suddenly on the universe!

The eternal silences were broken;
Hell became Heaven as I passed –
What shall I give you as a token,
A sign that we have met, at last?

I'll break and forge the stars anew,
Shatter the heavens with a song;
Immortal in my love for you,
Because I love you, very strong.

Your mouth shall mock the old and wise,
Your laugh shall fill the world with flame,
I'll write upon the shrinking skies
The scarlet splendour of your name.

Till Heaven cracks, and Hell thereunder

Dies in her ultimate made fire,
And darkness falls, with scornful thunder,
On dreams of men and men's desire.

Then only in the empty spaces,
Death, walking very silently,
Shall fear the glory of our faces
Through all the dark infinity.

So, clothed about with perfect love,
The eternal end shall find us one,
Alone above the Night, above
The dust of the dead gods, alone.

Having found his feet and many new friends, and established his popularity, the Brooke of 1907 was a quantum leap from the freshman of 1906 who had written to St John Lucas on his arrival, '. . . this place is rather funny to watch; and a little wearying. It is full of very young people, and my blear eyes look dolefully at them from the lofty window where I sit and moan . . . my room is a gaunt yellow wilderness . . .'

On top of Rupert's dramatic commitment and studies, he was writing poetry and reviewing it. He confessed to St John Lucas, '. . . in my "literary life" I have taken the last step of infamy and become – a reviewer! I have undertaken to "do" great slabs of minor poetry for *The Cambridge Review* . . . Cambridge is terrible, slushy and full of un-Whistlerian mists.'

Rupert's increasing enthusiasm for exploring England took him along the South Downs of Sussex through the sleepy villages of Amberley, Arundel, Duncton and Petworth and along the River Arun in a walking tour with Hugh Russell-Smith, which he picturesquely embellished in a letter to St John Lucas: '. . . we slew a million dragons and wandered on unknown hills. We met many knights and I made indelicate songs about them . . .' This was the heart of Hilaire Belloc country: Belloc had started many of his own walking tours from his house, Kings Land at Shipley. It must have crossed Brooke's mind to call unsolicited; even though he did not, the two were to meet within a couple of months. The marathon ramble ended at the Green Dragon, Market Lavington, over the Easter weekend of 1907, during which time Rupert was proclaiming himself, through Hugh Dalton's influence, a committed Fabian and was allegedly trying to write Fabian hymns, although one suspects they were more fancy than fact, as Rupert had little musical talent. For one who was so taken with the image and character of Belloc – who would write many songs whilst walking the downs and the Arun Valley, through which Brooke had just travelled – if he were trying to compose, it would undoubtedly be in Belloc style. Possibly something in the vein of Belloc's 'On Sussex Hills'.

On Sussex Hills

On Sussex hills where I was bred,
When lanes in Autumn rains are red,
When Arun tumbles in his bed,
And busy great gusts go by;
When branch is bare in Burton Glen
And Bury Hill is a-whitening, then,
I drink strong ale with gentlemen; . . .

Brooke and Belloc eventually met at King's in the spring of 1907:

> . . . last night I went to a private small society in Pembroke where Hilaire Belloc came and read a paper and talked and drank beer – all in great measure. He was vastly entertaining. Afterwards Gow [Andrew Gow, who had been at Rugby with Rupert, and was now at Trinity] and I walked home with him about a mile. He was wonderfully drunk and talked all the way . . . you can tell Ma if you see her; but for God's sake don't say he was drunk, or she'll never read him again.

During May, Brooke played many games for King's Cricket XI, under the captaincy of H.F.P. Hearson, returning bowling figures of three wickets for 16 runs against Queen's on 16 May, one of 13 matches played during a four-week period. The following month the King's College magazine *Basileon* printed three of Brooke's poems: 'Dawn', 'The Wayfarers' and 'My Song'.

My Song

They are unworthy, these sad whining moods.
Shall I not make of Love some glorious thing? –
A song – and shout it through the dripping woods,
Till all the woods shall burgeon into Spring?
Because I've a mad longing for your eyes,
And once our eager lips met wonderfully,
Men shall find new delight in morning skies,
And all the stars will dance more merrily.

Yes, in the wonder of the last day-break,
God's Mother, on the threshold of His house,
Shall welcome in your white and perfect soul,
Kissing your brown hair softly for my sake;
And God's own hand will lay, as aureole,
My song, a flame of scarlet, on your brows.

At the beginning of June, whilst knee-deep in exams and late nights, Brooke was informed by the Chapel Clerk that he had to read in chapel every morning that week, at the un-student-like hour of 8.00 a.m. However, a respite from duties came in the shape of the summer vacation, which ran from June to October. Chapel, drama, studies and his new life were put on hold while he went to stay at Grantchester Dene in Bournemouth, with his aunts Lizzy and Fanny. The latter was at one time the honorary secretary of the Church Missionary Society for the parish, and insisted on Rupert accompanying her and her sister to the local Holy Trinity Church when he stayed with them. While at his aunts' house, he pored over maps to find somewhere suitable to go off to with friends for a few days, and was captivated by the name of the Mupe Rocks near Lulworth Cove, Dorset. Later that month he wrote to his old schoolfriend Hugh Russell-Smith, 'You know I always like to keep you *au fait* (as our Gallic neighbours would have it) with my latest literary activity. This *came to me* as I was sitting by the sea the other day. I don't know what it was – perhaps it was the rhythm of the waves. But I felt *I must sing*. So I sang:

'I love a scrabbly epithet
The sort you can't ever forget,
That blooms, a lonely violet
In the eleventh line of a sonnet.

I know one such; I'm proud to know him.
I'll put him in my next GREAT POIM.
He plays the psack-butt very well:
And his Aunt was a Polysyllable.'

The night is purple with a weariness older than the stars;
and there is a sound of eventual tears.'

A week or two later Brooke dashed off a few flippant lines of verse to Andrew Gow:

A Song, Explanatory of Strange Sense of Incompatibility between Self and Universe and,

In Praise of Decease, written to a Fellow Sufferer

I Things are a brute,
    And I am sad and sick;
    Oh! You are a Spondee in the Fourth Foot
    And I am a final cretic
    (I hope the technical terms are right.)

II Things are beasts:
    Alas! and Alack!
    If life is a succession of Choreic Anapaests,
    When, O When shall we arrive at the Paroemiac?

Later in June, he described the atmosphere at Grantchester Dene to St John Lucas:

> Here in the South it is hot. In the mornings I bathe, in the afternoons lie out in a hammock among the rose-beds and watch them [his aunts] playing croquet (pronounced kröky) . . . My evangelical aunts always talk at meals like people in Ibsen. They make vast symbolic remarks about Doors and Houses and Food. My one aim is to keep the conversations on Foreign Missions, lest I scream suddenly. At lunch no

West Lulworth post office, nicknamed 'Pimpinella Palace' by Brooke, photographed the month before his stay there. Mrs Chaffey stands in the middle of the group

one spoke for ten minutes! Then the First Aunt said, '. . . The Sea? . . .
The Sea! . . .' And an Old Lady Visitor replied, 'Ah!'

The intriguingly named Mupe Rocks hadn't been forgotten. It transpired
that they were at Bacon Hole, a little east of Lulworth Cove. Rupert informed
Hugh Russell-Smith, who was to holiday with him, 'Mrs Chaffey, of the Post
Office, West Lulworth, thanks me for my card and will reserve rooms "as
agreed". (She thinks my name is Brooks, and therefore she is P.P. [puce Pig].
She is no Woman of Business, for she doesn't say what is agreed (Doric for
agreed) and I don't know . . . The effort of conducting a correspondence in
the Arcadian variety of the Doric dialect, with Mrs Chaffey, P.P. is exhausting.'
Unbeknown to Rupert, Emily Jane Chaffey was barely able to read or write,
so her communications with him about the holiday arrangements were, in
the light of that knowledge, highly commendable. She had been so illiterate
at the time of her wedding to Henry J. Chaffey that she had signed her
marriage certificate with a cross.

Rupert and Russell-Smith were joined there by a new friend who was also
studying at Cambridge, Dudley Ward. In his excitement Brooke exclaimed to
a friend: 'In a week I'm going to the most beautiful place in England,
Lulworth Cove . . .' Brooke, of course, wasn't the first wordsmith to wax
lyrical about the village of West Lulworth. John Leland, the earliest chronicler
of Lulworth and chaplain, librarian and antiquary to Henry VIII, wrote:

I saw the shore
A little fisher town
Caulled Lilleworth
Sumtyme longgings to the Newborows
Now to Poynings
Wher a gut or crek
Out it the se into the land
And is a socour for small shippes

The area is one of natural beauty; the rocks which form the cove, Stair
Hole, and the surrounding coastline are over 150 million years old, fossils
having been found there that predate the evolution of reptiles and birds. To
the east is the Isle of Purbeck, a spectacular ridge of chalk hills that were
once continuous with the Isle of Wight, while to the west are rugged cliffs,
including Durdle Door, the more inaccessible crags providing ideal nesting
grounds for puffins and guillemots. Not surprisingly, the natural beauty and
idyllic charm of Lulworth has attracted its fair share of artists and writers,
including John O'Keefe, who stayed at the Red Lion, now Churchfield
House, for six weeks in 1791, Sir John Everett Millais, who is reputed to

have painted his *Departure of the Romans from Britain* at Oswald's Wall, and John Keats, who is believed to have written his sonnet 'Bright Star' while berthed in the cove. Thomas Hardy, who lived at Bockhampton and Dorchester from 1890 to 1928, used a thinly disguised Lulworth in several of his novels; Bertrand Russell often stayed at Newlands Farm between 1916 and 1934; and actor Laurence Olivier would spend his first honeymoon there at a house called Weston. Brooke was yet to meet and fall in love with Olivier's cousin, Noel.

On 21 July 1907 Rupert wrote to his mother from the Chaffeys' post office at Albion Villas, West Lulworth:

> Sometimes we go in a boat in the Cove, or outside, for exercise, and sometimes walk on the downs or ramble about the cliffs and rocks. This last pastime is extremely destructive to shoes. Where we are is really Lulworth Cove, West Lulworth being half a mile further up from the sea, East Lulworth three miles to the NE . . . The sea is always different colours, and sometimes there are good sunsets . . . The lodgings are quite nice but rather free and easy!

The lines written to his mother differ wildly from the contents of a letter sent the same day to Geoffrey Keynes, written with deliberate affectation:

> Lulworth is a tiresomely backward & old-fashioned place. There are no promenades, nor lifts, nor piers, nor a band; only downs & rocks & green waters; & we sit & bathe & read dead & decaying languages. Very dull . . . on Tuesday we sat on seagirt rocks & read J. Keats. When I leapt from rock to rock J.K. fell from pocket into swirling flood beneath; &, ere aught could be done, was borne from reach on swift current. We rushed to the harbour, chartered a boat, & rowed frantically along the rocky coast in search of it. The sea was —. At length we spied it close in, by treacherous rocks – in a boat we could not get to it alive. We beached our barque (at vast risk) half a mile down the coast & leapt lightly over vast boulders to the spot . . . I cast off my garb, & plunged wholly naked into that 'fury of black waters & white foam' – Enough. J.K. was rescued, in a damaged condition.

Four years later he discovered that Lulworth was the last place in England that Keats had been to, before going to Italy. Brooke's stay at Lulworth inspired five untitled verses, which feel as if they should be sung. Again one feels the influence of Belloc creeping in.

Verse I

> Oh give our love to Lulworth Cove
> And Lulworth Cliffs and sea
> Oh! Lulworth Down! Oh! Lulworth Down!
> (The name appeals to me)
> If we were with you today in Lulworth
> How happy we should be!

Verse II

> The Lulworth Downs are large and high
> And honourable things
> There we should lie (old Hugh and I!)
> On the tombs of the old sea kings;
> If you lie up there, with your face on the grass
> You can hear their whisperings

Verse III

> And each will sigh for the good day light
> And for all his ancient bliss
> Red wine, and the fight, song by night
> Are the things they chiefly miss
> And one, I know (for he told me so)
> Is sick for a dead lad's kiss

Verse IV

> Ah! they're fair to be back for many things
> But mainly (they whisper) these;
> England and April (the poor dead kings!)
> And the purple touch of the trees
> And the women of England, and English springs
> And the scent of English seas

Verse V

> But a lad like you, what has he to do
> With the dead, be they living or dead
> And their whims and tears for what can't be theirs?
> Live you in their silly stead
> With a smile and a song for the live and strong
> And a sigh for the poor old dead

Verses VI to LX

> Still simmering

On 8 July he wrote 'Pine Trees and the Sky: Evening', while at Lulworth.

Pine Trees and the Sky: Evening

I'd watch the sorrow of the evening sky
And smelt the sea, and earth, and the warm clover
And heard the waves, and the seagull's mocking cry

And in them all was only the old cry
That song they always sing – 'The best is over!
You may remember now, and think, and sigh
O silly lover!'
And I was tired and sick that all was over
And because I
For all my thinking, never could recover
One moment of the good hours that were over
And I was sorry and sick, and wished to die

Then from the sad west turning wearily
I saw the pines against the white north sky
Very beautiful, and still, and bending over
Their sharp black heads against a quiet sky
And there was peace in them; and I
Was happy, and forgot to play the lover
And laughed, and did no longer wish to die;
Being glad of you, O pine-trees and the sky!

After Lulworth, Rupert headed up to the Russell-Smiths at Brockenhurst, writing from there to St John Lucas, on 4 August. He again affected a different stance and writing style, attempting to convey a world-weariness beyond his years. He clearly adored the Russell-Smiths but wrote with obvious exaggeration and suitable embellishment:

> . . . Now I am staying with this foolish family again till about next Saturday. They are delightful, and exactly as they were last year . . . A few days ago they found I was exactly 20; and congratulated me on my birthday, giving me a birthday cake, and such things. I hated them, and lost my temper. I am now in the depths of despondency because of my age. I am filled with a hysterical despair to think of fifty dull years more. I hate myself and everyone. I have written almost no verse for ages; I shall never write any more . . . The rest are coming back from church. They want to tell me what the sermon was about . . .

Rupert was spared the 50 dull years, as within eight, he, Hugh and Hugh's brother Denham, would all be dead, and Brockenhurst church where the Russell-Smiths worshipped would fill rapidly with First World War graves. For now, though, no shadow cast itself over the exuberant years of youth, where the summers seemed longer than the winters, and the countryside was there for the taking.

His travels around the south of England during the summer of 1907 included a stay with the Cotterills at Godalming. In his bedroom there he found a copy of William Morris's Utopian classic, *News From Nowhere or an Epoch of Rest*, a book which he had never read, but which had been on his list to track down ever since fellow student Ben Keeling had told him that a poster in his rooms at Cambridge had been inspired by it. The poster depicted a worker with clenched fist and the legend, 'Forward the Day is Breaking'. Morris's book and the piece of vivid artwork and slogan were to inspire Brooke to write in 1908 his only socialist poem, 'Second Best'.

Second Best

Here in the dark, O heart;
Alone with the enduring Earth, and Night,
And Silence, and the warm strange smell of clover;
Clear-visioned, though it break you; far apart
From the dead best, the dear and old delight;
Throw down your dreams of immortality,
O faithful, O foolish lover!
Here's peace for you, and surety; here the one
Wisdom – the truth – 'All day the good glad sun
Showers love and labour on you, wine and song;
The greenwood laughs, the wind blows, all day long
Till night.' And night ends all things.
                              Then shall be
No lamp relumed in heaven, no voices crying,
Or changing lights, or dreams and forms that hover!
(And, heart, for all your sighing,
That gladness and those tears are over, over . . .)

And has the truth brought no new hope at all,
Heart, that you're weeping yet for Paradise?
Do they still whisper, the old weary cries?
'Mid youth and song, feasting and carnival,
Through laughter, through the roses, as of old
Comes Death, on shadowy and relentless feet,

Death, unappeasable by prayer or gold;
Death is the end, the end!'
Proud, then, clear-eyed and laughing, go to greet
Death as a friend!

Exile of immortality, strongly wise,
Strain through the dark with undesirous eyes
To what may lie beyond it. Sets your star,
O heart, for ever! Yet, behind the night,
Waits for the great unborn, somewhere afar,
Some white tremendous daybreak. And the light,
Returning, shall give back the golden hours,
Ocean a windless level, Earth a lawn
Spacious and full of sunlit dancing-places,
And laughter, and music, and, among the flowers,
The gay child-hearts of men, and the child-faces,
O heart, in the great dawn!

Of William Morris's book he said, 'I found *News From Nowhere* in my room
and read it on and on all through the night till I don't know what time! And
ever since I've been a devoted admirer of Morris and a socialist, and all sorts
of things!' Rupert was allowed to keep his uncle's copy. Although the Utopian
ideas it embraced were delightfully idealistic, he wholeheartedly embraced
Morris's socialist ideology in his day-to-day life.

**NEWS FROM NOWHERE
OR AN EPOCH OF REST**
BEING SOME CHAPTERS FROM
A UTOPIAN ROMANCE BY
WILLIAM MORRIS

LONGMANS, GREEN AND CO.
39 PATERNOSTER ROW, LONDON
NEW YORK, BOMBAY, AND CALCUTTA
Price One Shilling Net

CHAPTER III

Apostle or Apollo?

Rupert's return to King's in the autumn of 1907 saw his pen in vitriolic mood towards the university town: 'Cambridge is less tolerable than ever . . .'; 'I pine to be out of Cambridge, which I loathe . . .'; 'Cambridge is a bog . . .'; '. . . in Cambridge the hard streets are paven with brass and glass and tired wounded feet of pilgrims flutter aimlessly upon them'. In a letter to his cousin Erica he was also disparaging about George Bernard Shaw: '. . . it was the same speech as he made the night before in London and the night after, somewhere. Mostly about the formation of a "middle-class party" in Parliament: which didn't interest me much.'

As well as being a member of the Carbonari and acting in the ADC, Brooke became a co-founder of the Marlowe Society, formed with the object of staging Elizabethan plays. By October, the finishing touches were being put to their debut production, Marlowe's *Tragical History of Doctor Faustus*, due to be performed on Monday, 11 November, and Tuesday, 12 November. Rupert was not only playing the part of Mephistopheles but had agreed to take on the role of President of the Society. Among the first-night audience were Prince Leopold of Belgium, the former Cambridge don E.J. Dent, who would become an eminent publisher, and Rupert's mother. Hugh Russell-Smith played one of the Seven Deadly Sins, Gluttony; Geoffrey Keynes, the Evil Angel; Justin Brooke, Doctor Faustus; W. Denis Browne, Rugby's star music pupil, Lucifer; and George Mallory, who was later to lose his life on Everest, the Pope. The chorus was directed by Clive Carey, of Clare College.

Later that month, Brooke was elected to the Fabian Society, as an associate member. As such he had not as yet signed the Basis (a commitment to the party), but his interest in politics was increasing. His Uncle Clem, an advanced socialist, had just published *Human Justice for Those at the bottom, An Appeal to Those at the Top*, prompting Brooke to write to him, whilst

44

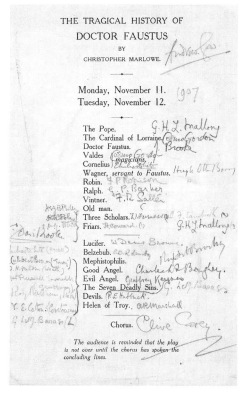

The programme signed by the cast

Rupert being tested on his lines by Jacques Raverat and Dudley Ward

staying with his aunts in Bournemouth, with the news that socialism was making great advances at the universities of Oxford and Cambridge. He had read his uncle's book and wondered whether 'this Commercialism or Competition or whatever the filthy infection is, hasn't spread almost too far, and that the best hope isn't in some kind of upheaval'. Despite being 'an Associate (not an actual member) of the Cambridge Fabian Society I have lately been coming across a good many Socialists, both at the University and without, as well as unattached sympathisers like Lowes Dickinson. I wish I could get more of these, especially among the Fabians, to accept your definition of Socialism. Most of them, I fear, would define it as "Economic Equality" or the "Nationalisation of Land and Food Production", or some such thing.'

The one Society that was decidedly ambivalent about Brooke was the Apostles. Founded in 1820 by a group of friends dedicated to working out a philosophy for life, its hierarchy would mark out suitable young men, undergraduates mainly from Trinity and King's, to swell its ranks by two or three a year – if that. The Society was intimate, secretive and often predominantly homosexual. 'Born' into the inner circle at various times before Brooke's day were: Bertrand Russell, Eddie Marsh, Maynard Keynes, G.E. Moore, Leonard Woolf, Oscar Browning, Clive Bell, Saxon Sydney-Turner and Lytton Strachey. James Strachey had suggested Rupert to Lytton

James Strachey (standing) *and Lytton Strachey*

as a possible candidate, before Brooke even came up. The Society meetings, invariably on Saturday evenings, were often graced by the occasional appearance of an 'angel' or retired Apostle, but it was Lytton and Maynard Keynes who were the main deliberators in the decision as to whether to enlist Brooke. Lytton felt that Rupert's influences at Rugby – Arthur Eckersley and St John Lucas – had not helped his literary style, expression or quality of thought, and the idea that the young Rugbeian had not read the novels of the celebrated American writer Henry James, was too abhorrent to Strachey for him to further consider the application.

It was at this time that Lytton, who had met Brooke briefly, dubbed him 'Sarawak', as there was some talk of his family being related to James Brooke, the British administrator who became the 'White Rajah of Sarawak'. This led to Brooke referring to his mother as 'The Ranee', a nickname that he was to use for the rest of his life.

By 30 October 1907, Maynard Keynes, too, was still undecided about electing Rupert to the Apostles. Of the others who were in on the discussion, Harry Norton didn't really know Brooke, although he'd met him briefly, Jack Sheppard was faintly opposed, while James Strachey was enthusiastic. Maynard wrote to Lytton: '. . . I'm damned if I know what to say. James's judgements on the subject are very nearly worthless; he is quite crazy. I have been to see R. again. He is all right I suppose and quite affable enough – but yet I feel little enthusiasm.' During November, Rupert went to Oxford with the Fabians, for a debate at the university. Despite referring to his own party as 'An indecorous, aesthetical, obscene set of ruffians', Brooke was elected by a large majority to the committee. He was also elected, in January 1908, to the Apostles. He was the first new member for two years, and membership meant membership for life, to a fraternity that hermetically sealed itself from outside forces. This led to, or was often because of, the insecurities of many of its members – brilliant intellectuals, who were often awkward in day-to-day situations or with ordinary people. For some, membership of the Apostles became a way of life; for Rupert there was a wider world waiting.

Strachey, as well as being an Apostle was also a member of the Bloomsbury group, a circle of friends who'd began meeting a couple of years previously at the Bloomsbury home of Virginia and Vanessa Stephen. The arts-orientated coterie would include amongst others Strachey, Maynard Keynes, Duncan Grant, Saxon Sydney-Turner, Roger Fry and Leonard Woolf, several of whom would figure in Brooke's life, although he would never be a member of their circle.

During the Christmas break, he went with friends on a skiing holiday in Andermatt, staying at Danioth's Grand Hotel; whilst there they rehearsed and performed Oscar Wilde's *The Importance of Being Earnest*. Then he went back to the grind of exams and his continued disenchantment with living in

Cambridge. His apparent despondency continued into 1908; a letter to St John Lucas ended with the gripe, '. . . I pine to be out of Cambridge which I lathe', and to Jacques Raverat he wrote, '. . . it is not from the Real England that I write. It is from the Hinder Parts. The faeces or crassamentum or dregs, the Eastern counties; a low swamp; a confluence of mist and mire; a gathering-place of darkness and mud and fever; where men's minds rot in the mirk like a leper's flesh and their bodies grow white and soft and malodorous and suppurating and fungoid and so melt in slime . . .' These exaggerated lines intended to amuse or create a dramatic air for his friend to marvel at are earthed by the line; 'I have a cold.'

In early April, Brooke escaped from Cambridge to Torquay to read Greek for Walter Headlam – a fellow of King's – who had introduced Brooke to the plays of John Webster and the poetry of John Donne. Headlam was to become a friend and mentor. Brooke's lodgings were on the east side of the bay at 3 Beacon Terrace, facing Beacon Quay.

Beacon Hill itself had been quarried away during the 1860s to provide the requisite limestone to infill the new Haldon Pier – not surprisingly causing a storm of protest from the locals. The pier had been completed by 1870. Beacon Terrace itself, hard by Beacon Hill, had been completed in 1833, when it was deemed to be 'a fine example of Regency marine building, with its crisp stucco facade and projecting cast-iron balconies'. In Brooke's day the Bath Saloons, originally the Medical Baths, were to his left, looking from his apartment window, and a little nearer stood the Electricity Generating Station, inaugurated in March 1898 – not pretty, although not blocking this view over the bay. At the time of Brooke's stay in Torquay, the town had just changed its public transport system from 15-seater steam buses to trams, and the town's first public library had just opened.

On 8 April, Rupert wrote from Beacon Terrace to Hugh Dalton, a devout Fabian, about his decision to sign the Fabian basis: 'I have decided to sign even the present Fabian basis and to become a member (if possible) of the central Fabian society. The former part I suppose may wait till next term, as I have no basis with me, spiritually, the thing is done (not without blood and tears).'

During his ten-day sojourn in Torquay he was moved to take time out from his political thoughts and Greek studies to write the sonnet 'Seaside'.

Seaside

Swiftly out from the friendly lilt of the band,
The crowd's good laughter, the loved eyes of men,
I am drawn nightward; I must turn again
Where, down beyond the low untrodden strand,

There curves and glimmers outward to the unknown
The old unquiet ocean. All the shade
Is rife with magic and movement. I stray alone
Here on the edge of silence, half afraid,

Waiting a sign. In the deep heart of me
The sullen waters swell towards the moon,
And all my tides set seaward.
                                        From inland
Leaps a gay fragment of some mocking tune,
That tinkles and laughs and fades along the sand,
And dies between the seawall and the sea.

Highlights of his stay there were an invitation from his cousin Erica, who had asked him to go with her to see George Bernard Shaw's new play, *Getting Married*, the following month at the Haymarket Theatre in London, and a play of hers that she had sent to him. He replied, 'Thanks for the play. Its market value would be higher if you had written "from the authoress to her adorable cousin" or words to that effect, inside. I carry it about with me and sit on it at intervals, so that it often lies quite flat now.' His thoughts were also on a chance meeting and conversation he had with the author H.G.Wells in London, *en route* to Torquay. He was more than happy to let his friends know about it, including the fact in letters to both Hugh Dalton and Geoffrey Keynes, to whom he wrote, 'Shall you be in London on Thursday or Wednesday? I am at my club. Last time I was at it I met Wells and talked with him – a month ago. Did I tell you? If not, you're a bright, bright green.' In the same letter, written from 3 Beacon Terrace on 17 April, he wrote, 'I am not a poet – I was, that's all. And I never, ah! never was a superman – God forbid.' The sea brought back fond memories of Lulworth, necessitating a postcard to Geoffrey, who was staying there: 'I hope you're still there [Lulworth Cove]. Give my love to the whole lot, downs and all, and especially the left-handed boy, who dwells in the coastguards' cottages, and the village idiot, and all the Williamses . . .'

From Torquay, Rupert returned to the inn on the western edge of Salisbury Plain, where he and Hugh Russell-Smith had stayed during a walking tour the previous Easter. This time the Green Dragon at Market Lavington was the venue for a gathering organised by Geoffrey Keynes's eldest brother Maynard, later to become one of the century's most eminent economists. Among those present were Desmond MacCarthy, hailed as his generation's greatest drama critic, Lytton Strachey and the philosopher G.E. Moore, whose revolutionary ethical concepts were woven into his *Principa Ethica*, published in the autumn of 1903. The novelist E.M. Forster was also present, and that Brooke was reading his *The Celestial Omnibus* at the time was either an interesting

High Street, Market Lavington. The Green Dragon is on the right

coincidence or well-organised public relations by Rupert. The weather was bitter and the food ghastly, according to Strachey, but it clearly didn't deter Moore from accompanying himself on the piano. He sang many of Schubert's songs during the temporary lulls in a weekend that swung from intellectual jousting to overt flirtation, in the maze of lofty rooms with their fine views towards the Plain and along the narrow high street. Brooke was younger than the others at the gathering, and one wonders whether the invitation would still have been forthcoming if he hadn't looked as he did. He appeared to cope with the homosexual proclivities of many of the Apostles, without either becoming involved or being rejected for not doing so.

In May 1908, a shaft of sunlight fell on King's when Brooke met Noel Olivier, the youngest daughter (then 15) of Sir Sydney Olivier, the Governor of Jamaica, at a dinner held in Ben Keeling's rooms in his honour. The dinner guests included H.G. Wells, Newnham students Amber Reeves and Dorothy Osmaston, and Noel's sister Margery. Rupert and Noel got on famously and he was clearly taken with her: the young girl becoming the object of his affections for several years. Her family lived at Limpsfield Chart, in Surrey, where she and her three sisters, Bryn, Daphne and Margery, would often spend all day in the local woods and fields leading a tomboy existence. The fact that Noel was still a schoolgirl (at Bedales in Hampshire) did not deter Brooke from pursuing her with dogged determination.

50

Noel Olivier

Your Eyes

Your eyes are a black lake
Where the moon always shines,
Her white fires make
Sound in the close black pines.

Deep in those waters old
One finds fantastic things,
– Strange cups, and gold
Crowns of forgotten Kings,

Cracked mirrors, jewelled pins
That bound dead harlots' hair,
Old monstrous sins
That once the world found fair . . .

Dark little shadows creep
Dumbly, in wait to kill
What voices weep
Dead hearts beneath the hill.

Glares one great star, a wound
Blood-red in the night's womb,

51

The woods around
Whisper; and wait – for whom?

After finding a little time for sport – 'I had my first game of tennis and found myself quite bad' – the majority of his time was taken up with the organisation of a production of John Milton's *Comus*, which was to be staged at the New Theatre in Cambridge to celebrate the poet John Milton's tercentenary. Brooke played the Attendant Spirit and stage-managed the production. The organisation was indeed enormous. He dealt with H. & M. Rayne, the theatrical stores opposite Waterloo Station: 'We received your letter today and note you require 17 more animal masks . . . we cannot give you a definite price until we have seen the sketches.' They also offered him '. . . anything in Wigs, Tights, Shoes, or Costumes . . .' In mid-June, there was a flurry of letters and post-office telegraphs between Rupert and the set designer Albert Rothenstein, who informed him, '. . . you will see from the drawing that it is perfectly possible to make use of scaffold or telegraph poles as trees . . .' and, 'When ordering clothes don't forget they must be sized and prepared for working on . . .' Rothenstein, groggy from having had his tonsils removed a few days before, was still full of enthusiasm: '. . . don't forget that we shall want two Back Cloths, ready primed & prepared for painting on . . .' Brooke's workload was eased mentally by the workforce being joined by Noel Olivier, on holiday from Bedales. The telegrams, letters and notes increased as members of the cast checked rehearsal times, sent apologies for absence and made endless enquiries.

A picnic party near Byrons pool during the May term of 1908. (Left to right) Frances Darwin, Francis Cornford, Eva Speilman, Margery Olivier, Rupert Brooke

52

*Rupert on the Cam with a rather intense-looking Dudley
Ward (left), Jerry Pinsent paddling and Dorothy Osmaston*

Comus had first been presented in the Great Hall at Ludlow Castle on Michaelmas Day, 29 September 1634, with music by Henry Lawes, who, like Brooke, played the Attendant Spirit. Lawes, born in Salisbury in 1600, and a close friend of Milton, is credited with having been the first musician to introduce the Italian style of music into England. As the Spirit, Brooke had the task of handling both the prologue and the epilogue, so the first words the audience would hear would be Rupert's, declaring:

> Before the starry threshold of Jove's court
> My mansion is, where those immortal shapes
> Of bright aerial spirits live insphered
> In regions mild of calm and serene air.
> Above the smoke and stir of this dim spot
> Which men call earth . . .

Francis Cornford, a 33-year-old don, undertook the title role. It was during rehearsals for *Comus* that fellow student Frances Darwin, a granddaughter of the naturalist Charles Darwin, who was to later marry Cornford, composed her famous lines on Brooke:

> A young Apollo, golden-haired
> Stands dreaming on the verge of strife
> Magnificently unprepared
> For the long littleness of life.

Although she later rather regretted having written it, Brooke himself confessed to not minding the Apollo image. Those two words of hers, 'young Apollo', were to change people's perception of Rupert for decades. In 1953, 38 years after his death she wrote:

Certainly there was something legendary about Rupert Brooke's appearance. He might have been born a youth in any century. It was easy to see him as one of Socrates' young men, listening and frowning in the Athenian sun. Again he would have been entirely happy with Chaucer, noticing everything about the Canterbury Pilgrims, in that English mood of laughing at what you care about most. He would have been especially at home in Elizabethan times as a young poet about Court.

Frances saw Brooke as the pivotal figure in their circle of friends, which in effect he had become, having learned the knack of how to be the centre of attention and the central attraction. Bizarrely, he made all those associated with *Comus* solemnly promise that they wouldn't get engaged or married during or within six months of the production – nonsense, of course, and impossible to impose upon anyone. In fact, Frances Darwin and Francis Cornford were the first to break the so-called pact by getting engaged.

Comus, using the original music by Lawes, was repeated at a public matinee on the following day at the New Theatre, Cambridge. Ticket prices ranged from one to three shillings. The reviews for the first night were mixed, though Lytton Strachey, writing kindly of it in *The Spectator*, felt that it was '. . . happily devoid of those jarring elements of theatricality and false taste which too often counterbalance the inherent merits of a dramatic revival'.

Scott & Wilkinson, art photographers who were based at Camden Studio adjoining the New Theatre at Cambridge, wrote to Rupert asking him to '. . . make an appointment with us to be photographed in your character in Milton's *Comus*'. They added that the photographer would 'consider it a personal favour' if Brooke would be willing to pose for them. He posed.

The production of *Comus* was a major feather in Brooke's cap; the Milton tercentenary celebration was attended by such luminaries as the Poet Laureate Alfred Austin, Robert Bridges, who was to become Laureate after Austin's death five years later, the author Edmund Gosse, Lytton Strachey and Thomas Hardy. The production was followed by a dance at Newnham Grange with the whole cast in costume, including Rupert in a rather short, spangled, sky-blue tunic that was far too skimpy to sit down in.

The only shadow cast over the success of *Comus* was the death, during the dress rehearsals, of Brooke's friend and mentor at King's, Walter Headlam, who had encouraged him to undertake a production of the play. Headlam had been taken ill while watching a cricket match at Lord's and later died in hospital of strangulation of the bowels. Rupert was devastated, pouring out his feelings to his mother: '. . . it made me feel quite miserable and ill for days . . . he was the one classic I really admired and liked . . . what I loved so in him was his extraordinary and loving appreciation of all English poetry.'

Hugh Dalton

In the summer of 1908, Brooke and several of his Cambridge friends, including Hugh Dalton, Noel's sister Margery, Ben Keeling, Dudley Ward and James Strachey, attended a Fabian summer school on the Welsh coast, in Merionethshire, some three miles south of Harlech. The first of the Society's summer schools in Llanbedr had taken place the year before, following a suggestion by Fabian member Mabel Atkinson after she had been inspired by a German summer school. At the same time, a similar suggestion had arisen, and Frank Lawson Dodd had devised a scheme by which a large house could be procured for the education and recreation of Fabians during the holidays. The Society put their heads together and came up with a solution: Dodd discovered a house at Llanbedr called Pen-yr-Allt (top of the cliff), while Mabel Atkinson laid down a blueprint for an educational programme. A management committee of 12 was formed, all of whom pledged their own money in ten-year loans, at five per cent interest. They included George Bernard Shaw and his wife, H.G. Wells, and socialists Sydney and Beatrice Webb. On the way to the camp Brooke and the others stayed with Beatrice at Leominster, after which the whole party went to Llanbedr via Ludlow Castle.

Before setting off, Rupert had sent Dalton a postcard claiming he was going to bring 'a blanket, chocolate and 19 books, all in a bag'. Dalton carried a torch for Rupert and was always eager to be in his presence, even though his feelings were not returned. Brooke's rebuffs fired Dalton's passions to greater heights and although no relationship was forthcoming, Dalton was still inspired enough to quote Brooke's poem 'Second Best' in his political speeches, both as Labour MP and as Chancellor of the Exchequer in 1935. When he went down from Cambridge, he pointedly burned all his correspondence, keeping only communication from Rupert. News of Rupert's death some seven years later would find Dalton inconsolable and in floods of tears. Thus Brooke moved people. Brooke also repelled James Strachey's advances and suggestions with gentle humour during the period at Llanbedr.

Pen-yr-Allt became their temporary home for almost a fortnight. The origins of the house go back further than 1869, when a Mr Humphreys converted the old Welsh farmhouse into a fine, family residence complete with its Caernarvon arches, an architectural feature not usually found that far south. It was later inhabited by the Williams family with their 17 children, before becoming a school. Four years before Brooke's arrival, another future poet, Robert Graves, attended the establishment for a term, at the age of eight and three-quarters. It was there that Graves chanced upon the first two poems he remembered reading: the early English ballads of 'Chevy Chase' and 'Sir Andrew Barton'. Here Graves was caned by the headmaster for learning the wrong collect one Sunday, and was terrified by the head's daughter and her girlfriend, who tried to find out about the male anatomy by exploring down his shirt. It was not only girls who frightened him: '. . . there was an open-air swimming bath where all the boys bathed naked, and I was very overcome by horror at the sight.' Brooke had the benefit of the same swimming facilities, which were more like a small plunge bath than today's conception of a pool. The changing hut had a small coal fire, to enable the boys to dry off properly before walking the quarter of a mile back to the house.

During his ten days at Pen-yr-Allt, Rupert attended lectures on Tolstoy and Shaw, long walks, daily exercises and evening dances – a formidable mixture. Fees were set at 35 shillings a week, with half a crown extra for Swedish drill. Despite these, and his comment, 'Oh, the Fabians, I would to God they'd laugh and be charitable', Rupert was not deterred from returning the following year. In between studies, there were not only Fabian meetings, football, rugby and cricket matches, drama societies, and poems to write, but also Carbonari gatherings. These are a few entries from Brooke's Cambridge pocket diary for 1908–9.

Sat 12th Sept 1908	Cornford
Tues 20th Oct 1908	G.L.K. [Geoffrey Langdon Keynes]
Thurs 22nd Oct 1908	Carbonari
Sat 14th Nov 1908	Tea-party – Keynes
Sun 15th Nov 1908	Supper – Justin
Mon 7th Dec 1908	Fabians
Sun 2nd May 1909	Darwins 7.45
Thurs 13th May 1909	Noon – tennis
Mon 7th June 1909	Picnic

Eddie Marsh

It was at one of the Carbonari gatherings that Brooke was properly introduced to Eddie Marsh, then a civil servant at the colonial office, who had first seen Rupert in 1906 in *Eumenides*. A former Apostle of the 1890s and the great-grandson of the assassinated British Prime Minister Spencer Perceval, he was extremely well connected both politically and socially and was later to introduce Brooke into the rarefied atmosphere of these circles. At breakfast, the morning after meeting Marsh, Brooke, who had just won a prize in *The Westminster Gazette* for 'The Jolly Company', showed an impressed Marsh his poem 'Day That I have Loved'.

Day That I Have Loved

Tenderly, day that I have loved, I close your eyes,
And smooth your quiet brow, and fold your thin dead hands.
The grey veils of the half-light deepened; colour dies.
I bear you, a light burden, to the shrouded sands,

Where lies your waiting boat, by wreaths of the sea's making
Mist-garlanded, with all grey weeds of the water crowned.
There you'll be laid, past fear of sleep or hope of waking;
And over the unmoving sea, without a sound,

Faint hands will row you outward, out beyond our sight,
Us with stretched arms and empty eyes on the far-gleaming
And marble sand . . .

Beyond the shifting cold twilight,
Further than laughter goes, or tears, further than dreaming,

There'll be no port, no dawn-lit islands! But the drear
Waste darkening, and, at length, flame ultimate on the deep.
Oh, the last fire – and you, unkissed, unfriended there!
Oh, the lone way's red ending, and we not there to weep!

(We found you pale and quiet, and strangely crowned with flowers,
Lovely and secret as a child. You came with us,
Came happily, hand in hand with the young dancing hours,
High on the downs at dawn!) Void now and tenebrous,

The grey sands curve before me . . .
From the inland meadows,
Fragrant of June and clover, floats the dark, and fills
The hollow sea's dead face with little creeping shadows,
And the white silence brims the hollow of the hills.

Close in the nest is folded every weary wing,
Hushed all the joyful voices; and we, who held you dear,
Eastward we turn and homeward, alone, remembering . . .
Day that I loved, day that I loved, the Night is here!

At the beginning of the Michaelmas term of 1908, a Trinity man who had been at Cambridge two years earlier returned for another year. He was Vyvyan Holland, Oscar Wilde's son, who had recently, at a friend's behest, experimented with using his real surname. He found it an embarrassment, and indeed had dropped the experiment, and by the time he came up again, was using the family's adopted name. 'I got to know Rupert Brooke and A.C. Landsberg, and he used to hold poetry recitals in Firbank's rooms.' When Wilde's close friend Robert Ross, who had done much to try to redeem Wilde's reputation, came to Cambridge on business, Holland and his old Cambridge chum Ronald Firbank threw a supper for him, retaining the menu signed by those present, including Ross and Brooke. They drank Möet et Chandon, 1884.

During 1908, Methuen & Co. published *The Westminster Problems Book*, which included three of Brooke's contributions to the problem page of *The Westminster Gazette*. Two of these were in verse.

A Nursery Rhyme

Up the road to Babylon,
Down the road to Rome,
The King has gone a-riding out
All the way from home.

There were all the folks singing,
And the church-bells ringing,
When the King rode out to Babylon,
Down the road to Rome.

Down the road from Babylon,
Up the road from Rome,
The King came slowly back
All the way back home.

There were all the folks weeping.
And the church-bells sleeping,
When the King rode back from Babylon,
When the King came home.

Fragment Completed

What of the voyage (the Dreamer saith)?
How shall the brave ship go?
Bounding waters to lift her keel,
Winds that follow with favouring breath –
Shall she come to her harbour so?
Up the shimmering tideway steal
To the flying flags, and the bells a-peal,
And the crowds that welcome her home from Death,
And the harbour lights aglow?

What at the end of her seafaring,
What will her tidings be?
Lands in the light of an unknown star?
Midnight waves, and the winds that bring
Scents of the day to be?
Lost little island in seas afar,
Where dreams and shadowy waters are,

And the winds are kindly, and maidens sing,
To the throb of an idle sea?

What of the voyage (the Dreamer saith)?
How hath the good ship come?
(They answered) The Sea is stronger than Dreams,
And what are your laughter and Hope and Faith
To the fury of wind and foam? –
Wreckage of sail, and shattered beams,
An empty hulk upon silent streams,
By the Tides of night to the Harbour of Death,
So hath your Ship come Home.

While he continued to develop as a poet, his passion for Noel Olivier grew. He became infatuated with her, although a strong will, sense of caution and independence instilled in her by school and family kept him firmly at arm's length. Her unavailability fanned the flames of desire to such an extent that Rupert even wrote to Dudley Ward on 20 October, 'Can't she be kidnapped from Bedales?'

The spirit of the pioneering establishment at which she was studying was to affect Brooke via some of the pupils who passed through it. In 1900, the founder of the co-educational Bedales School, J.H. Badley, moved his expanding establishment from Haywards Heath in Sussex to a new home in Hampshire. A 150-acre site just to the north at Petersfield and close to the village of Steep was selected. It has fine views of the Downs towards Butser and Wardown to the south, while to the north, rising to 800 feet, the Beech Hangers from Stoner Hill to the Shoulder of Mutton mark it is a dramatic area of England. The main house on the estate, Steephurst, built in 1716, initially housed the seven girls at the school (compared to 67 boys who had their dormitory in another building), while the architect and former pupil, Geoffrey Lupton, designed a new school building as an addition to the establishment. Badley's creed, still praised by the Bedalians and staff alike in autonomous retrospection, was integrated into his initial prospectus: '. . . to develop their powers in a healthy and organic manner rather than to achieve immediate examination results; and thus to lay a sound basis for subsequent specialisations in any given direction. With this view, body, mind and character as subjects for training are regarded as of equal importance!' Badley, 'the Chief', was, in short, building an alternative to the imperialist sausage machine of the public schools (he, like Brooke, was a Rugbeian), with the focus more on the individual.

Several of the circle that were to become Brooke's friends were Bedalians – Justin Brooke, Jacques Raverat and Noel Olivier – and their way of life and attitude towards it instilled the spirit of the school so strongly in him that he almost felt he had been partially educated there. Bedalian-style camps became a way of life for the group of friends for years. J.H. Badley had laid down the rules for the school camps:

> The camp is always pitched near a bathing place, for Bedalians, like fish, cannot live long out of water. The camp itself consists of four tents – the cook tent, one sleeping tent for the girls and two for the boys. Bedding of straw, bracken or heather is provided, and each camper brings with him three blankets, one of which is sewn up into a sleeping bag. Pillows most of us scorn; the most hardened do without, the others roll up their clothes, and this makes a good substitute . . . Every other day, at least, is spent in a good tramp across the country – ten or fifteen miles at first to get into training, but this may be increased to twenty or even twenty-five later on . . .

Rupert and Noel formed part of a crowd who went skiing at Klosters, Switzerland, at the end of 1908; the 11-day holiday cost him 11 guineas, which he was able to borrow from his mother. While there Brooke helped to compose a melodrama, *From the Jaws of the Octopus*, in which he played the hero, Eugene de Montmorency. They saw the new year in with a whirligig of skiing, tobogganing and youthful exuberance, before Rupert returned to King's, a round of Carbonari meetings, political and social debates, and to take up his role of president of the Cambridge Fabians for the year 1909–10.

Hilaire Belloc – one of Brooke's literary inspirations

61

On 9 February, he entertained in his own rooms, with Hilaire Belloc as the main guest and speaker. Belloc was a good catch, as he had already written some 28 books stretching back to 1896, and 1909 would see another five published, including his epic *Marie Antoinette*. His books were discussed by King Edward VII; and he was the subject of cartoons in *Punch*. Rupert knew many of Belloc's poems by heart and certainly some of his songs. The outpourings of the beer-loving Anglophile from La Celle St Cloud in France had far-reaching influences on Brooke's poems. These lines from Belloc's 'West Sussex Drinking Song'

> They sell good beer at Hazelmere
> And under Guildford Hill
> At little Cowfold as I've been told
> A beggar may drink his fill;
> There is good brew at Amberley too,
> And by the bridge also;
> But the swipes they sell in the Washington Inn
> Is the very best beer I know.

with their naming of places in Sussex and Surrey villages, are not dissimilar in their roots to sections of a poem Brooke would write in 1912: 'The Old Vicarage, Grantchester', in which he used place names local to Cambridge.

> Strong men have run for miles and miles,
> When one from Cherry Hinton smiles;
> Strong men have blanched, and shot their wives,
> Rather than send them to St Ives;
> Strong men have cried like babes, bydam,
> To hear what happened at Babraham.
> But Grantchester! ah Grantchester!
> There's peace and holy quiet there, . . .

As well as Belloc's words, Brooke was clearly impressed by the exhilarating manner, uproarious humour and powerful gift of speech of this larger-than-life character, who appeared to exist on a diet of beer and cheese.

The Athenian comic dramatist Aristophanes was not so much of an influence. Brooke declared his play *The Frogs*, written around 400 BC, to be a farce after seeing it in Oxford during February 1909, declaring to his mother that it was 'quite extraordinarily bad'. Notwithstanding his opinion, *The Frogs*, *The Birds* and *The Wasps*, three of Aristophanes most famous plays have certainly achieved a certain amount of durability!

With the spring approaching, Rupert was temporarily without holiday plans. There were thoughts of Wales, Devon, Cornwall, and even Belgium and Holland, when he realised that he could get from London to Rotterdam for just 13 shillings. 'In April,' he declared, 'I shall be God let loose!'

A Saint

I left the tomb where pilgrims prayed
To walk upon the hills apart,
And in the blackest of the shade,
I thought of Evil in my heart.

What were the prayer and praise to me,
The shrine, and many lights therein?
One night of all eternity
I know the lonely truth of sin.

For I was tired of all the chaunting
And all the chaunting dreary grew,
And always I felt something wanting,
That my perfection never knew.

So, from the world most far apart,
In the blind darkness only I,
I thought of Evil in my heart,
Alone between the earth and sky.

There was no light; And no thing stirred.
I thought, and chuckled. Suddenly
I crouched in fear, because I heard
A sound of music near to me;

A music many players made,
Of flutes and lutes and of timbrels;
And I knew that somewhere in the shade,
God was dancing on His hills.
And all the night He leapt and trod,
To the courtly flute and mad timbrels;
God whirling and pacing, a stately God;
God's lonely dance among the hills!

CHAPTER *IV*

The Dew-dabblers

The plan of driving a donkey cart through Holland was forgotten as Rupert discovered Becky Falls, on the edge of Dartmoor. On 25 March, he extolled the virtues of the local topography in a letter to his cousin Erica: 'My view from the window before me includes a lawn, flower-beds with many flowers, a waterfall, rocks and trees, forests, mountains and the sky. It covers some twenty miles of country and no houses.'

From under the shadow of Hound Tor to the south-west, Becky, or Becka, Falls, tumbles and plunges some 70 feet over vast granite boulders becoming the Becca Brook, which eventually joins the River Bovey to the east of the Falls. The stamp of the Iron and Bronze Age inhabitants on the area is very marked, with burrows, cairns and hut circles littering an area rich in natural and spectacular beauty. Manaton, a derivation of Maleston – Robert de Maleston having been given the manor by Edward I – is the parish in which the Falls lie, and at the time when Rupert Brooke, Lytton Strachey and their circle came to write here, there were just 300 or so people living in the area. From late Victorian times Becky Falls farmhouse, with its 60 acres, was occupied by Mr and Mrs Hern and their son Bob, the buildings comprising a sixteenth-century stone farmhouse with three bedrooms, a cowshed, milking parlour and Beechwood cottage, a two-bedroom Victorian structure.

Lytton Strachey was already staying at the Falls at Rupert's suggestion, when Brooke and Hugh Russell-Smith arrived, following advice that Rupert should terminate his studies of Classics and concentrate on English Literature for his fourth year at Cambridge. Strachey was working on *Landmarks in French Literature*. In letters to friends, descriptive passages about this part of Devon which he had just discovered flowed from Rupert's pen, with almost the speed and majesty of the Falls themselves. To Erica he wrote, 'I am leading the healthy life. I rise early, twist myself about on a kind of pulley that

Looking up to the farm house at Becky Falls where Brooke waxed lyrical about the
'. . . rocks and trees, forests, mountains and the sky'

is supposed to make my chest immense (but doesn't), eat no meat, wear very little, do not part my hair, take frequent cold baths, work ten hours a day and rush madly about the mountains in flannels and rainstorms for hours.' And to his close friend Dudley Ward, 'Here it rains infinitely. But I – I dance through the rain, singing musically snatches of old Greek roundelays. Have you ever seen me in my mackintosh walking-cape dancing seventeen miles in the rain?' Jacques Raverat also received a missive: 'We walked for hours a day. On one side were woods, strangely covered with green and purple by spring, and on the other great moors. The sunsets were yellow wine. And the wind! – oh! there was never such a wind to take you and shake you and roll you over and set you shouting with laughter.'

The author John Galsworthy lived at Wingston Farm near Manaton for 18 years until moving into Bury House, Sussex, in 1926. It was here he wrote *The Forsyte Saga* and other works, but there is no record of Brooke having visited him, although his friend David 'Bunny' Garnett did in 1914, just before the outbreak of war.

The Herns, the farmhouse tenants who played host to Brooke, were described by another visitor, Peggy Cornwell: 'Mr and Mrs Hern were lovely people. Mrs Hern used to come up each morning with a tray of tea for mother and wedges of that home-made bread, spread with clotted cream for us little ones.' The Herns' son Bob continued to run the place until the 1950s, when it was described as a 'large tea garden – set in surroundings of majestic beauty'.

By April 1909, Rupert was further west, at another gathering of the Apostles on the furthest tip of the Lizard, Cornwall. It was essentially a reading party, organised by G.E. Moore, who had been at Trinity with Edward Marsh and had become an Apostle in the early 1890s, at the same time as Bertrand Russell. Moore, in his early thirties at the time of this 'coming together' at the Lizard, was certainly a great influence on Brooke, who found the older man's philosophies and attitude to life absorbing, and his personality infectious, despite his dislike of Fabianism. Moore was also a gifted pianist and singer. Their base, Penmenner House ('Pen' meaning headland and 'menner' standing stones) is one of Britain's most southerly houses and was built around 1860 by Thomas Rowe. On his death in 1881, his Irish wife, Grace, lived there until her death in 1914. The eight-bedroomed dwelling that she was running at the time of Brooke's visit afforded panoramic sea views in all directions and views of the Lizard Lighthouse, as well as access to the path across the cliffs. This idyllic setting proved to be a great attraction to writers. It is said that Oscar Wilde came here to read to the locals, but the members of G.E. Moore's reading party offered no such public declamations, keeping their philosophies, poetry and readings within the confines of their own circle. Among the Cambridge Apostles at the gathering were the drama critic Desmond MacCarthy, barrister and author C.P. Sanger, author Leonard Woolf, poet and playwright R.S. 'Bob' Trevelyan (another leading Fabian), James Strachey, and Lytton Strachey. Strachey, some years before, had described the setting of Penmenner House in a letter to his mother as being 'nose to nose with the sea'. Brooke described the house in a letter from there to Dudley Ward: '. . . the house is twelve miles from a station and the posts are said to be irregular . . .' To Jacques Raverat he enthused that he went '. . . luggageless, and strange, and free, to The Lizard; and stayed some days. Cornwall was full of heat and tropical flowers: and all day I bathed in great creamy breakers of surf, or lay out in the sun to dry (in April!); and all night argued with a philosopher, an economist, and a writer. Ho, we put the world to rights!'

The bays of Kynance and Housel were just a short stroll from the house, low tide revealing hundreds of rocky outcrops, and at Kynance a beautiful expanse of sandy beach. The extraordinarily warm weather and subsequent swimming activities brought pressure to bear on the desires of James Strachey, who had longed for an active relationship with the uninterested Brooke. James wrote to his brother, Lytton, '. . . for the first time in my life, I saw Rupert naked. Can't we imagine what *you'd* say on such an occasion? . . . but *I'm* simply inadequate of course. So I say nothing, except that I didn't have an erection – which was fortunate as I was naked too. I thought him – if you'd like to have a pendant – "absolutely beautiful".'

After the brief sojourn by the Cornish sea, the peripatetic Brooke was off

Margery Olivier, Dudley Ward and Rupert at Beech Shade – April 1909

again, this time to the depths of the New Forest, the main attraction being the presence of the object of his desires, Noel Olivier. Although Brooke's letters and correspondence from there are headed 'Bank, Lyndhurst', the hamlet in which the house Beech Shade is situated is deeper into the forest, past Bank, in a cluster of some half dozen cottages called Gritnam, at the end of a track deep in the forest. Initially discovered by leading Cambridge University socialist Ben Keeling, the area may have been brought to his attention through Virginia Woolf, who stayed at Lane End House in Bank during 1904 and 1905. Bank, and nearby Lyndhurst, attracted many writers during the 1880s, as well as the inspiration for one: Alice Liddell, the model for Lewis Carroll's *Alice's Adventures in Wonderland* and *Through the Looking Glass*, lived at Bank, after marrying a local man, Reginald Hargreaves. Gritnam, small as it is, is mentioned in the 'Domesday Book' as Greteha (the Great Homestead) – its area being 'half a hide', some 120 acres, and the whole being held by the romantically named Waleron Hunter.

Noel's sister Margery had organised a Newhamite reading party at Beech Shade, which included not only Noel, but also Cambridge friends Evelyn Radford and Dorothy Osmaston. The rooms were let to them by Alice Primmer, née Hawkins, and her new husband, former army officer, Harry, who was a stud groom at Wilverly Park, Lyndhurst, at the time of the reading party, later becoming Master of the Hounds before his death in 1925. Learning that Noel would be at Bank, Rupert contrived, through Dudley

Ward, who let him know the exact location, to drop in on the party as if by chance. Full of the joys of spring, he recounted his arrival in the New Forest in a letter to Jacques Raverat, liberally spiced with flights of poetic fancy:

> But then, after the Lizard, oh! then came the Best! And none knows of it. For I was lost for four days. I was, for the first time in my life, a free man, and my own master! . . . For I went dancing and leaping through the New Forest, with £3 and a satchel full of books, talking to everyone I met, mocking and laughing at them. Sleeping and eating anywhere, singing to the birds, tumbling about in the flowers, bathing in the rivers and in general behaving naturally. And all in England, at Eastertide! And so I walked and laughed and met many people and made a thousand songs – all very good – and in the end of the days, came to a woman who was more glorious than the Sun and stronger than the Sea and kinder than the Earth, who is a flower made out of fire, a star that laughs all day, whose brain is clean and clear like a man's, and her heart is full of courage and kindness and whom I love. I told her that the Earth was crowned with wind flowers and dancing down the violet ways of Spring; that Christ had died and Pan was risen; that her mouth was like sunlight on a gull's wing. As a matter of fact, I believe I said 'Hullo! Isn't it rippin' weather! . . .'

Although Margery had been the instigator of the reading party, her presence did not make for an easy passage for Rupert, as a little jealousy, combined with her dual roles of guardian and older sister, meant that she watched over them. Despite that, Noel and Rupert managed walks in the woods together and some time alone, although it seems that his frustration with her 'cheerful, clear, flat platitudes' came through clearly at the end of 'The Voice', a poem inspired by the few days at Beech Shade.

The Voice

Safe in the magic of my woods
I lay, and watched the dying light.
Faint in the pale high solitudes,
And washed with rain and veiled by night,

Silver and blue and green were showing.
And the dark woods grew darker still;
And birds were hushed; and peace was growing;
And quietness crept up the hill;

And no wind was blowing . . .

And I knew
That this was the hour of knowing,
And the night and the woods and you
Were one together, and I should find
Soon in the silence the hidden key
Of all that had hurt and puzzled me –
Why you were you, and the night was kind,
And the woods were part of the heart of me.

And there I waited breathlessly,
Alone; and slowly the holy three,
The three that I loved, together grew
One, in the hour of knowing,
Night, and the woods, and you –

And suddenly
There was an uproar in my woods,
The noise of a fool in mock distress,
Crashing and laughing and blindly going,
Of ignorant feet and a swishing dress,
And a voice profaning the solitudes.

The spell was broken, the key denied me,
And at length your flat clear voice beside me
Mouthed cheerful clear flat platitudes.

You came and quacked beside me in the wood.
You said 'The view from here is very good!'
You said 'It's nice to be alone a bit!'
And 'How the days are drawing out!' you said.
You said 'The sunset's pretty isn't it?'

By God! I wish – I wish that you were dead!

During the few days at Bank, one of the party was extremely camera-happy
– presumably Dorothy Osmaston, as she does not appear in any of the many
photographs taken outside Beech Shade.

'The Voice' was tidied up and completed at Sidmouth, where Rupert, after
his few days in what he termed 'Arcady', at last arrived joining his parents and
Aunt Fanny at the holiday hotel where they were staying. Aunt Lizzie, with

Rupert outside Beech Shade – April 1909

whom Fanny shared Grantchester Dene in Bournemouth, had died on 9 April and this was by way of a recuperative holiday for her.

Long considered a 'fashionable watering place' for the wealthy in the eighteenth and nineteenth centuries, Sidmouth became a health resort for the old and sickly, despite the street being deep in mud during the winter, and carts moving around to lay the dust in the summer. The roadways were made of cracked flints bonded with clay and flattened with a horse-drawn roller, the horses creating their own form of pollution which ended up on the municipal manure dump on Bedford Lawn – on a hot day, too close for comfort to the Esplanade. When Rupert came to the resort at the mouth of the River Sid in April 1909, the fishing fleet had 23 'drifters' in which the local fisherman would drift for mackerel; on fine evenings the town turned out to watch them sail away, as Brooke may well have done from his bedroom window at Gloucester House on the Esplanade, a part of York Terrace. The following winter brought a sudden disappearance of the herring, due partly to severe weather and more industrial methods being employed; the fishing industry was never the same again in Sidmouth. During Rupert's stay, the beach was decorated with a dancing bear, barrel organ, hurdy-gurdy, crab, cockle and nougat vendors, a penny photographer, pony rides and bathing machines.

Lines on a monument to Mary Lisle (d. 1791) in Sidmouth churchyard:

Blest with soft airs from health restoring skies
Sidmouth! to thee the drooping patient flies
Ah! not unfailing is thy poet to save
To her thou gavest no refuge, but a grave!
Guard it mild Sidmouth, and revere its store
More precious, none shall ever touch thy shore

The rooms Rupert's parents had taken were often favoured by the actor/manager and builder of His Majesty's Theatre, Herbert Beerbohm Tree. The proprietor of Gloucester House was a Miss Couling and the Brookes' fellow guests were a Mrs and Miss Sitzer. Rupert stayed from 13 to 20 April. Before he arrived, he wrote to Dudley Ward, '. . . if I am going to join my people at Sidmouth (the bloody latest!) on Tuesday morning, pretending to have arrived from Cornwall that moment, I must be up on their last letters to me.' The elaborate deception seems to have passed off without a hitch, his parents remaining totally oblivious to the fact that he had spent four days in the New Forest.

The visitors list in the *Sidmouth Observer* mentioned the Brookes staying

Sidmouth in Brooke's day. Gloucester House, the hotel where he stayed with his parents and his Aunt Fanny, is on the left

there for several weeks, the page on which their name appeared also displaying an advertisement for the latest popular air, 'A New National Song' called 'Wake Up England'.

While at Sidmouth Rupert finished a sonnet, the seeds of which had been sown during the three days at Bank. In it his feelings for Noel shine through.

Sonnet

Oh! Death will find me, long before I tire
Of watching you; and swing me suddenly
Into the shade and loneliness and mire
Of the last land! There, waiting patiently

One day, I think, I'll feel a cool wind blowing
See a slow light across the Stygian tide
And hear the Dead about me stir, unknowing
And tremble. And I shall know that you have died

And watch you, a broad-browed and smiling dream
Pass, light as ever, through the listless host

Quietly ponder, start, and sway, and gleam
Most individual and bewildering ghost!

And turn and toss your brown delightful head
Amusedly, among the ancient Dead.

Brooke wrote from Sidmouth to fellow King's man Geoffrey Fry, who would later be knighted for his work in the Civil Service, 'yet England, My England (Henley) is to use an old-fashioned word, nice' and, 'there is a grey sea like this . . . and a grey sky like this . . . and I have just read *Cymbeline*'. On 15 April he wrote to Eddie Marsh, 'Returning on reluctant and bare feet from a long period of fantastic roaming, to the bosom of my sad family in their present seaside resort, I have found documents from King's that passionately demand my presence earlier than I had thought.' The following day he wrote to Hugh Dalton:

> You will wonder why Simple Life ends in a Seaside Resort and lined paper. It looks a little like Second Childhood, doesn't it? I think it is merely the first, revenant, but it is all too difficult to explain. I play a great deal on the beach. On reluctant and naked feet I turned from the violet wilderness to the sad breast of my family in their present seaside resort. For the first time in three weeks I wear a tie; almost a collar. This is a bloody place. And in this house Mr Joseph Hocking was staying a week ago; and, last year, Mr Beerbohm Tree and family! I move, as ever, you see, among the tinsel Stars.

Other 'tinsel stars' associated with Sidmouth included Elizabeth Barrett Browning, who lived there with her family from 1832 in Fortfield Terrace and Cedar Shade (then called Belle Vue), before moving to Wimpole Street in London in 1835. Jane Austen and William Makepeace Thackeray were two other eminent authors with strong Sidmouth connections. Gloucester House where the Brookes stayed is still as much as it was, only no longer bearing the name, and now incorporated into the Royal York and Faulkener Hotel, which began as the York, the first purpose-built hotel in Sidmouth – the 'Royal' prefix emanating from Edward VII's presence there when he was still Prince of Wales.

Having received a welcome financial prize from *The Westminster Gazette* for his poem 'The Voice', Rupert headed back to Cambridge via London, staying at 5 Raymond Buildings, Gray's Inn, with Eddie Marsh. By now Marsh was becoming an increasing influence in artistic circles, as well as in London's social and political arena, into which he was beginning to introduce Rupert.

In the ancient manor of Portpoole, Old Gray's Inn was bounded to the south by Holeburn Street, the Roman road which entered the City of London at New Gate, while to the east lay the town residence of Bishopric, later known as Ely Palace. To the north open fields stretched to Highgate, and to the west there was more country landscape, known as Jockey Fields. Raymond Buildings, on the west side of Gray's Inn, were built in the early 1800s on part of the gardens formerly known as the black walks, the southerly end of the impressive six-storey terrace rising on Bacon's Mount, where Francis Bacon had once constructed a 30-foot-high mound topped by a summerhouse. As others, including Brooke, would come to also, Bacon the philosopher loved the tranquillity of the walks; he wrote of them in his essay on gardens, 'God Almighty first planted a garden and indeed it is the "Pursuit of Human Pleasure".' The buildings were named after Sir Robert Raymond, as they were originally to be erected in 1725 when he was Chief Justice, although fate decreed they were not to grace the site until, as it proclaims over the door of number five, 1825, when George IV was halfway through his ten-year reign.

Brooke had become the pin-up of Cambridge and Marsh, like others, was captivated by the Old Rugbeian's looks and charisma. He kept a close watch on the young poet, inviting him to stay whenever he liked at 5 Raymond Buildings, which he did frequently as Rupert's gravitational pull towards London became stronger, so adding to the already colourful history of the area. But however much the literary and social activities lured him to the capital, they would never surpass his love of the English countryside.

The gatehouse at King's College Cambridge

74

Three years later, in his poem 'The Old Vicarage, Grantchester' Brooke would write, '. . . At Over they fling oaths at one . . .', but in May 1909 the locals may have had good reason to fling oaths, when Rupert and a crowd of Cambridge friends packed into Justin Brooke's German Opel motor car – surely a terrifying sight in any sleepy hamlet at that time – and nearly crashed the car there on the way to Overcote.

For centuries, Over depended on the River Ouse and the Fens for its existence, in Norman times the river being full of fish and wild fowl plentiful in the area (although now the closest point to the River Ouse, which at one time flowed much nearer to the actual village, is at Overcote, two miles over the fields). Catches were dispatched daily to many cities, including London. In 1630 the Earl of Bedford appointed the Dutch engineer Vermuyden to drain the Fens, causing angry locals who feared for their livelihood to wreck the dykes as fast as they were being built. Despite this opposition, 21-mile-long canals, known as the Old and New Bedford Rivers, were successfully constructed as well as red-back houses in the Dutch style being erected in Over. Woad, the blue dye with which the ancient Britons daubed themselves, was grown extensively around Over in the tenth century, which brought the cloth trade to the area. Architecture of the thirteenth, fourteenth and fifteenth centuries is still in evidence there.

On 2 May, the near-accident avoided, the Opel, with Justin Brooke at the wheel, Rupert, Geoffrey Keynes, Gwen and Margaret Darwin from Newnham Grange, and Ka Cox and Dorothy Lamb from Newnham College, rumbled down the track from Over to Overcote, where there was nothing more than a ferry and a small inn on the other side of the river. They laid out their breakfast at the edge of a meadow, where a crab apple was in bloom and a nightingale sang – an idyllic scene, despite only a watery sun and damp grass, inspiring Rupert to read aloud from Robert Herrick's poem 'Corinna's Going a-Maying':

> Come let us goe, while we are in our prime
> And take the harmlesse and follie of the time.
> We shall grow old apace, and die
> Before we know our liberty.
> Our life is short: and our dayes run
> As fast away as does the summer.

Through such early-morning escapades, at Cambridge they swiftly earned themselves the nickname of 'dew-dabblers', running barefoot through the grass at dawn, and making wreaths of apple blossom and chains of cowslips and daisies. The 'dew-dabbling' was so successful that it was repeated later that month, the party this time including Rupert, Justin Brooke, Keynes,

Trinity scholar Jerry Pinsent, Dudley Ward, Donald Robertson and three women thought to be the Darwins – Margaret, Frances and Gwen – although 43 years on, Donald Robertson, who was photographed wrestling with Rupert at the gathering, and Dudley Ward could not agree on their identity when writing to Geoffrey Keynes in 1952. He thought the women could have included Dorothy Osmaston and Evelyn Radford, confessing, '. . . the kneeling man defeats us all . . .'

Rupert and Donald Robertson wrestling during a picnic at Overcote, Cambridgeshire. The onlookers include (standing right to left) Dudley Ward, Geoffrey Keynes, Justin Brooke and Jerry Pinsent

CHAPTER V

First of May 1933

Before sitting for his Tripos in May, Rupert's thoughts turned to taking rooms out of King's, a few miles upstream, at Grantchester. The village was a key locality in pre-Roman times, as the River Granta could be forded there, the Fens circumvented and the dense forest leading south-west to the Chilterns avoided. In Roman times the Icknield Way, the Ermine Street and the Akeman Street all passed close enough to Cambridge to make the crossing of the Granta a position of importance. Grantabrycge is mentioned in a chronicle of AD 875 and is on the site of an early Roman settlement. The small cluster of houses had been known by at least 24 names or variants of spelling by the time it acquired its present name during the fourteenth century. A.C. Benson, a friend of Brooke's and student at Magdalene College, wrote of the village in an article 'Along the Road' for the church family newspaper:

> There is a little village near Cambridge called Grantchester, with an old church and pleasant homely houses among orchards and gardens. The hamlet dips down to the river by Trumpington Mill – the scene of one of Chaucer's tales which solidly and sturdily bestrides the Leat, that flows from the upper waters of the Cam, here called the Granta. It is a place of perfect English charm. The long high-towering woods of Trumpington Hall fringe the stream and the water-meadows and the pool where Byron used to bathe; the great clear mill-pool swirls and eddies below the mill.

Brooke's intimacy with the Granta was such that he became adept at paddling in a small boat the three miles from Cambridge to Grantchester, even on a moonless night and through overgrown stretches of the river. One of his

Mrs Stevenson and her team eager to prove that there is '. . . honey still for tea'

friends Sybil Pye recalled how '. . . he would know, he said, when we were nearing home by the sound of a certain poplar tree that grew there: its leaves rustled faintly even on such a night as this, when not a breath seemed to be stirring . . .' He had walked there on several occasions and taken tea at the Orchard. First planted in 1868, the Orchard became a popular place for taking tea purely by chance in 1897, after a Cambridge student, having punted up the Granta from the area behind the colleges known as 'the backs', asked Mrs Stevenson of Orchard House if she could possibly serve him and some fellow students tea, beneath the apple trees. She assented, and the students, so enjoying the experience, spread the word; and their enthusiasm turned it into a popular 'up-river resort' for all the colleges. The late-Victorian students of 1897 weren't the first to grace the area. For over 700 years Cambridge scholars had ventured to Grantchester by boat, foot, or horse, including such eminent names as Cromwell, Milton, Wordsworth, Coleridge, Newton, Darwin, Marlowe and Spenser. A frequent visitor to the Orchard was the philosopher, mathematician and essayist Bertrand Russell who, for ten years, lived two doors away, the other side of the Old Vicarage, at the Mill House; his Austrian pupil, the suicidal Ludwig Wittgenstein, was often to be seen working off his excess mental energy by running along the banks of the river. Rupert idly wondered whether there was a possibility of taking rooms in Grantchester.

In cavalier fashion he wrote to Noel Olivier:

At eleven o'clock in the morning I finished the last of my Classical Tripos. There were 108 other candidates in the room, but they all stayed the full time, till noon. They write longer, better papers than mine. (They all wear spectacles) . . . I screamed with laughter, suddenly; and the hundred & eight turned round and blinked. I nodded at the hairless don who was in command, & ran cheerily out of the room, tearing the examination paper to bits as I went . . .

No sooner was the exam over than his romantic side sprang into action. 'Oh lo! The South! The lakes of Surrey! They call me! And I shall possibly see Noel in the distance! . . . And then to have to pack a bag! And even that is a ritual of infinite joy and calm splendour . . .'

His destination was again the Cotterills' house at Godalming, although Noel and Bedales was his real goal. His infatuation with Noel continued unabated, while she exercised a natural caution and independence. She maintained a distance that continually fuelled his verbal passions and outpourings. He wrote to Noel at Bedales on 28 May 1909, 'Why should I do more than observe you in a distant crowd? Why, rather, come to Bedales at all? . . . I want to see you; and, as things are at present, I shall come over to Bedales, under the high protection of an OB [Old Bedalian], wander about, talk with Badley [the headmaster], and, ultimately, find out if I am allowed to talk to you. You can, and may, evade or stop me. (Surely we have got beyond the last insult of politeness?)' Noel responded on 1 June, 'I too always have the fear of you – the outsider – looking a fool and my feeling one; but as the last depends on the first, and the first depends on you, I am willing to risk owning your acquaintance, if you like?' Her postscript adds, 'She wishes you weren't coming; but she daren't say so outright, for fear of offending your pride!'

Writing from Coombe Field, Godalming, Rupert responded furiously on 2 June: 'You're a devil! Beginning by assigning a time, going on to water it down . . . and ending with a postscript in the third person, but referring, as far as the meagre wit classics have left me can discover, to you, and changing the whole thing, and leaving me cr-r-rushed!' He wrote as an adolescent lovesick schoolboy, although nearly 22, while Noel, at 17, responded with measured adult caution, sometimes her tone being incredibly brusque, as at the end of a letter written to Rupert from Bedales: 'I'm sorry – I'm in a very bad rage because I've been doing easy exams badly – a thing you never did, so you can't sympathise. Don't try . . . from Noel.'

In amongst the angst there was light relief. The King's magazine *Basileon* carried Gerald Shove's tongue-in-cheek freshers' guide to the college clubs and societies, including the Carbonari.

THE CARBONARI
Objects: The production of minor poets and strong silent politicians.
Subscriptions: All payments are made in kind – verse and epigrams preferred.
Qualifications: Culture: long hair; old pumps (or carpet-slippers).

The magazine also sent up the first Carbonari Ball, claiming that various unlikely performances would occur during the evening, culminating with the news that 'Mr RUPERT BROOKE will perform a dream-dance on tip-toe'. The organ also carried two of Brooke's poems, 'Day and Night' and 'Sonnet'.

Sonnet

All night the ways of Heaven were desolate,
Long roads across a gleaming empty sky.
Outcast and doomed and driven, you and I,
Alone, serene beyond all love or hate,
Terror or triumph, were content to wait,
We, silent and all-knowing. Suddenly
Swept through the heavens, low-crouching from on high,
One horseman, downward to the earth's low gate!

Oh! perfect from the ultimate height of living,
Lightly we turned, through wet woods blossom-hung,
Into the open. Down the supernal roads,
With plumes a-tossing, purple flags far-flung,
Rank upon rank, unbridled, unforgiving,
Thundered the black battalions of the Gods.

During the summer of 1909, socialising, poetry and the Fabian Society were making such an increasing demand on Brooke's time that his tutor suggested that he should not only give up Classics to concentrate on English Literature during his fourth year, but also move out of King's – preferably out of town altogether, away from the temptations of the social scene. So by June, Rupert had fulfilled at least one desire – to take rooms at the Orchard in Grantchester.

Having settled in to his new home, Rupert wrote from there to Noel:

I am in the country in Arcadia; a rustic. It is a village two miles from Cambridge, up the river. You know the place; it is near all picnicking

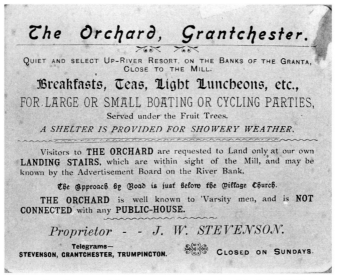

Brooke moved into rooms at the Orchard in July 1909

grounds. And here I work at Shakespeare and see very few people . . .
I wander about barefoot and almost naked, surveying nature with a
calm eye. I do not pretend to understand nature, but I get on very
well with her in a neighbourly way. I go on with my books, and she
goes on with her hens and storms and things, and we're both very
tolerant. Occasionally we have tea together . . . I live on honey, eggs
and milk, prepared for me by an old lady like an apple (especially in
face) and sit all day in a rose garden to work. Of a morning Dudley
Ward and a shifting crowd come out from Cambridge and bathe with
me, have breakfast (out in the garden, as all meals) and depart.

Noel dealt Brooke a curt, sarcastic, down-to-earth response to this latest
epistle, which was adorned with exaggerations about his surroundings and
lifestyle:

I don't quite see how it is you can enjoy breakfast – and all meals – but
especially breakfast in a rose garden in this sort of weather, I should
think the butter would be too hard and frozen and the coffee – I beg
your pardon, of course you don't drink such poisonous stimulants, but
milk – the milk too diluted with dirty rain water – dirty with
Cambridge soots – to be enjoyable. But no doubt you have a
tremendous capacity for enjoyment, only I wish you wouldn't talk
about Nature in that foolish and innocent tone of voice – you call it
making jokes, and I suppose you think it's nice, but I don't like it a bit
– I've told you why lots of times.

Breakfast at the Orchard (left to right) Brooke, Bryn Olivier,
A.Y. Campbell, Jacques Raverat and Geoffrey Keynes

The breakfast table from the other direction (clockwise)
Campbell, Raverat, Keynes, Hugh Morgan, Dudley Ward
with Ethel Pye in the foreground

He also wrote to his cousin Erica with a description of his new abode.

> I've been home for ten days and came here on Friday. It is a lovely village on the river above Cambridge. I'm in a small house, a sort of cottage, with a dear plump weather-beaten kindly old lady in control. I have a perfectly glorious time, seeing nobody I know day after day. The room I have opens straight out onto a stone verandah covered with creepers, and a little old garden full of old-fashioned flowers and crammed with roses . . .

That July, the eminent Welsh-born painter Augustus John camped by the Orchard, in the field by the river, prompting Brooke to write to Noel:

> Augustus John (the greatest painter) (of whom I told you) with his wife and seven children (all ages between 3 and 7 years) with their two caravans and a gypsy tent, are encamped by the river, a few hundred yards from here – I go and see them sometimes and they come here for meals . . . yesterday Donald Robertson, Dudley Ward and I took them all (the children) up the river in punts, gave them tea and played with them. They talked to us of an imaginary world of theirs, where the river was milk, the mud honey, the reeds and trees green sugar, the earth cake, the leaves of the trees (that was odd) ladies' hats, and the sky Robin's blue pinafore . . . Robin was the smallest . . .

The arrival of John, with his gypsy-like countenance, immense stature, earrings and long red beard, caused such a stir in Grantchester and Cambridge that expeditions were organised by the likes of Jacques Raverat to the field in which John was camping. Their intrigue and fascination at the unusual sight moved John to comment: '. . . we cause a good deal of astonishment in this well-bred town.' At a time when gypsies were being persecuted, John was desperately trying to imitate their lifestyle and become a non-blood brother. Eddie Marsh had already bought one of his·paintings and Rupert himself was 'quite sick and faint with passion' on seeing another of his works, and decided to set aside enough money to buy two A.J. drawings. While Augustus John was causing a stir in the meadows of Grantchester, Rupert was creating his own ripples at King's. This profile on him appeared in *The Granta* written by Hugh Dalton:

> Rupert Brooke came into residence at Cambridge in October 1906. The populace first became aware of him when they went to see the Greek play of that year, *The Eumenides*, and many of them have not yet forgotten his playing of the Herald.

He brought with him to Cambridge a reputation both as an athlete and as a poet, a combination supposed by vulgar people to be impossible.

He represented Rugby at cricket and football, rose to high rank in the Volunteer Corps, and was not unknown as a steeplechaser. He also won a prize poem . . .

At Cambridge he has forsaken a few old friends and entered many new ones. While a Freshman he used on occasions to represent his college in various branches of athletics, but soon dropped the habit, in spite of protests. On his day he is still an irresistible tennis player, preferring to play barefooted, and to pick up the balls with his toes.

As an actor *The Eumenides* provided him with not only his only triumph. He was one of the founders of the Marlowe Dramatic Society, which still flourishes, and among his later successes may be counted his performances in Marlowe's Faustus and in Comus during the Milton celebrations.

He has continued to write poems, some of which should be familiar to readers of *The Westminster Gazette* and *The Cambridge Review*. But the rest and certain other writings, not in verse, are known as yet only to a few, and mainly to certain King's Societies of which he is a member.

Some of us hope that the world will one day know more of them.

He is also a politician. His public utterances have indeed been few, though he once made a speech at the joint meeting of the Fabian Society and the Liberal Club, which two ex-presidents of the Union may still remember. But public speaking is not the only function of the politician, though the contrary opinion is sometimes held. For two years he has been a prominent member of the Fabian Society, of which he is now President. He is sometimes credited with having started a new fashion in dress, the chief features of which are the absence of collars and headgear and the continual wearing of slippers.

He will tell you that he did not really begin to live till he went out of college at the end of his third year and took up his residence at the Orchard, Grantchester.

It is said that there he lives the rustic life, broken by occasional visits to Cambridge; that he keeps poultry and a cow, plays simple tunes on a pan pipe, bathes every evening at sunset, and takes all his meals in a rose garden.

On the academic side of his Cambridge activities, Brooke achieved a second in his Classical Tripos in the summer of 1909, after which, in July, he was off again, 'restless as a paper scrap that's tossed down dusty pavements by the wind', for a second visit to the Fabian summer school at Llanbedr. The general manager of the school was Mary Hankinson, who was very popular with the students but felt that the set-up should be more focused on dancing, sports, walks and pastimes, punctuated by some educational facilities and lectures; Sidney and Beatrice Webb, on the other hand, felt that it should be a learning establishment, with leisure activities available when time allowed. The main thrust of the Webbs' lectures was centred on the outdated Poor Law of 1834. For months Rupert had read and reread the Fabian Society's book, *The Minority Report of the Poor Law Commission*, which set out the Fabian views. These differed from those in a review which had been set up by Balfour's government in 1905. The basic Fabian premise was that each case of poverty should be considered on its merit and treated accordingly, unlike the outdated Victorian approach of lumping together the infirm, dissolute, mentally ill, old and unemployed as 'the poor'.

For this and the previous summer, the summer school had proved so popular that a further Llanbedr house was secured. Caer-meddyg (the doctor's house in the field) was relatively new, having been built in 1905 as a retreat for the elderly and infirm, as the on-site spring allegedly possessed restorative properties. Were there no ailing ageds during the Fabian occupation, or was the good doctor's apparent altruism temporarily affected by hard Fabian cash? It was here that the famous photograph of Brooke and other young Fabians clustered around an ornate fireplace was taken. There were strict rules governing meals, lecture times, 'lights out', noise after hours and times that musical instruments and phonography could be played, and there was a total ban on alcohol. Owen, the gardener at the other summer-school house at Pen-yr-Allt, would have been a familiar sight to Rupert, as he undertook odd jobs, as well as ensuring that the garden was in good order for the early morning Swedish drill classes that were held before the morning dew had evaporated. The activities of the Fabians worried the locals, who were concerned that a revolutionary uprising was being organised in their village. The ghost of the Roman general Quintus Fabius Maximus, from whom the society took its name, would have been proud – as long as the uprising was non-confrontational. Sexual segregation was the order of the day, although Beatrice Webb was becoming increasingly alarmed by the close friendship between H.G. Wells and the brilliant young Cambridge student Amber Reeves. Amber would, however, eventually marry another Fabian, 'Blanco' Rivers White. The Utopian ideal of the summer school was beginning to tarnish a little in the Webbs' eyes, especially as news of evening parodies of daytime lectures reached the ears of Beatrice. Lytton Strachey recalled that he and Brooke upset her as they 'tried to explain Moore's ideas to Mrs Webb while she tried to convince us of the efficacy of prayer'.

After a surfeit of talks, lectures and discussions on the Welsh coast, Rupert headed south, to a riverside camp in Kent. An idyllic location had been discovered by a close neighbour and friend of the Oliviers, David Garnett, who had found it when cycling with Bryn and Daphne Olivier to Penshurst for a picnic, with colleagues Godwin Baynes, the giant rowing blue later to become a physician at St Bartholomew's Hospital, London, and fellow student doctor Maitland Radford, who late in life would become Chief Medical Officer of Health for St Pancras in London. Garnett recalled the outing in his autobiography *The Golden Echo*:

> . . . when we reached Penshurst we found a little road crossing the river Eden and above a narrow old bridge was a wider pool with water lilies, in which we bathed. Nearby was a little weirhouse over the river. I was enchanted by the place and came back there alone with camping things. When I had been living there a week Godwin came back and joined me, and then the Oliviers came with Harold Hobson and Dorothy Osmaston, a lovely blue-eyed girl who is now Lady Layton . . .

Over the field stood the magnificent Penshurst Place, built during the first half of the fourteenth century for the wealthy John de Pulteney (four times Lord Mayor of London) on his recently acquired 4,000-acre estate at Penshurst, which had belonged to Sir Stephen de Penchester in the previous century. By the early part of the fifteenth century Henry IV's third son John, Duke of Bedford, was in residence, the property on his death passing to his younger brother Humphrey, Duke of Gloucester, founder of the Bodleian library at Oxford. The next incumbent Humphrey Stafford, 1st Duke of Buckingham, entertained Henry VIII there, the King repaying his host's hospitality by beheading him and letting Anne Boleyn's brother run the property. Henry VIII's successor Edward VI eventually bequeathed the house and estate to his tutor and steward of his household Sir William Sidney. It soon passed to his son Henry who, although related by marriage to the doomed Guildford Dudley and Lady Jane Grey, escaped implication in the 'plot' against the eventual Queen Mary. Henry Sidney's first child was Philip Sidney, later to become Sir Philip, soldier, scholar, poet and the personification of everything that was virtuous, chivalrous and noble. After Brooke's death, his name would often be linked with that of Sidney; both poets died while serving as soldiers. The family built a London house, twice the size of Penshurst, but it was a white elephant pulled down 100 years later; the Empire, Leicester Square, now stands on the site. Many years later Sir Bysshe Shelley married into the family, his grandson Percy Bysshe Shelley becoming one of England's most famous poets, who, like Brooke and Sidney, was to die tragically young.

At Penshurst the party in the long meadows flanking the river Eden was soon joined by Noel Olivier, when her summer term at Bedales ended, and then by Brooke and Dudley Ward, Rupert again knowing fully Noel's movements. It was the first meeting between Brooke and Garnett, whom Rupert nicknamed 'Bunny'. Garnett's memory of his encounter with Brooke remained crystal clear:

> The following night, just after we'd all retired to sleep, there were gay shouts of greeting as we all emerged from sleeping bags and tents to find two young men from Cambridge had come to join us. They were Rupert Brooke and Dudley Ward. Rupert was extremely attractive. Though not handsome, he was beautiful. His complexion, his skin, his eyes and hair were perfect. He was tall and well built, loosely put together, with a careless animal grace and a face made for smiling and teasing and sudden laughter. As he ate in the firelight I watched him, at once delighted by him and afraid that his friendliness might be a mask. What might not lie below it?

The meadows by the River Eden, where the young Edwardians laughed, swam, talked and walked as July turned into August in that summer of 1909, were approached by turning off the Penshurst Road along the lane to Salman's Farm. Just before the hill leading to the farm itself, a small bridge crossed the River Eden, to the left of which some 50 yards away the river opened out into an ideal spot for bathing just above the old weirhouse. During his sojourn there Brooke went for walks along the river with Noel and they all swam, even at night, by the light of bicycle lamps, amidst, in Garnett's words, 'the smell of new-mown hay, of the river and weeds'. He recalled vividly this time at Penshurst in his autobiography:

> . . . soon we were sitting round the blazing fire, Noel's eyes shining in welcome for the new arrivals and the soft river water trickling from her hair down her bare shoulders. And on the white shoulders, shining in the firelight, were bits of duck weed, which made me love them all the more. The moon rose full. Soon we crawled back into our sleeping bags and slept, but Rupert, I believe, lay awake composing poetry.

Intrigued by the spectacle of a group of young people behaving in what they would deem an erratic, and probably erotic, manner the locals lined the little bridge by the wider part of the river where they were about to bathe. Undeterred, they continued to swim, Noel picking her way through the assembly on the bridge to effect a perfect dive into the Eden.

In a letter to Brooke, written some 18 months later, on 10 February 1911, Noel admitted, '. . . at camp at Penshurst I was driven silly with love and it was perhaps at that time that I felt it most strongly. Since then I have gradually began to know him [Rupert] better, and would, I think, have looked on him as a friend, a person whom I loved better than anyone else but for whom I neither needed nor expected more than to see him at times and talk to him; I wanted him to prefer me to others, but not to everything . . .'

The delightful spot by the River Eden that so enchanted Garnett, and where Noel's feelings for Rupert were at their height, remains unchanged, with its tranquil meadows, winding waterway soon to flow into the River Medway, views to Penshurst Palace and little arched bridge. The weirhouse has disappeared, although the weir still falls, and in the wide pool where Brooke and his friends swam, the occasional fisherman waits patiently for an obliging dace or chubb.

The round of summer activity continued, as Rupert, his family and his friends headed west. A part of Avon since the shuffling of the counties in 1976, Clevedon, on the Severn Estuary, was firmly in the more delightfully named Somerset in the summer of 1909, when Brooke persuaded his parents to rent a large Victorian vicarage there. Clevedon was once referred to as 'the brain-workers' paradise'; local postcards proudly proclaimed its best features as 'unrivalled sunsets, daily steamer services to Devon and delightful inland and coastal scenery'. The literati had always been drawn to the town. Samuel Taylor Coleridge was the first poet to write about the area when he resided in Old Church Road, describing the cottage and the view from Dial Hill in the Valley of Seclusion: 'dim coasts, and cloud-like hills, and shoreless ocean'. Minor poets associated with the area include Charles Abraham Elton (of the Elton family of Clevedon Court), Alfred, Lord Tennyson's friend Arthur Hallam (buried in the Elton vaults), H.D. Rawnsley and Hallam's second cousin Charles Isaac Elton, who wrote the following lines on Clevedon in 1885 about his childhood memories of the place:

> Come out and climb the garden path
> Luriana Lurilee
> The China rose is all abloom
> And buzzing with the yellow bee
> I'll swing you on the cedar bough
> Luriana Lurilee
> How long since you and I went out
> Luriana Lurilee
> To see the kings go riding by
> Over lawn and daisy lea
> With their palm leaves and cedar sheaves
> Luriana Lurilee

Clevedon's literary magnetism is borne out in the street names, acknowledging the likes of Thackeray, Tennyson, Hallam and Coleridge. The literary history of the area would have appealed to Brooke, who would undoubtedly have been familiar with the poem, 'In Memoriam', Tennyson's poetic epitaph to his friend Arthur Hallam.

> The Danube to the Severn gave
> The darkened heart that beat no more
> They laid him by a pleasant shore
> And in the hearing of the wave
>
> There twice a day the Severn fills
> The salt sea-water passes by
> And hushes half the bubbling Wye
> And makes a silence in the hills.

It was to All Saints Vicarage in Coleridge Road that the Brookes came that summer. The incumbent, the Reverend Richard A. Arden-Davis, had taken up his position seven years earlier in 1902, five years after the building was erected. In a letter dated 10 November 1902, Miss Elizabeth Teulon, writing to her daughter Margaret, asked, 'Have I described the new vicar? I think not. He is short, very bald, with quite light hair, a well-developed forehead and penetrating eyes, no nose worth mentioning, an expressive mouth, and chin denoting power and will. He has a most pleasant voice and I like him very much.'

Rupert and his friends' predilection for walking and the open road would have been truly sated by the coastal clifftop path leading to Portishead, with its wide distant views to South Wales. But Rupert affected a dislike of the place: 'Clevedon is insufferable. I have followed up all the rivers for miles around and they are all ditches.' For the first fortnight of the holiday Rupert was ill: Dudley Ward kicked him by accident, and the injury laid him up. His chums started arriving in dribs and drabs, as was his plan in suggesting the Cleveland Vicarage; it enabled him to invite his friends down as opposed to being subjected to obligatory seclusion at home in Rugby. Paradoxically, though, he enjoyed the role of one appearing to sequester himself from the world, whilst really encouraging visitors. A mixed assortment of Cambridge friends and associates appeared for varying lengths of time, including Margery and Bryn Olivier, Dudley Ward, Maynard Keynes, Gerald Shove, Hugh Dalton, Francis Birrell, Gwen Darwin (who was to marry Jacques Raverat), A.Y. Campbell, Eva Spielman, Bill Hubback and Eddie Marsh. Mrs Brooke clearly was not sure what to make of Rupert's new friends, commenting, 'I have never met so many brilliant and conceited young men'.

She was none too pleased at their bad timekeeping and general behaviour; Rupert wrote to Ka Cox from the Vicarage, 'Oh, poor Mother's Experiment of having some of my Acquaintances in a House in the Country this Summer! They've come and gone, singly and in batches, and the Elder Generation couldn't stand *any* of them . . .' Mrs Brooke was generally aware of several of her son's friends, especially the Olivier girls, Bryn, Margery, Daphne and Noel. About whom an acquaintance had exclaimed, 'My, yes, the Oliviers! They'd do anything those girls!' Her major misgiving was about the attitude of Bryn (who, she wrongly assumed, was the object of Rupert's affection) and her seemingly deliberate flaunting of normal convention and etiquette, although her attitude was in accordance with the freedom of her upbringing and education. In reality it was, of course, Noel who inflamed Rupert's passion, but Margery ensured that Noel didn't come to Clevedon and went as far as to tell him on arrival that his feelings weren't returned – clearly out of a mixture of jealousy, complicity and concern on Margery's part.

Of the girls in Rupert's circle, his mother admitted, 'I prefer Miss Cox, her wrists are very thick, and I don't like the expression of her mouth, but she's a sensible girl. I can't understand what you all see in these Oliviers; they are pretty, I suppose, but not at all clever, they're shocking flirts and their manners are disgraceful.' Despite these shortcomings, Daphne co-founded the first Steiner School in England and Noel became an eminent physician.

Margery and Bryn Olivier, Dudley Ward and Bill Hubback joined Rupert on one particular walk along the cliffs to Portishead, where, looking out over the Severn Estuary, the company fell into conversation about the poet John Davidson, who had recently drowned himself in Cornwall at the age of 51, and conjectured as to whether he had merely faked death to escape to another life elsewhere. Davidson's dictum that life on the road to anywhere was preferable to a long-drawn-out downhill slide into old age appealed to the five friends. Discussing it during the walk back to Clevedon, they made a pact to cast off their old lives at a certain point in the future and start afresh elsewhere, thereby denying any of their acquaintances the opportunity of watching them slip into senility. The plan was firmed up – to meet on 1 May 1933, the venue, the dining-room, Basle station, where they would meet for breakfast. Back at the All Saints Vicarage they decided on others who would get the call and be an essential part of their plan; these included Godwin Baynes, Ka Cox and Jacques Raverat. Rupert wrote to the latter:

> We are twenty-something. In 1920 we shall be thirty no-something. In
> 1930 we shall be forty no-something . . . still going to the last play,
> reading the last book; passing through places we've been in for twenty
> years . . . having tea with each other's wives; 'working' 10–5; taking a

carefully organised holiday twice a year, with Ruskin, luggage and a family, to Florence, disapproving of rather wild young people . . . my dear Jacques, think of 1940, 50! . . . we shall become middle aged, tied with more and more ties, busier and busier, fussier and fussier; we shall become old, disinterested, peevishly or placidly old men; the world will fade to us . . . the idea, the splendour of this escape back into youth fascinated us . . . Will you join us? Will you, in twenty years, fling away your dingy wrappings of stale existence, and plunge into the unknown to taste Life anew? . . . it's the greatest grandest offer of your life, or of ours . . . This is an offer. A damn serious and splendid offer . . . We'll be children seventy years instead of seven . . .

Twenty-one years old when they made the Clevedon pact, Rupert would have been 45 if he had made it to Basle station in 1933.

During the sojourn at Clevedon *The English Review*, vol. III no. 2, September 1909, published five of Brooke's poems – 'Blue Evening', the 'Song of the Beasts', 'Sleeping Out', 'Full Moon' and 'Finding'.

Finding

From the candles and dumb shadows,
And the house where love had died,
I stole to the vast moonlight
And the whispering life outside.
But I found no lips of comfort,
No home in the moon's light
(I, little and lone and frightened
In the unfriendly night),
And no meaning in the voices . . .
Far over the lands, and through
The dark, beyond the ocean,
I willed to think of *you*!
For I knew, had you been with me
I'd have known the words of night,
Found peace of heart, gone gladly
In comfort of that light.

Oh! The wind with soft beguiling
Would have stolen my thought away
And the night, subtly smiling,
Came by the silver way;

And the moon came down and danced to me,
And her robe was white and flying;
And trees bent their heads to me
Mysteriously crying;
And dead voices wept around me;
And dead soft fingers thrilled;
And the little gods whispered . . .

But ever
Desperately I willed;
Till all grew soft and far
And silent . . .
And suddenly
I found you white and radiant,
Sleeping quietly,
Far out through the tides of darkness,
And there in that great light
Was alone no more, nor fearful;
For there, in the homely night,
Was no thought else that mattered,
And nothing else was true,
But the whole fire of moonlight,
And a white dream of you.

Of 'Blue Evening', the American George Edward Woodberry, who would later write the preface for Brooke's first ever book of *Collected Poems*, was moved to comment, 'It is original and complete. In its whispering embraces of sense, in the terror of seizure of the spirit, in the tranquil euthanasia of the end by the touch of speechless beauty, it seems to me a true symbol of life whole and entire. It is beautiful in language and feeling, with an extraordinary clarity and rise of power; and above all, though rare in experience, it is real . . .'

Blue Evening

My restless blood now lies a-quiver,
Knowing that always, exquisitely,
This April twilight on the river
Stirs anguish in the heart of me.

For the fast world in that rare glimmer
Puts on the witchery of a dream,

The straight grey buildings, richly dimmer,
The fiery windows, and the stream

With willows leaning quietly over,
The still ecstatic fading skies . . .
And all these, like a waiting lover,
Murmur and gleam, lift lustrous eyes,

Drift close to me, and sideways bending
Whisper delicious words.
But I
Stretch terrible hands, uncomprehending,
Shaken with love; and laugh; and cry.

My agony made the willows quiver;
I heard the knocking of my heart
Die loudly down the windless river,
I heard the pale skies fall apart,
And the shrill stars' unmeaning laughter,
And my voice with the vocal trees
Weeping. And hatred followed after,
Shrilling madly down the breeze.

In peace from the wild heart of clamour,
A flower in moonlight, she was there,
Was rippling down white ways of glamour
Quietly laid on wave and air.

Her passing left no leaf a-quiver.
Pale flowers wreathed her white, white brows.
Her feet were silence on the river;
And 'Hush!' she said, between the boughs.

While at Clevedon, Rupert discussed his love for Noel with her sister Margery, who later touched on the subject in a letter to him: '. . . do be sensible! . . . she is so young . . . You are so young . . .' She also informed him that women shouldn't marry before 26 or 27, that Rupert was to be shut out of Noel's existence and warned him, 'if you bring this great terrible, terrible, all absorbing thing into Noel's life now . . . it will stop her intellectual development'. Margery was soon to begin suffering from delusions, during which she would invariably imagine every young man she met to be in love with her. Sadly she became increasingly unmanageable, and was eventually, in 1922, committed to an institution.

The Vicarage in Coleridge Road has been less affected by the ravages of time, although the tennis lawn on which Brooke and his friends played in the summer of 1909 has reverted to its natural state, and the only plans drawn up today are those for the Sunday sermon.

CHAPTER VI

Unrequited Love

Before returning to Cambridge, Brooke called in at School Field. While there he made Fabian plans with Hugh Dalton to whom he indicated a place on the wall in the Poet's Corner of the Rugby Chapel: 'There is a vacant space reserved for me between Matthew Arnold and Arthur Hugh Clough.' His prophecy would come true within a few short years.

More immediate plans included a visit to the Champions, the Oliviers' home at Limpsfield Chart in Surrey – not somewhere he could be completely at ease, because of the unfulfilled relationship with Noel. He was there not at Noel's invitation, but strangely at the behest of Margery – compensation of a sort for Brooke being refused permission to take Noel to see *King Lear*. It was clear that most of the family, probably including Noel herself, felt that she was too young to be subjected to Rupert's unswerving fixation. Their home was on the Surrey/Kent border, the Chart (as Limpsfield Chart is known) – Anglo-Saxon for stony ground – now belies its name with its woods and verdant setting, as indeed it already did by the time Sydney Olivier and his family settled there. Olivier, who held a high position on the staff of the South African Department, began to reconstruct the joined cottages at the Champions he had acquired in a wonderful position 600 feet above the weald in 1891. His wife, Margaret Olivier, recalled, 'We had already spent two summer holidays there in a tiny cottage near the common, a mile from Oxted station. The cottage we acquired later was a mile further on, near the Chart woods.' The family found it enchanting, with its woods, commons, scent of the fir trees and stunning southerly views. The area had a magnetism that drew others to it, including the Peases (Edward Pease was the founding father of the Fabians), the literary Garnetts (Edward, Constance and David), and the Pye family, whose daughters Sybil (a bookbinder) and Ethel (a sculptress) would become close friends of Brooke. In 1905, H.G. Wells first came to the house, where he taught the Olivier girls to play croquet on the small and highly unsuitable lawn; another visitor, Prince Kropotkin, the Russian anarchist, helped the girls to collect frogs, beetles and other creatures that fascinate children. George Bernard Shaw was also a regular at the Champions. The Oliviers extended the building in many directions, including building a long playroom for the girls in which they used to put on plays for, and with, their friends; George Bernard Shaw once politely sat through a performance of *The Admirable Bashful*, in which a 12-year-old David Garnett portrayed the Zulu King, Cetewayo.

The Oliviers wholeheartedly and actively supported the local commons preservation society, successfully fighting several right-of-way and enclosure battles with domineering landowners and the lord of the manor. The family often were abroad in Jamaica, and when in England Sydney was invariably based in London, occasionally going down to the Champions, which was looked after by a caretaker and her husband. The other occupant of the house was the Oliviers' grey parrot – a gift from an African friend. Sydney Olivier embraced the Utopian principles of the Fabian Society when Fabianism was still in its infancy, helping to establish the movement for radical but passive social reform. It was Rupert becoming a young Fabian that led to that meeting with Sir Sydney Olivier and his daughters Margery and Noel at Ben Keeling's supper party back on 10 May 1908.

The Champions was one of many venues that witnessed the cat-and-mouse tale of Rupert's unrequited love for Noel, Rupert vacillating between open devotion and an assumed sang-froid, Noel wary and holding his frisky boyishness at arms' length. While there, they walked in the garden and discussed the 1 May pact, which Rupert reminded her about weeks later:

> Well do you remember as I drove away from the Champions in a strangely stuffy cab, weeping a little out of the left-hand window, I indistinctly cried through the cheering of the multitudes, 'I shall write a letter about it.' But I expect you never heard. Anyhow you foresaw it when we discussed – or rather when you asked questions among the flower pots, and I could not reply, because my mouth was full of biscuit, and my tongue burnt by the hot milk (which I dislike). By now, perhaps you have answered your own questions, or discovered new difficulties, or worked out the Scheme further than I.

In the middle of December, Rupert attended the Slade School of Art fancy dress ball, dressed, with a little help and advice from Gwen Darwin, as Shelley's 'West Wind', before leaving England for a short holiday in Switzerland. From the Hotel Schweizerhof, at Lenzerheide, on Christmas Eve, he posted greetings to Noel: 'I send a book you know because tomorrow is your and Jesus' birthday

. . . there are more trees than at Klosters: fewer people.' On the way back, Rupert, Jacques and a couple of others stopped at what was their intended destination for 1933, sending a postcard to Ka: 'We passed through Basle this morning while you slept. Ha, Ha!' – before travelling to Paris, where Rupert fell ill, having eaten 'green honey' that disagreed with him. He fainted at the Louvre, and was so ill on returning to School Field that his face turned a bright orange and his tongue, mouth, throat and stomach were raw: 'The skin peels off like bad paper from a rotten wall.' From his sickbed, Brooke tidied up a poem that had been sketched out in Switzerland, having been inspired by a rough crossing from England to France. Initially titled 'A Shakespearean Love Sonnet', it became 'A Channel Passage', and was somewhat controversial because of the way it dealt with seasickness in such an overt way.

A Channel Passage

The damned ship lurched and slithered. Quiet and quick
My cold gorge rose; the long sea rolled; I knew
I must think hard of something, or be sick;
And could think hard of only one thing – *you*!
You, you alone could hold my fancy ever!
And with you memories come, sharp pain, and dole.
Now there's a choice – heartache or tortured liver!
A sea-sick body, or a you-sick soul!

Do I forget you? Retchings twist and tie me,
Old meat, good meals, brown gobbets, up I throw.
Do I remember? Acrid return and slimy,
The slobs and slobber of a last year's woe.
And still the sick ship rolls. 'Tis hard, I tell ye,
To choose 'twixt love and nausea, heart and belly.

During January illness was plaguing the Brooke household. Rupert was still under the weather and his father beginning to suffer from acute neuralgia. Parker Brooke's condition soon gave cause for alarm as his sight began to fail and he suffered increasingly from lapses of memory. A local doctor diagnosed a clot on the brain, an oculist found nothing wrong with his eyes while a nerve specialist concurred with the doctor that there was something amiss in the brain. His condition was giving the family so much cause for concern, that it looked certain that Rupert wouldn't be able to participate in the Marlowe Society's production of *Richard II*, or W.B. Yeats's play, *The Land of Hearts Desire*. Hugh Dalton took on Rupert's Fabian work on the Minority Report.

A still feverish Brooke wrote another poem on 11 January.

The One Before the Last

I dreamt I was in love again
With the One Before the Last,
And smiled to greet the pleasant pain
Of that innocent young past.

But I jumped to feel how sharp had been
The pain when it did live,
How the faded dreams of Nineteen-ten
Were Hell in Nineteen-five.

The boy's woe was keen and clear,
The boy's love just as true,
And the One Before the Last, my dear,
Hurt quite as much as you.

*

Sickly I pondered how the lover
Wrongs the unanswering tomb,
And sentimentalizes over
What earned a better doom.

Gently he tombs the poor dim last time,
Strews pinkish dust above,
And sighs, 'The dear dead boyish pastime!
But this – ah, God! – is Love!'

– Better oblivion hide dead true loves,
Better the night enfold,
Than man, to eke the praise of new loves,
Should lie about the old!

Oh! bitter thoughts I had in plenty.
But here's the worst of it –
I shall forget, in Nineteen-twenty,
You ever hurt a bit!

For a while, it was thought that Rupert may have typhoid. It turned out to be a false alarm, but he was undoubtedly susceptible to illness and appeared to have a weak immune system. Some 45 years after his death, a nurse saw, amongst other photographs, a picture of Brooke. Without knowing who he was, she was moved to comment, 'Well, that young man won't see 25, he's tubercular.'

As Rupert's condition improved, so his father's deteriorated. Parker Brooke's sight began to fail, and on 24 January he had a stroke. Rupert wrote to Dudley Ward from School Field: 'Father has had a stroke. He is unconscious. We sit with him by turns. It is terrible. His face is twisted half out of recognition, and he lies gurgling and choking and fighting for life.' Later that day his father died and a great sadness descended on the family. Rupert, still weak from his own illness, caught influenza at the funeral. There was still work to be done though, and 54 boys returning from the Christmas holidays. Rupert stepped into the breach and became Acting Housemaster, until the end of term. His Aunt Fanny came up from Bournemouth to lend a hand with the arrangements and Rupert's friends sent him messages of condolence. He missed Grantchester, but soon warmed to his new role of pedagogue: 'Being Housemaster is in a way pleasant. The boys are delightful; & I find I am an admirable schoolmaster . . . they remember I used to play for the School at various violent games, & respect me accordingly.'

In March he completed a poem begun in December:

Dust

When the white flame in us is gone,
And we that lost the world's delight
Stiffen in darkness, left alone
To crumble in our separate night;

When your swift hair is quiet in death,
And through the lips corruption thrust
Has stilled the labour of my breath –
When we are dust, when we are dust! –

Not dead, not undesirous yet,
Still sentient, still unsatisfied,
We'll ride the air, and shine, and flit,
Around the places where we died,

And dance as dust before the sun,
And light of foot, and unconfined,
Hurry from road to road, and run
About the errands of the wind.

And every mote, on earth or air,
Will speed and gleam, down later days,
And like a secret pilgrim fare
By eager and invisible ways,

Nor ever rest, nor ever lie,
Till, beyond thinking, out of view,
One mote of all the dust that's I
Shall meet one atom that was you.

Then in some garden hushed from wind,
Warm in a sunset's afterglow,
The lovers in the flowers will find
A sweet and strange unquiet grow

Upon the peace; and past desiring,
So high a beauty in the air,
And such a light, and such a quiring,
And such a radiant ecstasy there,

They'll know not if it's fire, or dew,
Or out of earth, or in the height,
Singing, or flame, or scent, or hue,
Or two that pass, in light, to light,

Out of the garden, higher, higher . . .
But in that instant they shall learn
The shattering ecstasy of our fire,
And the weak passionless hearts will burn

And faint in that amazing glow,
Until the darkness close above;
And they will know – poor fools, they'll know! –
One moment, what it is to love.

By the middle of the month he was, he informed Gwen Darwin, longing to
return to Grantchester: 'I shall be at the Orchard next term. Will you have a

meal in the Meadows in May with me – i.e. honey under the Orchard apple-blossom?' While he dreamed of his idyllic home near the Granta he was facing the practicalities of moving from School Field and finding another family home. After 15 years there, leaving was a wrench for Mrs Brooke, who was praying that they wouldn't be turned out overnight. Noel asked, 'Will you have to go and build a house for your mother to live in and then write nonsense to support yourself and her? Or will she be independent and let you go back and play and be distinguished in Cambridge?' She was independent, taking a rather solid, plain-looking house at 24 Bilton Road, Rugby, which would be their new home and a part-time base for Rupert. On 27 March 1910, a few days before their departure from School Field, he sent these nostalgic words to Dudley Ward:

> . . . Oh soon
> The little white flowers whose names I never knew
> Will wake at Cranborne. They've forgotten you
> Robin, who ran the hedge a year ago
> Runs still by Shaston. Does he remember? No
> This year the ways of Fordingbridge won't see
> So meaty and so swift a poet as me
> Mouthing undying lines. Down Lyndhurst way
> The woods will rub along without us
>
> Say,
> Do you remember the motors on the down?
> The stream we washed our feet in? Cranborne Town
> By night? And the two Inns? The men we met?
> The jolly things we said? The food we ate?
> The last high-toast in shandy-gaff we drank?
> And – certain people, under trees, at Bank?

Following his mother's move to Bilton Road, Brooke went to spend some time at Lulworth, staying this time a few yards across the road from the Post Office, at Cove Cottage, belonging to the Williams family. It was a pretty, typically English thatched house with a wonderfully wild garden that faced a peculiar cottage that had been constructed in Canada and transported to Lulworth during the nineteenth century. From Cove Cottage he wrote to Geoffrey Keynes on 8 April: 'Here (ecce iterum!) I roam the cliffs and try to forget my bleeding soul. Tonight some Stracheys join me – James for his journalist's weekend, Lytton for a week or so. After that – ie next Saturday or Sunday (or rather, Sat or Sun the 16th or 17th) – Jacques and Godwin Baynes *may* be joining me, or I them, somewhere for a day or two's walk.' Five days later he wrote from Cove Cottage, to Eddie Marsh, 'My dear Eddie, At length I am escaped from the world's great snare. This is Heaven – Downs, Hens, Cottages and the Sun.'

Rupert returned to the Orchard in time to celebrate May Day. It was now exactly 23 years away from the date that they all planned to meet at Basle station. On 1 May 1910 a crowd of friends, including Ka Cox and Geoffrey Keynes, came to have breakfast with Brooke at the Orchard, causing him to complain good-naturedly in a letter to Noel Olivier:

> . . . the thing is that they insist on 'dabbling in the dew' and being 'in the country' on the first of May. I had to get up at half-past seven to give them breakfast; though I had worked until two. It rained in the morning, yet they all turned up, thousands of them – men and women – devastatingly and indomitably cheery . . . when rain ceased we put on galoshes and gathered cowslips in the fields. We celebrate the festival with a wealth of detailed and ancient pagan ritual; many dances and song.

Amid the comings and goings of the tea garden, Brooke worked on an essay on Webster, which was to win him the Charles Oldham Shakespeare Prize, as well as working on a collection of his own verse and devoting some time to his campaign in support of Beatrice Webb's plans for Poor Law Reforms. Brooke's guests at the Orchard at various times included E.M. Forster and Lytton Strachey, both of whom received Mrs Stevenson's hospitality. Brooke loved the Orchard – '. . . golden and melancholy and sleepy and enchanted. I sit neck-deep in red leaves' – but the Stevensons were unhappy with his habit of wandering around the house, garden and village barefoot. As a result Brooke moved a few months later to the Old Vicarage next door. Prior to his departure he wrote to Noel Olivier from the Orchard:

> I've been finishing off a poem I began and planned in the spring. It's a bit out of date now. But illuminating. The position is this – I worshipped. I once ridiculously hoped you'd fall in love with *me*. But that was blasphemy . . . Oh, my cleverness! My poor grubby cleverness! That couldn't at all foresee you falling in love, and yet doing it in your own perfect & gracious manner. The poor poem is rather knocked on the head . . .

Success

I think if you loved me when I wanted;
If I'd looked up one day, and seen your eyes,

And found my wild sick blasphemous prayer granted,
And your brown face, that's full of pity and wise,
Flushed suddenly; the white godhead in new fear
Intolerably so struggling, and so shamed;
Most holy and far, if you'd come all too near,
If earth had seen Earth's lordlust wild limbs tamed,
Shaken, and trapped, and shivering, for *my* touch –
Myself should I have slain? or that foul you?
But this the strange gods, who have given so much,
To have seen and known you, this they might not do.
One last shame's spared me, one black words unspoken;
And I'm alone; and you have not awoken.

Virginia Stephen (later Virginia Woolf) came out of curiosity, to see the young poet living in the great outdoors at Grantchester and dubbed Brooke and his group of friends who frequented the Orchard and the Old Vicarage, the 'neo-pagans'. Her name was undoubtedly added to a long list of luminaries who nature would have called to the only 'small house' while taking tea at the Orchard. The privy in the garden with its two-hole bench still exists, as does the wooden tea pavilion.

That June, Rupert was back at Overcote, 13 miles north of Cambridge, camping with Geoffrey Keynes among the wildlife and communing with nature. While there he wrote a review of James Elroy Flecker's new volume *Thirty Six Poems*, commenting: '. . . too often seems to have been inspired with a few good lines and completed the poems with a few dull ones . . . the healthy human vulgar man's vulgar and mixed emotions made, somehow, beautiful by the magic of poetry . . .' Keynes and Brooke discussed the staging of a revival of *Faustus*, walked, read and swam in the Ouse. The day after their return to Cambridge, Rupert described his few days at Overcote with enthusiasm:

> I went into camp (a tent six feet each way) with Geoffrey on Monday . . . We had a very good time, with no rain at all. I slept out and Geoffrey slept inside the tent. We got extraordinarily red and brown. My nose is peeling, whilst Geoffrey's arms and ankles went quite raw the last few days. We bathed a good deal. I became quite an expert at cooking – especially fried eggs. We had one or two visitors in camp – the Batesons among others. But it was too far for many people to come. Overcourt (or more correctly Overcote) is a lovely place, with nothing but an old Inn and a ferry. There are villages round a mile or two away, but hidden. And there's just the Ouse, a slow stream, and some trees and fields and an immense expanse of sky. There were a lot of wild

birds about – wild duck and snipe and herons. I sat and wrote my
beastly essay most of the day. We rose about 6.30 on Friday yesterday,
made breakfast, washed up, packed everything up and rode off.

Four years later, while he was on board ship from the South Seas to the
United States in April 1914, Brooke wrote nostalgically of this time to Frances
Cornford (although addressing his letter to her six-month-old daughter
Helena): '. . . but you won't have gone dabbling in the dew in Justin's car at
Overcote. No indeed – you young folks don't do these things – these *were*
days . . . but I weary you . . .' Overcote is virtually unchanged to this day –
the Ouse still glides past the ferry, wild fowl still abound – but the sight of a
1909 Opel crammed with Edwardian 'dew-dabblers' from Cambridge is rare.

Rupert continued to feed his wanderlust, plotting a Fabian expedition to
the New Forest with Dudley Ward, where they would undertake a Poor Law
Reform tour, travelling by horse and cart and preaching from village greens.
Part of Rupert's agenda was that they would approach their route via
Froxfield, because of its proximity to Bedales and Noel. She had already
suggested a visit in a letter written several months earlier: '. . . you ought to
come down here in the Summer once, it is better then than in the Spring or
Winter, and there are downs; perhaps you have been already? If not, get
Jacques to invite you, or Lupton . . .' Rupert responded on 2 April, '. . . yes I
shall get Jacques to take me there once more (Petersfield I mean) and in the
Summer, or Dudley and I will come in our carriage . . .'

Known as little Switzerland, the area of Froxfield Green, Steep and Stonor
Hill, with its wooded heights and beech hangers, rises some 500 feet above the
western end of the Weald and the River Rother. Despite the steep nature of
Stonor Hill, the stage coaches from Petersfield to Winchester and Alton crawled
their way up the face of the slope, tacking patiently across it before the route
was replaced with a zigzag road in the 1820s. Brooke had been to the area in
June 1909, writing to Noel Olivier from his uncle's house at Godalming:

> . . . I shall go to Froxfield, Petersfield (address) on Thursday, talk to
> Jacques, meet Badley (perhaps, see Bedales, you by chance in the
> distance, or not) – & go back to London at six that evening . . . and if,
> if, there's anything more to be said, a letter here by tomorrow's first
> post, or to Froxfield, Petersfield (which I reach at noon) would find
> me. So if I even shan't see Bedales, you know where & how to stop me.
> Damn the rain!

This western tail-end of the North Downs had a resident writer in Edward
Thomas, who, at the time of Brooke's first visit to the area, was living at
Berryfield Cottage with his wife Helen, moving in December 1909 to the Red

The poet Edward Thomas in pensive mood near his home at Froxfield Green

Cottage (later the Red House), a William Morris-style dwelling commissioned by Old Bedalian and local furniture craftsman Geoffrey Lupton and built by Alfred Powell. Lupton's own house and workshops were just a few yards to the west, with equally commanding southerly views over Petersfield towards the South Downs. Both the Red House and Geoffrey Lupton's home next door were tucked in a far corner of Froxfield Green out on a limb in Cockshott Lane and almost in Steep, which began at the bottom of their gardens. Thomas wrote in a small room away from the house that looked 'through trees to a magnificent road winding up & round and a coombe among beeches, & to the Downs four miles away south'. Three years later Thomas would contemplate incorporating the name of the area into the pseudonym 'Arthur Froxfield', when planning a work of fiction about a Welsh household in London set in the 1890s.

In 1910 Rupert's plan was to break the journey and stop over at Froxfield Green, where he hoped to see Noel and converse with Edward Thomas. He revealed the plot to Jacques Raverat:

> Dudley and I are going to – or want to – go to Petersfield before we start off in our cart: in, that is, about ten days from now. It is enormously unfortunate that you'll not be there. For I, of course, daren't face Bedale's without you. But all, almost, we want to do is to

see the gorgeous Noel and talk with the tired Thomas. Thomas himself has a wife and babes, so we should not bother him as a hosts, I suppose. But what of Lupton? You know the world, and him, and us. Would it be possible for me to suggest that he gave us a bed (or, an outhouse) and, if necessary, had Noel to tea . . . or is he too quiet-loving, and does he hate us quick-tongued urbane people whom you have brought there too much? Tell me these things. For if it would be at all possible, I should like Dudley to see Life on a Hill, as well as Thomas. Is, if all's well, Lupton's address just Froxfield, Petersfield?

Despite Rupert's enthusiasm for the adventure, Noel was typically cautious.

. . . I cannot be sure about seeing you, but as Petersfield – its surroundings – *are* pleasant and as there is Thomas who you want to see, and also Lumpit, who provides such good teas, both of them live on a hill nearby, your efforts in reaching this district will not have been wasted, even if I have to spend the day in bed. Perhaps you had better find out from the two above mentioned people, whether they will be there . . . *Conclusion* come with your German friend by all means & camp in the cart in Lumpit's garden; I will try & intimate to you there if I can come, & arrange where, when & how . . .

Brooke, now hopeful of a meeting with Noel, put pen to paper to Lupton and then Dudley Ward: 'I've written to Lupton: yesterday. But, you know, he's one of those splendid, dour, natural, stupid men; who hates my dialectical skill and conversational wit, and would not scruple brutally to say to, or kick me in the stomach with his hobnailed boots. Still I've written him in a winning letter . . .' The letter won the day, despite Brooke's jokily disparaging remarks about Lupton to Ward. 'Lupton's answered, and will be alone and can manage us. So all is well.' The news was quickly passed on to Noel:

Lupton, in fact, *will* be there. And the German & I are going to stay with him . . . Well 'as things are' we shall leave London on Thursday & reach Petersfield 3:32 or 4:45 or some such ridiculous time. And will leave it again, no doubt, on Saturday morning . . . can you, if you *can*, come a walk or excursion on the Thursday or Friday, at any hour, and also to a meal? Or to one-developing-into-another? Or to which? I think, you know, you'd better make out, on the information I've given you, what can, may and shall be done and tell Lupton, or send a note to me up there . . .

Noel did get permission to join them for tea, bringing with her Mary Newberry, a close schoolfriend, who later married landscape painter Alix Riddell Sturrock, and lived to the ripe old age of 93, dying in 1985. So Brooke and Dudley Ward stayed with Lupton, amongst the furniture of the man who had studied under Ernest Grimson, and whom Nikolaus Pevsner called 'the greatest English artist-craftsman'. Rupert's mind, though, was more on Noel than on appreciating Lupton's expertise in fashioning small pieces of timber. Other diversions were the captivating southerly views and Edward Thomas, whose wife Helen was heavily pregnant with their third child Myfanwy, born just one month after Brooke's departure.

Eventually, Rupert and Dudley Ward set off on their tour, in a caravan borrowed from King's colleagues Hugh and Steuart Wilson, with a horse called Guy pulling it to various destinations. Armed with assorted utensils from the Orchard, including a Primus stove and kettle, Ward and Brooke travelled the New Forest area for a fortnight, handing out leaflets and making speeches on village greens or in market places and encouraging debate. Posters proclaimed the travellers prior to their arrival at each venue. The Poole poster read: 'Poole High Street, close to the free library. Principal speaker MR BROOKE. Questions invited. In support of proposals for Poor Law Reform. Sponsored by the NCPD.' At Wareham, their spirits were temporarily dampened by the weather, which caused them to check into the Black Bear Hotel.

The Black Bear at Wareham where Rupert and Dudley Ward stayed during their 'Poor Law Reform tour' of the New Forest area

107

The hotel dates back to the early 1700s, the first mention of it occurring in 1722. Forty years later, the old hostelry was destroyed and the elegant inn where Rupert and Dudley were to stay was built. In their day, the 'Emerald' stage coach departed from the hotel for London six days a week, and the owners advertised good accommodation for motorists, cyclists and yachtsmen, the town being situated between the Rivers Frome and Piddle. The Romans were at Wareham for five centuries; St Aldhelm, the first bishop of the West Saxons, founded a nunnery on the banks of the Frome about AD 700. The Anglo-Saxons knew the town as Werham – the homestead by the weir – and fished its salmon-filled waters. Beorlitic, the King of the West Saxons, is buried there. By 876, the Vikings held the town, until they were beleaguered by King Alfred, while King Edward (the Martyr) was buried there 150 years later. In 1066, the town boasted a population of over a thousand, whose offspring years later were to side with William the Conqueror's granddaughter over her brother Stephen in their tussle for the throne. As a personal thank-you, Stephen had the town razed to the ground. The town revived but Wareham's next major fire in 1762 again destroyed a major part, including the Black Bear, with its six-foot ursine character dominating the River Frome end of South Street. Local legend runs that 'if the bear falls from the porch, the world will end'. In case of accidents and him subsequently getting the blame for the ensuing Armageddon, he is securely fastened by a collar and chain.

From Wareham Rupert wrote to his cousin Erica at Godalming, 'The last week (& the next) I have been going round delivering it [the Minority report] at towns & villages in the New Forest & round here. We travel in a caravan & live like savages. As a public orator I am a great success. As a caravaner, less. It rains incessantly.'

At the end of the campaign, Rupert and Dudley Ward remained in the area, to join a crowd of their friends at Bucklers Hard on the Beaulieu River; which included, of course, Noel. Ships had been built on the spot where they set up camp, as early as the late seventeenth century, but in the 1740s Bucklers Hard became an important shipbuilding village, providing 50 ships for the British Navy between 1754 and 1822. Two of the four terraces were demolished, leaving a wide airy space between the remaining two, as by the mid-nineteenth century the workforce and output had been scaled right down, due to the change to iron constructed vessels and the onslaught of the cheaper and speedier railways. By the time Bryn Olivier and Ward discovered the place earlier in 1910, it looked much the same as it had done for the previous hundred years, with its two rows of old terraced houses and wide expanse of grass, and a clearing surrounded by extensive woodland running down to the peaceful Beaulieu River – an ideal place for a Bedalian-style camp.

The campers, in August 1910, included Noel and Bryn Olivier, Jacques Raverat, Ka Cox, the giant rowing blue and medical student Godwin Baynes,

In camp at Bucklers Hard on the Beaulieu River – August 1910.
Dudley Ward catches up on what the rest of the world is up to,
while Ka Cox and Ethel Pye look a trifle displeased with the
candid cameraman, and Brooke, unconcerned, is engrossed

Harold Hobson who was studying engineering at King's, Maitland Radford's cousin Arthur 'Hugh' Popham, the Cambridge diving champion who was later to become the Keeper of Prints and Drawings at the British Museum, Bill Hubback and Eva Spielman (by now engaged to each other), Sybil and Ethel Pye, their younger brother David and Bunny Garnett. Ethel Pye painted the neo-pagan camp during their stay; A.E. Popham later describing her painting to Bryn Olivier (whom he eventually married): 'On the extreme left the boat comes to her muddy mornings and I am seen unshipping the rudder, then Harold (Hobson) is seen grumbling on his way to fetch wood, then the big tent and Ka and you cooking, then Dudley (Ward) and *The Financial Times* and Rupert and all.' Choosing a moment when he and Noel were alone

Noel Olivier at Bucklers Hard

gathering wood together, Rupert plucked up the courage to ask her to marry him. Surprisingly, she agreed, but added the caveat that it was to be their secret, and he was not to tell a soul. Not surprisingly, it was soon common news in the camp. Jacques Raverat later summed up how the situation appeared to the other campers at Bucklers Hard: 'She accepted the homage of his devotion with a calm, indifferent, detached air, as if it were something quite natural. No doubt she was flattered by his attentions, for she cannot have failed to see something of beauty and charm. Also, she saw how he was sought out, admired, showered with adulation on every side. But he did not inspire respect in her; she found him too young, too chimerical, too absurd.' Brooke celebrated his twenty-third birthday in the clearing haunted by black-headed gulls, oyster-catchers, lapwings, redshanks and curlews on the very spot where three of Nelson's fleet were built.

On his return to Grantchester, he discovered that Mrs Stephenson had people staying in his rooms, so briefly he decamped to the Old Vicarage next door. During the previous September when he was looking for somewhere, Rupert had described the house, garden and inmates to Lytton Strachey.

> The Neeves are 'working people' who have 'taken the house and want lodgers' (beware of that plural). So far they have been singularly unsatisfied. Mr Neeve is a refined creature, with an accent above his class, who sits out near the beehives with a handkerchief

110

over his head and reads advanced newspapers. He knows a lot about botany. They keep babies and chickens: and I rather think I have seen both classes entering the house. But you could be firm. The garden is the great glory. There is a soft lawn with a sundial and tangled, antique flowers abundantly; and a sham ruin, quite in a corner . . . Oh, I greatly recommend all the outside of the Old Vicarage. In the Autumn it will be Ussher-like. There are trees rather too closely all around; and a mist. It's right on the river. I nearly went there: but I could find no reason for deserting our present place.

He eventually would live there, but that was in the future.

In the late summer, James Strachey, Hugh Dalton and Rupert were back at the Fabian summer school in Llanbedr, Brooke and Strachey sleeping under their own blankets on the floor of one of the stables. The Society was still using Pen-yr-Allt, Caer-meddyg and their associated outbuildings. By now Beatrice Webb, a prime mover in the setting up of the summer schools, was becoming disenchanted with them:

> We have had interesting and useful talks with these young men, but the weather, being detestable, must have made the trip appear rather a bad investment for them, and they were inclined to go away rather more critical and supercilious than they came. Quite clearly we must not attempt it again unless we can ensure the presence of twenty or thirty leading dons and attractive celebrities. 'They won't come unless they know who they're going to meet,' sums up Rupert Brooke . . . They don't want to learn, they don't think they have anything to learn . . . the egotism of the young unversity man is colossal. Are they worth bothering about?

Nevertheless Brooke 'We all loved Beatrice, who related amusing anecdotes about Mr Herbert Spencer over and over again . . . The Cambridge group teased her and founded an "anti-athletic league" when she tried to organise long, uphill walks, but at least they were eager to talk to her and explain their point of view.' The Oxford boys, however, appeared recalcitrant and antagonistic. Beatrice asked, 'Why must these young men be so rude?' On one occasion, the local police had to be called following unruly behaviour when the young Fabians vehemently supported each other against the hierarchy. If one of them was upbraided during a meeting, they would walk out as one body. After the summer school Rupert wrote to Geoffrey Keynes, 'I'm just back from doing my accursed duty at the Fabian Summer School. It was really rather fun. A thousand different people from different parts of life.' And to Ka Cox, 'I went to Llanbedr. You ought to go one year, to learn a little about life, and to teach them a little about what? Anyhow it's not so bad as you think . . . The Webbs too are very nice . . .'

By 1911 the lease on Pen-yr-Allt would expire and a decision taken to abandon North Wales and hold the schools at the Hotel Monte Movo at Saas Grund in the Swiss Alps, but Brooke would not be present.

Rupert's cousin Erica had become increasingly obsessed with George Bernard Shaw. Initially she sought advice from him, but her attentions were soon to become embarrassing, and Shaw suggested that she found someone of her own age to distract her from her hero worship. The fact that he had entered into a correspondence with her about his plays, and explained that the expressions and feelings of the characters weren't necessarily his own, served only to fan the flames. Her declarations of love became more intense and she even moved closer to the Shaws, to try to inveigle her way into their household. He lectured her on the fact that marriage was sacred and spoke of the 'iron laws of domestic honour', but it did little to discourage her. It is evident that Rupert knew nothing of the situation.

During October 1910, Edward Thomas stayed with Brooke at the Orchard, as did E.M. Forster who had just had his new novel, *Howard's End*, published. Rupert returned to Froxfield Green to spend some time with Thomas while his wife was away. It is hard to imagine the two poets gelling – Brooke gregarious and youthful, Thomas an often unhappy and depressed man weighed down with financial worries. Nevertheless they read aloud to each other Brooke's latest poems, including 'Flight', which would have sounded perfect read aloud in the beech hangers.

Flight

Voices out of the shade that cried,
And long noon in the hot calm places,
And children's play by the wayside,
And country eyes, and quiet faces –
All these were round my steady paces.

Those that I could have loved went by me;
Cool gardened homes slept in the sun;
I heard the whisper of water nigh me,
Saw hands that beckoned, shone, were gone
In the green and gold. And I went on.

For if my echoing footfall slept,
Soon a far whispering there'd be
Of a little lonely wind that crept
From tree to tree, and distantly
Followed me, followed me . . .

But the blue vaporous end of day
Brought peace, and pursuit baffled quite,
Where between pine-woods dipped the way.
I turned, slipped in and out of sight.
I trod as quiet as the night.

The pine-boles kept perpetual hush;
And in the boughs wind never swirled.
I found a flowering lowly bush,
And bowed, slid in, and sighed and curled,
Hidden at rest from all the world.

Safe! I was safe, and glad, I knew!
Yet – with cold heart and cold wet brows
I lay. And the dark fell . . . There grew
Meward a sound of shaken boughs;
And ceased, above my intricate house;

And silence, silence, silence found me . . .
I felt the unfaltering movement creep
Among the leaves. They shed around me
Calm clouds of scent, that I did weep,
And stroked my face. I fell asleep.

Thomas noted that Brooke '. . . stretched himself out . . . drew his fingers through his waved, fair hair, laughed, talked indolently and admired as much as he was admired. No one that knew him could easily separate him from his poetry . . . he was tall, broad, and easy in his movements. Either he stooped, or he thrust his head forward unusually much to look at you with his steady blue eyes. His clear rosy skin helped to give him the look of a great girl . . .' Brooke returned to Grantchester, inspired by his time with Thomas, just as Thomas himself was to be encouraged in his poetry by the American poet, Robert Frost.

On 5 November 1910, Rupert was at Ye Olde George Hotel at Chatteris, some 20 miles north of Cambridge, where he scribbled down and sent to Jacques Raverat a poem entitled 'Mummy' that was later published in *Poems 1911* as 'Mummia'.

Mummy

As those of old drank mummia
To fire their limbs of lead,
Making dead kings from Africa
Stand panders to their bed;

Drunk on the dead, and medicined
With spiced and royal dust,
In a short night they reeled to find
Ten centuries of lust.

So I, from paint, stone, tale and rhyme
Stuffed loves infirmity,
And sucked all lovers of all time
To rarify ecstasy.

Helen's the hair shuts out from me
Verona's livid skies;
Gypsy the lips I press; and see
Two Antony's in your eyes.

The unheard invisible lonely dead
Lie with us in this place,
And ghostly hands above my head
Close face to straining face;

Woven from their tomb and one with it
The night wherein we press;
Their thousand pitchy pyres have lit
Your flaming nakedness . . .

The following day Noel Olivier received a copy. 'This is a very rough unfinished copy of the sort of thing I shall send you *on a postcard* if you don't write to me, – even ten words to say you exist. Don't ask me how I got here. I leave in five minutes . . . Farewell. Imagine, most unapproachable, a little figure stumping across the illimitable Fens, occasionally bowing to the sun because it reminds him of you . . .'

Rupert continued his verbal bombardment to Noel, who, now almost 18, was usually confused by the ravings in his letters: 'If I could only talk to you & ask you things. Two sensible people can say anything, – anything in the world – to each other . . . I'm an infinitely vulgar nuisance . . . The world has given to you that you may have any emotion – violent lust, eternal hatred, infinite indifference, – to me or to anyone else in the world, for as long or as short a time, & at any moment, you like . . .' Noel had just returned from Prunoy, in France, where she'd been a guest of Jacques Raverat's family. During her stay, Rupert had sent Jacques a new sonnet.

The Life Beyond

He wakes, who never thought to wake again,
Who held the end was Death. He opens eyes
Slowly, to one long livid oozing plain
Closed down by the strange eyeless heavens. He lies;
And waits; and once in timeless sick surmise
Through the dead air heaves up an unknown hand,
Like a dry branch. No life is in that land,
Himself not lives, but is a thing that cries;
An unmeaning point upon the mud; a speck
Of moveless horror; an Immortal One
Cleansed of the world, sentient and dead; a fly
Fast-stuck in a grey sweat on a corpse's neck.

I thought when love for you died, I should die.
It's dead. Alone, most strangely, I live on.

Rupert kept up the onslaught, his frustration seeming to intensify with each letter: '. . . if I could only beat you suddenly on the nose, very hard, or pull your hair with painful and unexpected vehemence – Oh Noel, but I must see you. I weary you with another long slushy letter. I mistrust myself letter writing . . . I know I often fail to convey the effect I desire . . .' On 6 December, he enclosed a sonnet written the previous spring; '*Don't* go reading anything into it except itself. I've *never* seen you "cry & turn away".'

The Hill

Breathless, we flung us on the windy hill,
Laughed in the sun, and kissed the lovely grass.
You said, 'Through glory and ecstasy we pass;
Wind, sun, and earth remain, the birds sing still,
When we are old, are old . . .' 'And when we die
All's over that is ours; and life burns on

115

Through other lovers, other lips,' said I.
'Heart of my heart, our heaven is now, is won!'

'We are Earth's best, that learnt her lesson here.
Life is our cry. We have kept the faith!' we said;
'We shall go down with unreluctant tread
Rose-crowned into the darkness!' . . . Proud we were,
And laughed, that had such brave true things to say.
– And then you suddenly cried, and turned away.

Noel appeared ambivalent to his poetry: 'I liked the old Mummy poems better than this "we flung us" one.'

During November, Rupert dined at Magdalene College with his friend A.C. Benson, who recorded Brooke's physical attributes and countenance:

He was far more striking in appearance than exactly handsome in outline. His eyes were small and deeply set. It was the colouring of face and hair which gave special character to his look. The hair rose very thickly from his forehead, and fell in rather stiff arched locks on either side – he grew it full and over-long, it was of a beautiful dark auburn tint inclining to red, but with an underlying golden gleam in it. His complexion was richly coloured, as though the blood were plentiful and near the surface; his face much tanned, with the tinge of sun-ripened fruit. He was strongly built, but inclined to be sturdy, and even clumsy, rather than graceful or lithe . . . his voice was far from beautiful, monotonous in tone, husky and somewhat hampered in the throat.

Notwithstanding Benson's comments about his voice, Rupert was a convincing speaker, addressing the Cambridge Fabians a month later for the last time as their president. His lecture was on 'Democracy and the Arts', and included various interesting observations and thoughts: 'It seems to me that this century is going to witness a struggle between Democracy and Plutocracy' and:

Observe the situation and remember it's a real one, not one in a book. (1) Art is important. (2) The people who produce art at present are, if you look into it, nearly always dependent on unearned income. (3) We are going to diminish and extinguish the number of those dependent on unearned income. We shall also reduce the number of those rich enough to act the patron to artists, and change in a thousand other ways the circumstances of the arts and of the artists.

116

Brooke was clearly concerned that the systems which enabled artists, writers and musicians to live was being destroyed, debating how much literature would have been lost to us, had writers over the centuries not received patronage: 'Poetry is even worse off than the other arts. Even Mr Rudyard Kipling could not live on his poetry. Very few poets, perhaps one or two in five years, sell 1,000 copies of a volume . . . An experienced publisher tells me no one in England makes £50 a year by poetry – except perhaps Mr Kipling and Mr Noyes.' Brooke stressed the importance of contemporary art as opposed to excepting the standards of former generations: 'Beware for the generations slip imperceptibly into one another, and it is so much easier to accept standards that are prepared for you. Beware of the dead.'

CHAPTER VII

When You Were There, and You, and You

Rupert had also to beware of the living, in the shape of Mrs Stevenson at the Orchard, who had been getting increasingly disenchanted with the comings and goings at all hours of Rupert and his friends, and especially with his habit of going barefoot. The landlady and lodger reached an impasse, which concluded in him defecting to the Old Vicarage next door, with his beloved Granta running at the bottom of the garden.

In 1380 Corpus Christi College had appropriated the Rectory at Grantchester, appointing the first vicar, William Wendye, and establishing a building on the site of the Old Vicarage, built on a strip of land that ran down to the river at a place where the locals extracted gravel from a pit called Hog Hunch. The present dwelling was erected in the 1680s and remained as a vicarage until early in the 1820s, when it was advertised to be let, and was taken by the Lilley family who also owned Manor Farm. In the middle of the century Grantchester's new vicar, William Martin, had a new vicarage built, and the old one was bought by a local market gardener, Samuel Widnall, on the occasion of his marriage to Elizabeth Smith; Widnall lived there until his death in 1894. The house then passed to his sister-in-law and subsequently a niece; she, having decided not to live in the house, installed Henry and Florence Neeve and their son Cyril as tenants. The fourth member of the family was the bull terrier that Brooke nicknamed Pudsey Dawson. The dog seemed equally at home in the Orchard and the Old Vicarage.

No sooner had Rupert moved his things into the Old Vicarage than he announced that he was soon to leave for Germany and would return in May. Before going abroad, though, he returned to Lulworth early in the new year, staying again at Cove Cottage – with Gwen Darwin, Ka Cox and Jacques Raverat, the latter drawing Rupert's portrait. Ka tried to buy Rupert a belated Christmas present of a book, and when he seemed indifferent as to what it was she was clearly hurt, for he felt compelled to write, 'Oh tell me that you're unhurt, for I hurt you in such a way, and I was mean and selfish, and you're I think one of the most clear and most splendid people in the world.'

On 1 January 1911 he wrote 'Sonnet Reversed':

Sonnet Reversed

Hand trembling towards hand; the amazing lights
Of heart and eye. They stood on supreme heights

Ah, the delirious works of honeymoon!
Soon they returned, and, after strange adventures,
Settled at Balham at the end of June.
Their money was in Can. Pacs. B. Debentures,
And in Antofagastas. Still he went
Cityward daily; still she did abide
At home. And both were really quite content
With work and social pleasures. Then they died.
They left three children (besides George, who drank);
The eldest Jane, who married Mr Bell,
William, the head-clerk in the County Bank,
And Henry, a stock-broker, doing well.

Despite the seemingly one-sided relationship with Noel, Brooke was a frequent visitor to the Champions, where Bryn, Daphne and Margery all enjoyed his company. Prone to more than a little exaggeration on occasion, Rupert wrote to Ka Cox, 'I'm staying – I don't know how long, at the Champions. Till Wednesday afternoon or Thursday dawn . . . Limpsfield. It is very unpleasant. The atmosphere at Priest Hill [the home of the Oliviers' neighbours, the Pyes], and The Champions is too damned domestic. I love the people and cough the atmosphere,' although he would later write to Noel, saying, 'Limpsfield made me incredibly better. Could you let it get round to your mother how nice I found it?' Rupert later went through a period where he felt drawn to the sensuality and beauty of Noel's sister Bryn, but nothing ever came of it and seemed to be a fleeting fancy. Margery became temporarily obsessed with Rupert, which was attributed to her mental instability and her assumptions that many of the males she met were in love with her.

Rupert went to Europe for three months, writing to various friends, 'I shall be in Germany at peace', 'I shall be in Germany for ever' and 'It is a thousand years since I have seen you and it will be more before I can see you again, for in three days I go to Germany, and from there I shall wander South and East, and no one will hear of me more . . .' During January, February and March, Rupert resided in Munich, where he learned German, watched Ibsen plays and saw one of the first performances of Strauss's new opera, *Der Rosenkavalier*. Through an introduction from the publisher E.J. Dent, he stayed for some while with the painter Frau Ewald, through whom he was thrust into the social and artistic circles of the city. There was a part of Brooke, though, that couldn't shake off England completely, which diminished his ability to enjoy Munich to the full. Despite having been away for some while, he was still much talked about in Cambridge and London, one friend declaring to James Strachey, 'I'm not surprised people don't fall in love with Rupert, he's so beautiful that he's scarcely human.' By the end of this period, he had produced an excellent new poem, which he explained to Eddie Marsh. 'I spent two months over a poem that describes the feelings of a fish, in the metre of "L'Allegro". It was meant to be a lyric, but has turned into a work of 20 lines with a moral end.' He copied the original onto two separate postcards, which he sent to Ka; this was the version published later, containing several changes.

The Fish

In a cool curving world he lies
And ripples with dark ecstasies.
The kind luxurious lapse and steal
Shapes all his universe to feel
And know and be; the clinging stream
Closes his memory, glooms his dream,
Who lips the roots o' the shore, and glides
Superb on unreturning tides.
Those silent waters wave for him
A fluctuant mutable world and dim,
Where wavering masses bulge and gape
Mysterious, and shape to shape
Dies momently through whorl and hollow,
And form and line and solid follow
Solid and line and form to dream
Fantastic down the eternal stream;
An obscure world, a shifting world,
Bulbous, or pulled to thin, or curled,
Or serpentine, or driving arrows,
Or serene slidings, or March narrows.
There slipping wave and shore are one,

And weed and mud. No ray of sun,
But glow to flow fades down the deep
(As dream to unknown dream in sleep);
Shaken translucency illumes
The hyaline of drifting glooms;
The strange soft-handed depth subdues
Drowned colour there, but black to hues,
As death to living, decomposes –
Red darkness of the heart of roses,
Blue brilliant from dead starless skies,
And gold that lies behind the eyes,
The unknown unnameable sightless white
That is the essential flame of night,
Lustreless purple, hooded green,
The myriad hues that lie between
Darkness and darkness! . . .

                              And all's one,
Gentle, embracing, quiet, dun,
The world he rests in, world he knows,
Perpetual curving. Only – grows
An eddy in that ordered falling,
A knowledge from the gloom, a calling
Weed in the wave, gleam in the mud –
The dark fire leaps along his blood;
Dateless and deathless, blind and still,
The intricate impulse works its will;
His woven world drops back; and he,
Sans providence, sans memory,
Unconscious and directly driven,
Fades to some dank sufficient heaven.

O world of lips, O world of laughter,
Where hope is fleet and thought flies after,
Of lights in the clear night, of cries
That drift along the wave and rise
Thin to the glittering stars above,
You know the hands, the eyes of love!
The strife of limbs, the sightless clinging,
The infinite distance, and the singing
Blown by the wind, a flame of sound,
The gleam, the flowers, and vast around

The horizon, and the heights above –
You know the sigh, the song of love!

But there the night is close, and there
Darkness is cold and strange and bare;
And the secret deeps are whisperless;
And rhythm is all deliciousness;
And joy is in the throbbing tide,
Whose intricate fingers beat and glide
In felt bewildering harmonies
Of trembling touch; and music is
The exquisite knocking of the blood.
Space is no more, under the mud;
His bliss is older than the sun.
Silent and straight the waters run,
The lights, the cries, the willows dim,
And the dark tide are one with him.

After Munich he moved south to Vienna and then to Wien, before
continuing to Florence, to meet up with his godfather and Rugby schoolmaster,
Robert Whitelaw, who had journeyed south with Rupert's younger brother
Alfred. From there Brooke wrote to Eddie Marsh, 'I am thirsting for
Grantchester. I am no longer to be at the Orchard, but next door at the Old
Vicarage, with a wonderful garden.' And a letter to Gwen Darwin also showed
an element of homesickness: 'Oh my God! I do long for England!'

Although Noel and Rupert were technically engaged, there now seemed
to be a gulf between them preventing any real relationship from developing.
Rupert had been in Munich mingling with painters, psychologists and poets,
while Noel was mending underclothes with Miss Middlemore or making
dresses and blouses under the watchful eye of Miss Rice. While she attended
school dancing classes, and practised Irish jigs and Morris dancing, Rupert
was revelling at the 'Bacchus-Fest' and having a romantic dalliance with
Elizabeth Van Rysselbergh, the daughter of a neo-impressionist painter. But
on 10 February 1911, Noel's last letter to Rupert before leaving Bedales
shows that she had grown to understand him more and, although putting a
disclaimer on any jealousy on her part, following his other flirtations, and
writing about him in the third person, she does open up more about her
feelings. Doubtless her refusal to become involved in a physical relationship,
or even display interest in that direction, coupled with Brooke's own sexual
frustration led to his affair with Elizabeth in Munich. She wrote, '. . . and he
is very beautiful, everyone who sees him loves him . . . I fell in love with him
as I had fallen in love with other people before, only this time it seemed final

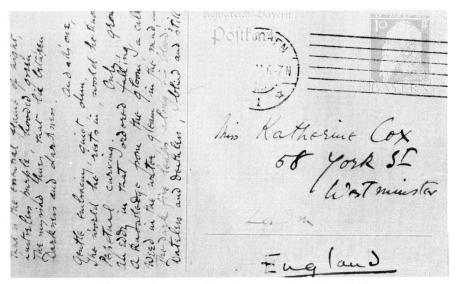

*Part of the original version of Brooke's poem The Fish sent by him on
two postcards from Munich to Ka Cox*

Katherine Laird Cox 1887–1938

– as it had, indeed, every time – I got excited when people talked of him and spent every day waiting and expecting to see him and felt wondrous proud when he talked to me or took any notice.' So what happened? They both approached the relationship from angles alien to the other; they did not always communicate with ease; and Noel never really opened up until later in life – by which time Rupert was dead, and she declared that she knew then she would 'never marry for love!'. Her school, Bedales, continues to thrive; many eminent citizens and household names emanating from the establishment founded by the still spiritually present J.H. Badley, 300 feet above the Rother Valley, where Noel Olivier received those tortuous love letters from Rupert.

By May he was back at Grantchester and settled in at the Old Vicarage, seeking solace in the tranquil atmosphere, and trying to sort out his emotions. In June he gave vent to his feelings in a letter to Ka. 'How many people can one love? How many people should one love? What is love? If I love at 6 p.m. do I therefore love at 7?' during May and June, Rupert was writing regularly from the Old Vicarage to both Noel and Ka. To Noel: 'Oh it is the *only* place, here. It's such a nice breezy first glorious morning and I'm having a hurried breakfast, half dressed in the garden, and writing to you. What cocoa! What a garden! What a you!' And to Ka: 'You *must* come this weekend. Then we'll talk: and laugh . . . Come! and talk! And love me – a little.' He also sent her his list of

> the best things in the world – a sketchy list: and, of course generalities
> have an unfair advantage –

(1)	Lust
(2)	Love
(3)	Keats
(4½)	Weather
(4)	go
(5)	Truth
(5½)	guts
(6)	Marrons glaces
(7)	Ka . . .
(29)	Rupert

During the third week of July, Rupert visited Oxford to see Noel, who was staying off the Banbury road, in north Oxford, at 2 Rawlinson Road, a large bulky house that Noel considered ugly. As inconsistent as Rupert in her own way, as now the warm side of her feelings for him shone through the invitation which, uniquely, began, 'Rupert, *darling!*' and continued, 'so please, if you come, be stern with me, because I should hate to find myself drifting into a relationship that I can not maintain with you . . .' And of Ka she says, 'Oh it would have been so much better, if you had married her ages 'ago!' while staying at Rawlinson Road, Rupert rose early, bathed in the Cherwell and worked in the Bodleian Library.

July saw the usual stream of visitors to the Old Vicarage, including Eddie Marsh, to whom Rupert wrote an exaggerated account of his primitive lifestyle of simple food, bathing, reading, talking and sleeping. The 'simple' lifestyle, though, did include beginning his dissertation and seeing in the Russian Ballet at Covent Garden performing *Sheherazade.*

During the summer of 1911, Virginia Stephen came to the Old Vicarage to spend five days with Rupert, and to revise her novel, begun in 1907 as *Melymbrosia,* and eventually published in 1915 as *The Voyage Out.* In between playing host to Virginia – the anticipation of her visiting having, by his own admission, made him a little nervous – he worked on his thesis and collection of poems.

Gwen Darwin captured the magic of the Grantchester era and even at the time wept for their impending and inevitable adulthood.

> I wish one of us would write a 'Ballade des beaux jours a Grantchester'.
> I can't bear to think of all these young, beautiful people getting old and tired and stiff in the joints. I don't believe there is anything compensating in age and experience – we are at our very best and most livingest now – from now on the edge will go off our longings and the fierceness of our feelings and we shall no more swim in the Cam . . . and we shan't mind much. I am still drunk with the feeling of

Brooke photographed in the garden of the Old Vicarage, Grantchester in the summer of 1911 by Estrid Linder, a Swedish student whom he was helping with some translation

Thursday afternoon. Do you know how one stops and sees them all sitting round – Rupert and Geoffrey and Jacques and Bryn and Noel – all so young and strong and keen and full of thought and desire, and one knows it will all be gone in 20 years and there will be nothing left. They will all be old and tired and perhaps resigned . . . If one of those afternoons could be written down, just as it was exactly, it would be a poem – but I suppose a thoroughly *lived* poem can't be written, only a partially lived one. Oh it is intolerable, this waste of beauty – it's all there and nobody sees it but us and we can't express it. We are none of us great enough to express a thing so simple and so large as last Thursday afternoon. I don't believe in getting old . . .'

In less than a year Rupert would capture those feelings in what would become one of the most endearing and enduring poems of the twentieth century.

As they, Brooke and Ka Cox, became closer, Brooke would often visit her home, Hook Hill Cottage just outside Woking in Surrey, with its panoramic vista of the North Downs to the Hogs Back and Stag Hill – the latter to become the site for Guildford Cathedral. Although a cottage in name, it was a sizeable dwelling, built in 1910 by Horace Field, who was responsible for erecting several of the neighbouring houses; Field himself lived next door at South Hill. Ka's father Henry Fisher-Cox, a wealthy stockbroker and a

Hook Hill Cottage, the home of Ka Cox

member of the Fabian Society, lived at Hook Hill House, which had been built in 1723 as a public house by the men working on the ladies' prison at Knaphill; the Yew Tree that had given the inn its name still stands to this day. Following Ka's mother's early death her father remarried, and he and her stepmother Edith and Ka and her two sisters Margaret and Hester lived there, until he too died suddenly in 1905 when Ka was just 18, leaving her a financially independent young woman when she went up to Cambridge, with her own home on the lower slopes of the old family house.

Brooke increasingly turned to Ka in his troubled moments or when he needed a comforting shoulder, and by the second half of 1910, Ka having been supplanted in Jacques Raverat's affections by Gwen Darwin, Rupert began to see the emotionally devastated woman in a new light. The platonic relationship began very gradually to develop into something more romantic in Rupert's mind, as her mature manner gave the volatile young poet a certain security and warmth – virtues that had been lacking in Noel. He wrote to Ka at Woking:

> Oh! Why do you invite responsibilities? Are you a Cushion, or a Floor? Ignoble thought! But why does your face invite one to load weariness upon you? Why does your body appeal for an extra load of responsibilities? Why do your legs demand that one should plunge business affairs on them? Won't you manage my committees? Will you

take my soul over entire for me? Won't you write my poems? . . . Ka,
what can I give you? The world? A slight matter . . .

He also went down to Woking in person to ask her to join an imminent
summer camp in Devon, having already persuaded Virginia Stephen. Being
worn down a little by Noel's continual rejections, he began to lean more
towards Ka, with her down-to-earth, straightforward manner. His
confidence, though, in her feelings towards him would be shattered by the
events at Lulworth Cove at the tail-end of 1911 and the New Year of 1912.

The Chaplain at King's had put a young Swedish student, Estrid Linder, in
touch with Brooke, suggesting that he help her with the colloquial English
she needed for her translation of Swedish plays. The assistance turned out to
be reciprocal, as she was to introduce him to, and help translate, the plays of
Strindberg, which he came to adore.

Another positive meeting during the summer was with the publisher Frank
Sidgwick, who was sufficiently impressed with Rupert's poems to agree to
publication. The deal was to be 15 per cent for the publisher, with the author
bearing the printing costs, which would amount to a little under £10, for 500
copies. Brooke's mother, rather decently, footed the bill, but there would be a
small difference of opinion between Sidgwick and Brooke over some of the
contents. As Rupert pointed out to Ka, he drove himself hard to achieve the

*The Beeches, Crediton, home of Paul Montague's parents, where Brooke and his friends
trooped over to have tea – taken in the dining-room (lower left window) which 'inspired
one of his greatest poems – Dining Room Tea*

desired result; 'I've been working for ten days alone at this beastly poetry. Working at poetry isn't like reading hard. It doesn't just tire and exhaust you. The only effect is that your nerves and your brain go . . . I had reached the lowest depths possible to man.'

At the end of August 1911 Rupert and several of his friends, including Justin Brooke, Oscar Eckhardt, James Strachey, Geoffrey and Maynard Keynes, Maitland Radford, Daphne, Bryn and Noel Olivier, Gerald Shove and others set up camp in a meadow at Clifford Bridge, Devon, on the banks of the River Teign. Ka Cox and Virginia Stephen joined them later. In fact, they turned up to find no welcoming party, as the others had gone to Crediton, leaving them only mouldy fruit pie for supper. One of the party, Paul Montague (known as Pauly), a zoologist and accomplished musician, had suggested they all go over to his parents at Crediton some ten miles to the north-east for afternoon tea, and the whole crowd of them descended on the residence of Colonel and Mrs Montague.

The Montagues' home, Penton (formerly Panton or Painton), a Georgian stucco house with superb south-eastern views over the town, had its origins in a dwelling owned by John Burrington in 1685, the property becoming the area's first Bluecoat School from 1804 to 1854. In 1860, Penton was rebuilt and enlarged by the Reverend George Porter, the property including parcels of land with the intriguing names of Three

Rupert at the Clifford Bridge camp looking decidedly more boyish than his 24 years

Cornered Close, Lame John's Field, Barn Close and Shooting Close. In 1878, Pauly Montague's grandfather Arthur purchased the estate, which passed to his son Leopold in 1887. A Justice of the Peace, Leopold rose to the rank of colonel; he also wrote plays which were performed in the double drawing-room, one end serving as a stage, and was a revered writer of Victorian farce. Colonel Montague was not at home when the Clifford Bridge campers arrived at Penton, but Mrs Montague received them and provided them with tea in the dining-room. It was this occasion that inspired Rupert Brooke to write 'Dining Room Tea' – one of his finest poems – where he, the observer, encapsulated a moment in time through the eyes of the writer. While the others are talking, laughing and eating, he takes a literary photograph, freezing a fleeting, but ultimately blissful, moment in his life – withdrawing to an objective plane before returning to the reality and normality of the situation. At the centrepiece of the poem were his feelings for Noel Olivier, and the security of a circle of friends who he loved, captured in a cameo that, ideally, he would liked to have preserved for ever:

Dining Room Tea

When you were there, and you, and you,
Happiness crowned the night; I too,
Laughing and looking, one of all,
I watched the quivering lamplight fall
On plate and flowers and pouring tea
And cup and cloth; and they and we
Flung all the dancing moments by
With jest and glitter. Lip and eye
Flashed on the glory, shone and cried,
Improvident, unmemoried;
And fitfully and like a flame
The light of laughter went and came.
Proud in their careless transience moved
The changing faces that I loved.

Till suddenly, and otherwhence,
I looked upon your innocence.
For lifted clear and still and strange
From the dark woven flow of change
Under a vast and starless sky
I saw the immortal moment lie.

One instant I, an instant, knew
As God knows all. And it and you
I, above Time, oh, blind! could see
In witless immortality.
I saw the marble cup; the tea,
Hung on the air, an amber stream;
I saw the fire's unglittering gleam,
The painted flame, the frozen smoke.
No more the flooding lamplight broke
On flying eyes and lips and hair;
But lay, but slept unbroken there,
On stiller flesh, and body breathless,
And lips and laughter stayed and deathless,
And words on which no silence grew.
Light was more alive than you.

For suddenly, and otherwhence,
I looked on your magnificence.
I saw the stillness and the light,
And you, august, immortal, white,
Holy and strange; and every glint
Posture and jest and thought and tint
Freed from the mask of transiency,
Triumphant in eternity,
Immote, immortal.

          Dazed at length
Human eyes grew, mortal strength
Wearied; and Time began to creep.
Change closed about me like a sleep.
Light glinted on the eyes I loved.
The cup was filled. The bodies moved.
The drifting petal came to the ground.
The laughter chimed its perfect round.
The broken syllable was ended.
And I, so certain and so friended,
How could I cloud, or how distress,
The heaven of your unconsciousness?
Or shake at Time's sufficient spell,
Stammering of lights unutterable?
The eternal holiness of you,
The timeless end, you never knew,

The peace that lay, the light that shone.
You never knew that I had gone
A million miles away, and stayed
A million years. The laughter played
Unbroken round me; and the jest
Flashed on. And we that knew the best
Down wonderful hours grew happier yet.
I sang at heart, and talked, and ate,
And lived from laugh to laugh, I too,
When you were there, and you, and you.

The paving stones, laid by Napoleonic prisoners of war a century before, still lead up to the house, dappled by the shade from the magnificent beech trees high above Crediton. The postal facilities at Clifford Bridge being non-existent, it has been deemed over the years most likely that Brooke posted his package of poems to publisher Frank Sidgwick from Crediton, thereby dating the 'Dining Room Tea' episode as 30 August *ex silentio*. They proved to be the only collection of his poems he saw published in his lifetime.

In the evening at Penton, Miss Montague suggested they all went to Crediton Fair, where a version of the popular drama *The Lyons Mail* was to be performed. The party took up the entire front row at a shilling a ticket, before

The dining-room at the Beeches. '. . . I saw the marble cup; the tea, hung on the air, an amber stream; I saw the fire's unglittering gleam . . .'

moving on to the fair, where they saw a girl who looked uncannily like Ka Cox – who at that moment was making her way with Virginia to the Clifford Bridge camp. Pauly Montague's sister Ruth, who was present at the tea, recalled:

> . . . in return for tea my Mother and I were invited to spend the day at the camp at Clifford Bridge – she rode her bicycle and I my pony – returning in the dark. As I was young Rupert and Justin decided that a ball game was the best way to entertain me. I remember an enormous meal of stew cooked by my brother Paul, in which someone discovered a button. Afterwards we watched Rupert looking very beautiful swimming up and down in the river.

Ruth was later befriended by Ka Cox while at the Slade School of Art, and Justin Brooke would propose to her but withdraw the offer after she decided she needed time to think about it. She married another, becoming Mrs Pickwoad, and surviving her brother Paul (who was killed in the First World War) by some 70-odd years, passing away in the late 1980s at the age of 90.

Today, the Beeches is much as it was in 1911, apart from having being divided in two by Maurice Webber in the mid-1950s; the dining-room is intact, complete with its fireplace – and the alabaster Buddahs, squatting on

Ka and Rupert at Clifford Bridge

the mantelpiece in the old picture, still preside over meal times.

Not everyone was a lover of the principles of Bedalian-style expeditions. James Strachey disappeared, to join his brother Lytton at nearby Becky Falls, after one night huddled in a blanket, sitting up especially to see the sun rise in an attempt to get into the mood of the camp. Rupert wrote the following couplet allegedly about him, although Noel Olivier felt it was written about Gerald Shove – either way it demonstrates that not all were willing or natural neo-pagans:

> In the late evening he was out of place
> And utterly irrelevant at dawn.

The more enthusiastic embarked on a 32-mile round walk to Yes Tor, to the north-west of the camp, and organised a manhunt on the return journey, in which Bryn Olivier became the quarry and succeeded in gaining the camp without being caught. At night there were songs around the fire as Pauly Montague played his Elizabethan gittern, possibly inspiring Rupert in his dissertation on 'John Webster and the Elizabethan Drama' at which he was working by day. Brooke used an apt quote for one at that time living a rough and ready outdoor existence from Webster's *Appius and Virginia*: 'I wake in the wet trench, loaded with more cold iron than a gaol would give a murderer, while the General sleeps in a field-bed, and to mock our hunger feeds us with the scent of the most curious fare. That makes his tables crack!' His dissertation argued both for and against *Appius and Virginia* being the work of John Webster, eventually reaching the conclusion that it was, in his opinion, from the pen of Thomas Heywood. The work, partly written in the meadow by the Teign at Clifford Bridge, won him his fellowship at King's College, Cambridge, and was published in book form in Britain and America in 1916.

Today the Clifford Bridge camp site plays host to far more than the handful of neo-pagan tents of 1911. The tranquil and idyllic area where Brooke read Webster, Keats's letters to Fanny Browne, and crafted 'Dining Room Tea' now bustles with holidaying families.

Rupert arrived back at the Old Vicarage to discover that Frank Sidgwick of Sidgwick & Jackson, who had agreed to publish his first book of poetry, was objecting to the title of one of the poems. 'Lust' wasn't the first of the works intended for inclusion that had raised Sidgwick's eyebrows. 'The Seasick Lover', which had originally been 'A Shakespearean Love Sonnet', he also found faintly objectionable. Against his better judgement, and having argued his points, Rupert conceded that if it were absolutely necessary the title 'Libido' could be substituted for 'Lust'. 'The Seasick Lover' became 'A Channel Passage'. He complained to friends of the enforced changes, but seemed to accept them with a degree of equanimity if any other course meant losing sales. The excitement of having his first volume of poetry published was tempered by Dudley Ward's betrothal to his German girlfriend Anne Marie, as this meant, in his eyes, that yet another friend was shedding their skin of youth to become domesticated. Francis and Frances Cornford were an item; so were Jacques Raverat and Gwen Darwin. His thoughts turned to Ka, as he still imagined Noel to be out of his reach – at least physically, while Ka might just not be . . .

The increasingly domiciliary attitude of his friends seemed only to fuel his restlessness; he implored Ka to join him doing something romantically exciting and interesting: 'I am getting excited. Lincolnshire? The Peaks? The Fens? East London? Lulworth, if you like, but *somewhere*.' In another spirited outburst to Ka, he declared that 'I'm determined to live like a motor car, or a needle, Mr Bennett [Arnold Bennett], or a planetary system, or whatever else is always at the keenest and wildest pitch of activity'. At the same time, he was still professing his love to an ostensibly ambivalent Noel.

In October 1911 he wrote to Ka Cox of a drama at the Old Vicarage, which happened in the middle of a letter he was writing to her: 'I've been the last half hour with my arms up a chimney. The beam in the kitchen chimney caught fire. "These old houses!" we kept panting. It was so difficult to get at, being also in part the chimney piece. Only Mrs Neeve, I and Mr Wallis at home. Mr W dashed for the brigade on his motorbike. An ever so cheerful and able British working man and I attacked the house with buckets and a pickaxe . . .'

During October, Rupert was becoming increasingly stressed, worrying about the lack of work he felt he had put into his dissertation on Webster, being in love in different ways with both Noel and Ka, and rushing backwards and forwards between Rugby, Grantchester, Cambridge and London. In the capital, he walked Hampstead Heath, stayed with James Strachey in Belsize Park, saw Wagner's Ring Cycle, ate at the National Liberal Club, talked with Eddie Marsh and moved into the second floor of the studio of the Strachey's cousin, the artist Duncan Grant, at 21 Fitzroy Square. He also took time to correct the proofs of his forthcoming poetry book.

Bizarrely, for someone not musically gifted, Rupert decided he would like to have singing lessons and asked Clive Carey, with whom he had worked on various Cambridge productions, if he would be available: '. . . if I was taught singing by some sensible person who understood all the time that I couldn't ever sing properly whatever happened, I might gain anyhow two things. 1. Be able to hear music . . . 2. Have a better and more manageable reading voice.' As late as 1957, while adjudicating at Bournemouth at a Music Competition Festival, Carey spoke warmly of Brooke and again in the 1960s commented, 'he was a very close friend of mine and a wonderful person in

65

MEMORANDUM OF AGREEMENT made this *Twelfth* day of *August* 1911
BETWEEN Rupert Brooke Esq, of The Old Vicarage, Grantchester,
Cambridge., hereinafter called the Author, his heirs, executors,
and assigns, of the one part, and Sidgwick & Jackson Limited, of
3 Adam Street, Adelphi, London, W.C., hereinafter called the Publishers, of the other part; WHEREBY it is agreed as follows:-

(1) The Author having supplied the Publishers with the M.S. of
his poems, the Publishers undertake at the Author's charge to print

R B an edition of ~~Eight~~ *five* hundred copies and bind and advertise the
same as required and publish the said work in the Author's behalf
and offer it for sale through the ordinary trade channels at the
published price of two shillings and sixpence net.

(2) The Publishers shall produce the said work in accordance
with the specimens and estimates submitted to and approved by the Au
Author, who undertakes to bear all costs of production in accordance with the Publishers' letters to him, together with the charges
for Author's corrections on the proofs.

(3) The Publishers shall render to the Author an account of the
sales of the said work, reckoning thirteen copies as twelve, and
shall pay over to him the net amounts derived therefrom as received
less their commission of fifteen per cent. on such amounts. Accounts
shall be rendered half-yearly as at June 30th and December 31st in
each year and shall be settled in cash within three months of the
said dates respectively.

(4) The Publishers shall include the said work in their lists
and catalogues free of further charge, but all costs of newspaper
advertising shall be borne by the Author and debited to his account;

R B but the sum so spent shall not exceed the sum of £ *3 three* pounds
without written instructions from the Author.

(Agreement continued to Folio 2.)

Brooke's publishing contract with Sidgwick & Jackson signed by Brooke
and witnessed by Virginia Woolf

65

Folio 2 of Agreement
Between Rupert Brooke Esq and Sidgwick and Jackson Ltd.

(5) If after two years from the date of publication the demand
for the said work shall in the Publishers' opinion have ceased, they
shall be at liberty to return to the Author the unsold stock of
the work, and this agreement shall thereupon determine.

(6) The Author undertakes to keep the Publishers indemnified
against all actions claims and demands which may be brought against
or made upon them by reason of the said work containing or being
alleged to contain any libellous or other actionable matter or to
be an infringement of any right or rights belonging to any other
party.

(7) The Publishers shall be allowed six free copies of the said
work for their file and travellers' use, and five copies for the
Statutory Libraries gratis.

SIGNED.

In the presence of

Virginia Stephen
29 Fitzroy Square
London W.

all respects'. He declined to comment on Rupert's singing ability, but did once persuade him to air his voice amongst others and take the part of a slave in a Cambridge production of Mozart's *The Magic Flute*.

Despite not being comfortable on stage, Rupert certainly worked hard on any role he had to take. There are two photographs of him reciting Faustus at the Old Vicarage to Jacques Raverat and Dudley Ward, who appear to be testing him on his lines. On another occasion he sat up in one of the chestnut trees reading aloud to Noel Olivier and Sybil Pye. Sybil remembered those moments with fondness.

> The peculiar golden quality of his hair. This hair escaping from under the crown, flapped and leapt . . . Our sitting-room was small and low, with a lamp slung from the ceiling, and a narrow door opening straight on to the dark garden. On quiet nights, when water sounds and scents drifted up from the river, this room half suggested the cabin of a ship. Rupert sat with his book at a table just below the lamp, the open door and the dark sky behind him, and the lamplight falling so directly on his head would vividly mark the outline and proportions of forehead, cheek and chin, so that in trying afterwards to realise just what lent them, apart from all expression, so complete and unusual a dignity and charm, I find it is to this moment my mind turns.

The romance of the house itself was tempered by the presence of an army of woodlice, about which Rupert was once moved to comment:

> . . . they will fall into my bed and get in my hair. The hot weather brings them out. They climb the walls and march along the ceiling. When they're above me they look down, see with a start – and a slight scream – that there's another person in the room and fall. And I never could bear woodlice. Mrs Neeves sprinkles yellow dust on my books and clothes, with a pathetic foreboding of failure, and says 'They're 'armless, poor things!' But my nerve gives.

Brooke's volume of poems was published in November although he was in no mood to be excited about the prospect as the long hours put in revising his dissertation on Webster had worn him out, and left him feeling run-down. His book didn't set the literary world on fire immediately but from a humble start it went on to sell almost 100,000 copies in the next 20 years alone.

A reading party was being organised at Lulworth Cove to begin after Christmas 1911 and run into the new year. The circle included Lytton and James Strachey, Ka Cox, Justin Brooke, Maynard Keynes, Duncan Grant,

Gwen Raverat and an old Bedalian and King's man, Ferenc Bekassy, a Hungarian with more than a passing passion for Noel. Henry Lamb was to join the party, but he was staying locally in Corfe Castle.

Before Lulworth, Rupert slept a night at Ka's flat at 76 Charlotte Street in London, before joining his mother in the Beachy Head Hotel high up on the cliffs looking down on Eastbourne, Sussex. It was here he completed his dissertation on Webster, but his restless mental state, workload and general ill-health were taking their toll. He was jaded and overwrought, and suffered from insomnia while staying at Beachy Head – a strangely wild, windy and remote setting for a December break.

Brooke's literary mentor Eddie Marsh was now Private Secretary to the First Lord of the Admiralty, Winston Churchill, and as such was becoming increasingly influential. So it was good news that he was enamoured with Rupert's volume of poems: 'I had always in the trembling hope reposed that I should like the poems . . . but at my wildest I never looked forward to such magnificence . . . you have brought back into English poetry the rapturous beautiful grotesque of the 17th century . . .' Rupert was delighted, writing to Marsh from his mother's house in Rugby just before Christmas, 'God! It's so cheering to find someone who likes the modern stuff, & appreciates what one's at. You can't think how your remarks and liking thrilled me . . .'

CHAPTER VIII

Monsters of the Darkest Hell
Nibbled My Soul

On 27 December 1911, Rupert and the others descended on Lulworth. Brooke himself stayed with Mrs Carter at Churchfield House, a dwelling that began as a simple cottage and was converted in the early seventeenth century by Lawrence Randall, in whose family it stayed until 1870. In the 1750s it became the Red Lion – the name being taken from the coat of arms of the local Duberville family. George III dined there in 1802 and sang its praises. After 1870 it became Churchfield House.

This was to be Rupert's most traumatic stay in Lulworth. Lytton Strachey was there, too, while others were at Cove Cottage; Henry Lamb arriving later, from Corfe, allegedly at Lytton's behest, as there seemed to be a potential dalliance in the air between Lamb and Ka Cox. Rupert was uncommunicative and reclusive, becoming increasingly paranoid as Ka revealed to him her feelings for Henry Lamb. Despite an understanding with Noel Olivier, Brooke's relationship with her seemed to be standing still, if not becoming cooler. Even so, Ka's revelations were not designed to provoke any latent jealousy in Rupert. They not only provoked but inflamed him swiftly, to the point of unreasonable paranoia; Brooke suddenly believed himself in love with Ka much in the same way that Lysander seemingly irrationally transferred his affections from Hermia to Helena in Shakespeare's *A Midsummer Night's Dream*. But who was the mischievous Puck at Lulworth? Rupert for a long time, and in retrospect unfairly, blamed Lytton Strachey for plotting the whole Ka Cox/Henry Lamb saga. In reality it was Lamb's weakness for women and overt flirtatiousness combined with Ka's susceptibility.

In depressed state he walked with James Strachey from Lulworth over the Purbeck Hills to Corfe Castle, where James caught a train to London and Brooke walked on further to Studland, before returning to Lulworth. His

Churchfield House, West Lulworth where Brooke's nervous breakdown began

state of mind worsened to such an extent that he had a nervous breakdown of sorts and became temporarily obsessed by Ka. He wrote from Churchfield House to Noel on 6 January, 'I have been ill and feeling very tired; and as the days go by I get worse. Also, I can't get my plans settled even for the nearest future, and I don't know what I shall be feeling in even two or three days. It isn't your "fault" this time! In addition to all the other horrors, there's now a horrible business between me and Ka – we're hurting each other . . .' Only the week before he had written to Noel proclaiming, 'I love you: any how. I love you. I love you. I wish you were here.'

In this run-down state, he was taken to Dr Craig, a Harley Street specialist, who recommended rest, a special diet and a holiday. Dr Craig confirmed his diagnosis to Mrs Brooke – 'Your son was obviously in a state of severe breakdown when I saw him. He was hypersensitive and introspective.' He was due to join his mother in Cannes anyway, but first he flew to Noel in Limpsfield, this time to counsel her about Ka. Breaking his journey to the south of France in Paris, he was looked after by his friend Elizabeth Van Rysselbergh, before heading to Cannes and the Hotel du Pavillion to join his mother. Rather than letting things lie, taking his time and regaining his mental equilibrium, he proceeded to bombard Ka with letters padded with declamatory overtures: 'Love me! Love me! Love me! . . . I love you so much'; 'I love you so . . . I kiss your lips'; 'I'm all reaching out to you, body and mind.' He described to her the view from his balcony overlooking the Mediterranean; 'Outside there are large numbers of tropical palms, a fountain, laden orange trees and roses. There's an opal sea and jagged hills with amazing sunsets behind . . .' He was also very descriptive about a moment some 18 months earlier when he'd first seen Ka in a different light: 'You'd for some reason got on a low dress. I looked at the firm and lovely place where your deep breasts divided and grew out of the chest and went down under your dress . . . and I was suddenly very giddy, and physically hit with a glimpse of a new sort of beauty that I'd not quite known of . . .' Would he have had such a sudden physical fixation for her were it not for her interest in Henry Lamb? Probably not, but he convinced her to meet him in Munich where they could be together: sleep together. In the meantime, he had to rub along with Mendelssohn, Ravel, Mozart and Saint-Saens at Cannes concerts.

Suspicious of the increasing correspondence arriving for Rupert, Mrs Brooke soon realised something was afoot. She felt he should spend more time recuperating and that he was not yet fit to travel, but her protestations fell on stony ground. Despite some 'awful scenes with the Ranee', it was arranged that Ka would meet him off the train at Verona and they would return a few days later to where she was staying in Munich. In the event they also visited Salzburg and Starnberg. In his agitated condition, which erupted spasmodically during their time there, he was becoming more and more dependent upon her, growing stronger from her supportive presence, while she became increasingly strained. They were clearly not 'in love', he desiring her for release from physical pressures and as a cushion, while she was willing to be submissive. Because of Rupert's delicate mental balance, she had to pick her moment to let him know that she had, in fact, been seeing Henry Lamb while Rupert was recuperating in Cannes.

He was unwittingly the cause of Rupert and Ka being forced together in a way that wasn't right for either of them. He liked her as a friend, and ended up believing he was in love with her, his protestations of love while his mind was a little unbalanced eventually convincing her. He soon realised that he did not *really* want the security of Ka but it was too late for her – she now believed that Rupert was the man for her and it was only his mental state that would make it sometimes appear otherwise.

Although it wasn't immediately apparent, Rupert began to cool by degrees towards Ka from the end of their time together in Germany. His manner towards her became more matter of fact and at times off hand, and, although he wrote to her five times in one weekend during March, from the Mermaid Inn at Rye, Kent, the letters had a different tone from those written in Cannes, and Noel's name crept into them more than once.

His feelings of guilt towards Ka, that he had used her, were to be with him for the rest of his life, but in the short term he played along with the facade until he was forced to be honest about his feelings later in the year. In May he was to confide to Jacques: 'I go about with the woman dutifully. I've a sort of dim, reflected affection for something in her . . . love her? Bless you, no! but I don't love anybody. The bother is I don't really *like* her. There is a feeling of staleness, ugliness, trustlessness about her . . .'

Before Rye, Rupert repaired to Rugby. Ka came to stay with him and great plans were laid to avoid Mrs Brooke's suspicions of a relationship or that they had met in Germany. Edward Marsh and Geoffrey Keynes also arrived, Rupert impressing on Keynes the importance of not letting his mother know too much about his personal life: 'Relations between the Ranee and me are very peculiar.' Then Rupert went to the Mermaid with James Strachey, a friend of Richard Aldington the owner's son, who was to become an eminent poet and writer.

The famous inn, which probably dates from 1156, certainly 'stood on this present site, built of wattle, daub, lath and plaster' in 1300, when the Mermaid brewed its own ale and charged a penny a night for lodging. It was rebuilt in 1920 using ships' timbers and baulks of Sussex oak, the fireplaces being carved from French stone ballast rescued from the harbour. Long associated with smugglers, it would now be referred to as a 'no-go' area, especially during the eighteenth century, when the 600-strong Hawkhurst gang openly flaunted their illicit activities without fear of reprisals, with consummate ease. By 1912, however, life at the Mermaid was a little more civilised, as Brooke revealed in one of his letters to Ka.

The Mermaid at Rye as it was when Brooke stayed in March 1912

We're in a Smoking Room. They're all in evening dress, and they talk – there are these people in the world – about Bridge, Golf and Motoring. They're *playing* bridge. But then the most extraordinary thing is about 'Colonel' Aldington, May, Anabel and Dick. Because – it turns out – *they* keep the Inn. (Very Old place – you see these beams?) She's written a book of poems and *several* novels. And Dick – but Dick's been a flame of James' for years. One's almost further from you among the upper classes than elsewhere. Oh Lord! And in the Dining Room . . . but James, or I'll, tell you all about it.

The following day (Sunday) he wrote again to Ka. 'I'm just out a walk to Winchelsea', obviously so mentally overwrought that he omitted the 'for'. He ends the letter, '. . . you'd better marry me before we leave England, you know. I'll accept the responsibility. And the fineness to come . . .' In yet another epistle written on Mermaid notepaper to Ka on the Sunday evening he complained: 'Oh God, we've been searching for rooms in Winchelsea. No luck,' but extolled the virtues of Rye's neighbour: 'Oh, and Winchelsea's so lovely. On the road back we met a small lady who was lost, and I was (nervously) kind to her and restored her, practically to her Mother. Ha! I read *The Way of All Flesh*, and talk to James and think of you.' Brooke's walk to Winchelsea, two miles of marshland away from Rye, ran between the road and the railway, Elsie M. Jacobs described it in 1947:

> . . . it was much used before people got too lazy to walk; old folk still speak of it as the shortcut. It is so seldom used now that the path is almost obliterated, but the bridges over the dykes are intact, a most important consideration on the marshes . . . Do not attempt this walk in mist or fog, as even a slight mist will ruin the view and cause endless worries about the path . . . The land on which you walk was once the bed of the sea and here in August 1350 sailed forty large Spanish ships. Edward III and the Black Prince commanded fifty good ships and pinnaces of the smaller type. A stirring naval battle was fought and fifteen of the enemy were sunk or captured!

Brooke also described to Ka an evening foray to Lamb House, just around the corner from the Mermaid in West Street.

> James and I have been out this evening to call on Mr Henry James. At nine. We found, at length, the House. It was immensely rich, and brilliantly lighted at every window on the ground floor. The upper floors were deserted: one black window open. The house is straight on the street. We nearly fainted with fear of a Company. At length I pressed the

Bell of the Great Door – there was a smaller door further along, the Servant's door we were told. No answer. I pressed again. At length a slow dragging step was heard within. It stopped inside the door. We shuffled. Then, very slowly, and very loudly, immense numbers of chains and bolts were drawn within. There was a pause again. Further rattling within. Then the steps seemed to be heard retreating. There was silence. We waited in wild, agonising stupefaction. The House was dead-silent. At length there was a shuffling noise from the Servants' door. We thought someone was about to emerge from there to greet us. We slid down towards it. Nothing happened. We drew back and observed the house. A low whistle came from it. Then nothing happened for two minutes. Suddenly a shadow passed, quickly, across the light in the window nearest the door. Again nothing happened. James and I, sick with surmise, stole down the street. We thought we heard another whistle, as we departed. We came back here shaking – we didn't know at what. If the evening paper, as you get this, tells of the murder of Mr Henry James – you'll know.

Despite Brooke's intriguing description of the mysterious scenario, the American author Henry James was actually in London at the time – at the Reform Club – so his life was never in danger from the chain-rattling whistler!

The arrival of Henry James at Lamb House in 1896 had seemed to herald the birth of a literary era for Rye, as his visitors included distinguished English contemporary writers Rudyard Kipling, Joseph Conrad, Ford Madox Ford and G.K. Chesterton, as well as French anglophile Hilaire Belloc and American literary luminaries Edith Wharton and Stephen Crane. The younger literati, not of his peer group, came too in the shape of Virginia Bell, Virginia Woolf (Virginia Stephen had by this time married Leonard Woolf), E.M. Forster and E.F. Benson – the latter eventually taking the property on three years after James's death in 1916.

Albert Edward Aldington, the owner of the Mermaid, wasn't actually a colonel, Anabel was Arabella – a nickname only, her real name was Dorothy Yorke – an American girlfriend of Dick's who lived until her eightieth year. He called he Dolikins. Even Dick was an adopted name, Edward Godfrey Aldington calling himself that from an early age. The mother, Jessie May, to whom Brooke refers, wrote five novels and two books of poems between 1905 and 1917, while the youngest daughter Patricia was only four years old at the time and spent her days in the garden, where the car park is now, climbing the big old tree that used to stand there. Patricia Aldington still lives in Rye, where she used to take an active role in the running of the museum, and still remembers Brooke's visit.

In 1919 'Dick' Aldington wrote to a friend, 'I am thinking of collecting all my war poems – I have about 60 or 70 – into a book. Do you think the USA would care for them? They are 70 – not popular – I mean they are bitter anguish-stricken, realistic, not like Brooke or Noyes or anybody like that. They are the stern truth and I have hesitated about publishing them.' The disparaging attitude that he had about Brooke's war poems was not entirely fair, as Aldington was to see the war out and therefore be in a position to write a more balanced view – a chance not afforded to Rupert.

On 31 March, Rupert wrote to Jacques Raverat; 'I leave here tomorrow evening. I go to Noel's then to Ka Wednesday evening? Till Friday? Then I don't know where: Winchelsea or the New Forest.'

He determined to call at Limpsfield Chart to see Noel, before going on to Ka at Woking. Still uncertain of his feelings he also wrote to Noel from the Mermaid. 'There is no doubt you're the finest person in the world. How dare I see you . . .' But Rupert wasn't Noel's only suitor. As well as Ferenc Bekassy, Adrian Stephen, Virginia Woolf's brother, was now making overtures to Noel and appeared at the Champions. From Ka's house Rupert wrote to Jacques Raverat: 'I'm going tomorrow to c/o Mrs Primmer, Beech Shade, Bank, Lyndhurst. I'm going to leave Ka alone till she's rested and ready for Germany. I found her (I came yesterday) pretty bad . . .'

This stay at Bank, in April 1912, found him in a totally different mood to the lovestruck 22-year-old who had gone 'dancing and leaping through the New Forest' in 1909. His nervous breakdown following the jealousy and paranoia over Ka Cox's dalliance with Henry Lamb, and his own subsequent affair with her, had left his nerves taut, his behaviour erratic and his state of mind irrational. Their love-making in Germany resulted in Ka becoming pregnant with Brooke's child, but a subsequent miscarriage circumvented any hurried talk of marriage plans; in any case, he continued to feel disenchanted with the relationship, seeing Ka as a 'fallen woman'.

Ka was attempting to be philosophical about the situation, while her friends feared for her general well-being. The relationship between Rupert and Ka was to be awkward for some time while before the channels of communication became a little more open. The potential threat of extra-marital parenthood with all its implications, although now averted, was clearly pushing him towards a second breakdown, causing him to escape to the solitude and happy memories of Beech Shade with the loyal James Strachey. On 6 April he wrote to Noel, 'I *say*, being here, you know; and precisely three years – Easter time – Oh Lord! Mrs Primmer is well. The trees are there. The black hut stands. Also the holly-bush. And the room. Oh! Dearest Noel, you *were* good. It's incredible – I didn't *know* there were such things as you in the world!' The black hut stood, until recent times, on a clearing near the house, and the holly-bush – which grew nearby, remained until it was taken down as late as the 1950s when the track was metalled. To Ka he wrote a more factual, conversational note.

James had to leave me to solitude . . . I sit and read and write . . . it is fine but not warm. The beeches are in bloom. Also the junipers and arbutuses and so forth. We went walks and enjoyed the scenery. James pointed to a clump of larches and said 'Birches! . . . ah! Birches! Birches are a wonderful tree' . . . Mrs Primmer is, of course, the *most* amazing cook in the world. Four-course dinners, absolutely perfect. One eats a lot. I think of staying here for ever . . .

Despite his apparent joy at the solitude that was now his, in reality he didn't want to be left alone, and following James's departure, his anxious entreaties to Bryn Olivier brought her to Bank – probably more out of concern for his state of mind than any other reason. Whether in a cry for help or a dramatic pose, he talked of suicide and of buying a revolver, apparently searching the shops at Brockenhurst for a suitable firearm, treading the pathway towards insanity one moment and relapsing into a sentimental lassitude the next. Almost as an automaton he wrote to Hugh Dalton:

Friend of my laughing careless youth, where are those golden hours now? Where now the shrill mirth of our burgeoning intellects? And by what doubtful and deleterious ways am I come down to this place of shadows and eyeless pain? In truth I have been for some months in Hell. I have been very ill. I am very ill. In all probability I shall be very ill. It is thought by those who know me best (viz myself) that I shall die . . . I do nothing. I eat and sleep and rest. My thoughts buzz drearily in a vacuum . . . I am more than a little gone in my head, since my collapse . . .

Probably kept sane by the excellent home cooking of Mrs Primmer, he waxed lyrical about her culinary expertise in a letter from Beech Shade to Maynard Keynes: 'I'm here, under the charge of Brynhild at present. Most charming. And about my intellectual level . . . Oh! Oh! Mrs Primmer's five-course dinner is on the table – funny she should be the best cook in England. Brynhild, a little nervously, sends you her love . . .' His black mood also came through in a letter to the poet James Elroy Flecker: 'I galloped down hill for months and then took the abyss with a leap . . . nine days I lay without sleep or food. Monsters of the darkest Hell nibbled my soul.'

April also brought the gloomy news that he had failed to obtain his fellowship. Rupert later confided to Bryn, 'I'd been infinitely wretched and ill, wretcheder than I'd thought possible. And then for a few days it all dropped away and – oh! – how lovely Bank was!' During those days at Bank, he must have seen her as a lifeline in his hour of need, and felt that closeness that a patient in hospital so often does with their nurse.

147

'The best cook in England' outlived Brooke by 30 years and her husband by 20, Mrs Primmer passing away in 1945 at Bridport, while Beech Shade and the rest of the hamlet of Gritnam nearly became a victim of the motor age when Royal Blue Coaches attempted to buy the clearing in which the handful of cottages stood, in order to demolish it and create a coach park. Fortunately the Gritnam Trust was formed which put paid to the plan, but Beech Shade and the adjoining cottage were pulled down and rebuilt in the late thirties after falling into the hands of the Forestry Commission. The new house bears the name of its predecessor and, although not dissimilar in style, is different – the best example of how Beech Shade looked during Brooke's day is its near neighbour Woodbine Cottage.

In a rootless and agitated frame of mind Rupert returned briefly to Limpsfield Chart, before heading to the anonymity of London. Ka was now convinced that Rupert's feelings for her were cooling. They met in Trafalgar Square, close to where he was staying at the National Liberal Club. She was in tears and he was comforting, but undoubtedly going through the motions of consoling her, as the beginnings of guilt gnawed at him. He escaped to Berlin to stay with Dudley Ward, who was about to marry his girlfriend Anne Marie Von der Planitz, on 11 May in Munich, but he did ask Ka to go and visit. No doubt her pragmatism detected a faint demurring in his suggestion. Nevertheless she agreed to join him at some point.

Near the station in the Berlin district of Charlottenburg, the Cafe des Westens was where Brooke took to sitting, reading and writing, well away from the wedding preparations, and leaving Dudley space to write his articles for *The Economist*. The cafe proved the unlikely setting for two major trains of thought for Rupert. First a friend of Dudley's told him a tale there. The action had allegedly taken place in Lithuania the previous year. A boy who had run away from there at the age of 13, returned as a man, unrecognised by his own family. They put him up for the night, and the daughter, encouraged by the parents, killed him for his money. When the truth was revealed, they were overcome with grief and remorse. Whether true or apocryphal, and the story is an old one, it was to sow the seed for his only play, *Lithuania*, which would be produced three and a half years later in America. The other work that germinated at the Cafe des Westens was the poem that eventually became 'The Old Vicarage, Grantchester'. Initially entitled 'Home', it then became 'Fragments of a Poem to be Entitled The Sentimental Exile'.

He was homesick not for England in general – after all, he had only just completed the circuitous route of Rugby, Rye, Limpsfield Chart, Bank, Limpsfield Chart, Rugby and London – but for Grantchester. In a letter to Ka on the train to Germany he admitted his unashamed nostalgia for the Old Vicarage, as fragments and ideas for a poem were clearly beginning to form themselves in his mind. 'I fancy you may be, just now, in Grantchester. I envy you, frightfully. That river and the chestnuts come back to me a lot. Tea on the lawn. Just wire to me and we'll spend the Summer there . . .' At the Cafe des Westens his ideas became notes, the notes became couplets and the couplets began to form what was to become one of his two most famous and enduring poems. On its completion he despatched it to the editor of the King's magazine, *Basileon*, preceded by a telegram: 'A masterpiece on its way.'

The Old Vicarage, Grantchester

Just now the lilac is in bloom,
All before my little room;
And in my flower-beds, I think,
Smile the carnation and the pink;
And down the borders, well I know,
The poppy and the pansy blow . . .
Oh! There the chestnuts, summer through,
Beside the river make for you
A tunnel of green gloom, and sleep
Deeply above; and green and deep
The stream mysterious glides beneath,
Green as a dream and deep as death.
– Oh, damn! I know it! And I know
How the May fields all golden show,
And when the day is young and sweet,
Gild gloriously the bare feet
That run to bathe . . .
                        Du lieber Gott!

Here am I, sweating, sick, and hot,
And there the shadowed waters fresh
Lean up to embrace the naked flesh.
Temperamentvoll German jews
Drink beer around; – and *there* the dews
Are soft between a morn of gold.
Here tulips bloom as they are told;
Unkempt about those hedges blows
An English unofficial rose;
And there the unregulated sun
Slopes down to rest when day is done,
And wakes a vague unpunctual star,
A slippered Hesper; and there are

149

Meads towards Haslingfield and Coton
Where *das Betreten's* not *verboten*.

ειθε γενοιμην . . . would I were
In Grantchester, in Grantchester! –
Some, it may be, can get in touch
With Nature there, or Earth, or such.
And clever modern men have seen
A faun a-peeping through the green,
And felt the Classics were not dead,
To glimpse a Naiad's reedy head,
Or hear the Goat-foot piping low: . . .
But these are things I do not know.
I only know that you may lie
Day-long and watch the Cambridge sky,
And, flower-lulled in sleepy grass,
Hear the cool lapse of hours pass,
Until the centuries blend and blur
In Grantchester, in Grantchester . . .
Still in the dawnlit waters cool
His ghostly Lordship swims his pool,
And tries the strokes, essays the tricks,
Long learnt on Hellespoint, or Styx.
Dan Chaucer hears his river still
Chatter beneath a phantom mill.
Tennyson notes with studious eye,
How Cambridge waters hurry by . . .
And in that garden, black and white,
Creep whispers through the grass all night;
And spectral dance, before the dawn,
A hundred vicars down the lawn;
Curates, long dust, will come and go
On lissom, clerical, printless toe;
And oft between the boughs is seen
The sly shade of a Rural Dean . . .
Till, at a shiver in the skies,
Vanishing with Satanic cries,
The prim ecclesiastical rout
Leaves but a startled sleeper-out,
Grey heavens, the first bird's drowsy calls,
The falling house that never falls.

God! I will pack, and take a train,
And get me to England once again!
For England's the one land, I know,
Where men with Splendid Hearts may go;
And Cambridgeshire, of all England,
The shire for Men who Understand;
And of that district I prefer
The lovely hamlet Grantchester.
For Cambridgeshire people rarely smile,
Being urban, squat, and packed with guile;
And Royston men in the far South
Are black and fierce and strange of mouth;
At Over they fling oaths at one,
And worse than oaths at Trumpington,
And Ditton girls are mean and dirty,
And there's none in Harston under thirty,
And folks in Shelford and those parts
Have twisted lips and twisted hearts,
And Barton men make Cockney rhymes,
And Coton's full of nameless crimes,
And things are done you'd not believe
At Madingley, on Christmas Eve.
Strong men have run for miles and miles,
When one from Cherry Hinton smiles;
Strong men have blanched, and shot their wives,
Rather than send them to St Ives;
Strong men have cried like babes, bydam,
To hear what happened at Babraham.
But Grantchester! Ah, Grantchester!
There's peace and holy quiet there,
Great clouds along pacifist skies,
And men and women with straight eyes,
Lithe children lovelier than a dream,
A bosky wood, a slumberous stream,
And little kindly winds that creep
Round twilight corners, half asleep.
In Grantchester their skins are white;
They bathe by day, they bathe by night;
The women there do all they ought;
The men observe the Rules of Thought.
They love the Good; they worship Truth;
They laugh uproariously at youth;

151

(And when they get to feeling old,
They up and shoot themselves, I'm told) . . .

Ah God! To see the branches stir
Across the moon at Grantchester!
To smell the thrilling-sweet and rotten
Unforgettable, unforgotten
River-smell, and hear the breeze
Sobbing in the little trees.
Say, do the elm-clumps greatly stand
Still guardians of that holy land?
The chestnuts shade, in reverend dream,
The yet unacademic stream?
Is dawn a secret shy and cold
Anadyomene, silver-gold?
And sunset still a golden sea
From Haslingfield to Madingley?
And after, ere the night is born,
Do hares come out about the corn?
Oh, is the water sweet and cool,
Gentle and brown, above the pool?
And laughs the immortal river still
Under the mill, under the mill?
Say, is there Beauty yet to find?
And Certainty? And Quiet kind?
Deep meadows yet, for to forget
The lies, and truths, and pain? . . . oh! yet
Stands the Church clock at ten to three?
And is there honey still for tea?

Ka joined Rupert in Berlin, but his physical passion for her was no longer there, as he told Dudley: 'I remain dead. I care practically nothing for any person in the world. I've anxiety, and a sort of affection, for Ka – But I don't really care. I've no feeling for anybody at all – except the uneasy ghosts of the immense reverence and rather steadfast love for Noel, and a knowledge that Noel is the finest thing I've ever seen in the world, and Ka – isn't . . .' Ka fell ill in Germany, and Rupert's mental equilibrium was still inharmonious and out of kilter, causing them to put the future on hold. She returned to her sister Hester in London, while Rupert, in a state of torpor, wrote to Jacques Raverat, '. . . my love for Ka was pretty well at an end – poisoned, dead – before I discovered she was after all in love with me . . .' Despite the finality of his feeling when writing to friends, his communications with Ka still gave

*Workings of the poem 'The Sentimental Exile' that
was to become 'The Old Vicarage, Granchester'*

her hope: 'Hadn't we better fix a date? The end of July? Would that do? It's madness for me to make up my mind now isn't it?' He also confesses to a 'mechanical dull drifting through the days'. He felt though, that he owed her something and was going through the motions of what he imagined to be doing the right thing by her.

James Strachey joined Rupert in Berlin and the two of them journeyed to the Hague. Rupert eagerly devouring Hilaire Belloc's new book *The Four Men* at the Hotel des Indes where they were staying. The tale – a journey under the downs of Sussex – was to have a profound effect on him, the verses at the end of the work eventually inspiring his most quoted poem, 'The Soldier'.

CHAPTER IX

Hope Springs Eternal . . . (*Alexander Pope*)

Back in London came a little occupational therapy for his confused mind: a play with the Cornfords, a gathering of the Apostles and a meet with E.M. Forster, who was also staying at Raymond Buildings with Eddie Marsh. From Gray's Inn, it was a fleeting visit to see his mother before retiring to his spiritual home, the Old Vicarage. He was glad to discover that God was in his heaven, and indeed all was right with the world – at least this little plot. Mrs Neeve was still there, so was the honey, and his poem had been published in *Basileon*. Bryn Olivier impressed the family at Champions when she read it to them over Sunday breakfast; while Eddie Marsh thought it 'the most human thing you've written, the only one that has brought tears to my fine eyes', and implored him to 'never write anything so good again without my knowing'. It was admired not only by friends: eminent poets Edmund Gosse and Austin Dobson were enraptured, as was the writer and fellow of King's, G. Lowes Dickinson.

Rupert's general misery was compounded in July by the news of the death of one of his oldest friends, Hugh Russell-Smith's brother Denham. He had written quite often to Denham, who usually answered his letters by return of post. The family that had made him envious with their obvious good nature were shattered by his early death in July 1912, aged just 23. It was only after Denham's death that he confessed, in a letter to James Strachey, to an experimental sexual dalliance that he and the younger Russell-Smith had had at the Orchard in the autumn of 1909.

> The Autumn of 1909! We hugged and kissed and strained Denham and I on and off for years – ever since that quiet evening I rubbed him, in the dark, speechlessly in the smaller of the two dorms. An abortive affair, as I have told you. But in the Summer holidays of 1906 and

1907 at Brockenhurst, he had often taken me out to the hammock after dinner, to lie entwined there . . .'

Of the one-off escapade at the Orchard he wrote, 'I wanted to have some fun, and, still more, to see what it was like and to do away with the shame (as I thought it was) of being a virgin.' He was, inevitably, disillusioned by what he believed was going to be a quantum leap from virginity to sexual knowledge. Despite the rushed, unsatisfactory night in his bedroom at the Orchard, the two remained good friends and did not speak of the moment again. As far as can be ascertained it was Brooke's only real homosexual experience, apart from schoolboy experimentation at Rugby.

In spite of being run-down, taking strong sedations to help him sleep and living with the knowledge that sooner rather than later he must address the situation with Ka, he joined a summer reading party at a hostelry situated on the extreme north-east edge of Salisbury Plain. Maynard Keynes attempted to go one better than the previous year's camp at Clifford Bridge by taking over the Crown at Everleigh for a few weeks and inviting a mixture of Apostles and Brooke's neo-pagan/old Bedalian circle. Keynes had recently become interested in riding, so maybe he discovered the Crown via Cobbett's *Rural Rides* or, less likely, through the knowledge that the 1897 (and 1898) Grand National winner, Manifesto, came from the stables at the Crown Inn! The Crown Inn at Everleigh was originally built as the Dower House, being converted to its present use around 1790. The journalist and reformer William Cobbett stayed at the Crown on 27 August 1826, commenting in his book, *Rural Rides*:

> This Inn is one of the nicest, and in Summer one of the pleasantest in England; for I think my experience in this way will justify me in speaking thus positively. The house is large, the stables good, the Landlord a farmer also, and therefore no cribbing your horses in hay or straw, and yourself in eggs and cream. The garden which adjoins the south side of the house is large, of a good shape, consists of well-disposed clumps of shrubs and flowers and of short grass very neatly kept. In the lower part of the garden there are high trees and amongst these a most populous rookery . . .

The area was once so open that one could ride from Everleigh to Salisbury, a distance of about ten miles, without jumping a fence or opening a gate.

Among Maynard's guests were his brother Geoffrey, Daphne, Bryn and Noel Olivier, Justin Brooke, Rupert, James Strachey, Apostles Gerald Shove and Gordon Luce and Frankie Birrell. The company rode, played croquet and walked, as they wished, and read from Jane Austen in the evenings. Noel's notes about the occasion reveal that Brooke was no horseman, and took no part in the riding side of the activities. The Crown possessing only some five or six bedrooms, the party took over the whole inn with the exception of the small bar for the locals. Maynard, whose inclinations were then exclusively homosexual, seemed disenchanted with the female contingent, and annoyed by Rupert's overtures to Bryn, confessing in a letter to Duncan Grant,

> I don't much care for the attitude these women breed and haven't liked this party nearly so much as my last week's [guests were coming and going at different times]. Noel is very nice and Daphne very innocent, but Bryn is too stupid and I begin to take an active dislike to her. Out of the window [his bedroom overlooked the garden] I see Rupert making love to her – taking her hand, sitting at her feet, gazing into her eyes. Oh these womanisers. How on earth and what for can he do it?

Rupert's nerves and emotions, coupled with the heavy medication, contributed to his irrationality and confusion while at Everleigh. He was flirting outrageously with Bryn – inviting her to go boating with him the following month – only to be told, when cornered, that she wanted to take Hugh Popham as well. Rupert's incredulity forced her to confess to him that she had, in fact, decided to marry Popham. Rupert was distraught, and not only reneged on the boating arrangements but refused to say goodbye to her when she left Everleigh. His feelings seemed to be all over the place as he wrote to Noel from the Crown after her departure.

> I had tea, sat a little, walked for miles alone, changed – I don't know what the time is, or where anybody is. There seems nothing to do but write to you . . . it's so damned full of you this place. There are many spots where we walked, the lawn where I saw you in so many attitudes, all you, there's this room – why shouldn't you swing round the door now? – You did yesterday, this morning, the day before yesterday . . . Oh Noel if you knew the sick dread with which I face tonight – that bed & those dragging hours – And the pointlessness of tomorrow, the horror that it might just as well be this evening, or Wednesday, for all the pleasure or relief from pain I get out of it. The procession of hopeless hours – That's what's so difficult to face; – that's why one wants to kill oneself. It's all swept over me. These last few days; & so much stronger and more certain than before – and rather different too. It seems deeper & better – Oh I can't explain it all . . . Remember those days on the river: and the little camp at Penshurst, next year, – moments then; & Klosters: and the Beaulieu camp: & our evenings by

that great elm clump at Grantchester: & bathing in early morning by Oxford: & the heights above Clifford Bridge camp: & a thousand times when we've gone hand in hand – as no two other people could . . . you must see what we are child – I cannot live without you. But remember, I'm not only in love with you, I'm very fond of you. Goodnight, child – in the name of our love . . .

Fine words, but to write them to Noel, who had watched Rupert openly flirting and making romantic overtures to her sister Bryn during the previous few days, points to him being close to a relapse following his nervous breakdown earlier in the year. In a further letter to Noel, written at the Crown, he reiterates his emotions and feelings for her: 'Noel, Noel, there's love between you and me, and you've given me such kindness and such sympathy in your own Noel way – I'm wanting your presence so much – I'm leaning on you at this moment, stretching towards you . . .' To complicate the issue even further, in the same letter he discussed his impending meeting with Ka, as she was awaiting a decision from him as to their future together. To Noel he confided: 'I couldn't ever live with her, I know from experience even, I should go mad, or kill her, in a few months. And – I love someone else. We've got to part. I suppose she really knows that by now. But I've got to tell her tomorrow . . .' And he did. Justin Brooke drove him away from Everleigh, the Crown, the Keynes' poker games and the croquet to a meeting place by the roadside at Bibury, where Ka was staying at the Swan. She and Rupert went off for three hours to discuss their relationship while Justin waited in his Opel. It was the end. Ka was inconsolable and Rupert riddled with guilt; it was the sour icing on the stale cake of his stay at Everleigh. His state of mind that weekend, and his being at such an all-time low, led to Frances Cornford suggesting that he go abroad for a while. Although he didn't eventually take her advice until the following May, with beneficial results, he never sank so low again.

Rupert was, though, overcome himself with his own grief and guilt about ending the relationship. He poured his anguish into a letter to Noel.

You see, child – Noel – there's been so much between Ka & me. We've been so close to one another, naked to each other in our good parts ·& bad. She knows me better than anyone in the world – better than you let yourself know me – than you care to know me. And we've given each other great love & infinite pain – and that's a terrible, unbreakable bond. And I've had her . . . it's agony, *agony*, tearing out part of one's life like that . . . You see I have an ocean of love & pity for her . . . I'd give anything to do Ka good. Only – she killed something in me. I can't love her, or marry her . . .

The visitors' book from the Crown, containing not only the signatures and comments of Keynes, Brooke and the rest of the party but also those of many other distinguished guests, including Montgomery of Alamein and General de Gaulle, disappeared some two or three years ago under mysterious circumstances.

During August, Rupert ricocheted from place to place like a pinball; from Witney in Oxfordshire he headed back to Rugby, before heading to the Cornfords' house at Cambridge and then up to Overstrand on the Norfolk coast, where he stayed at Beckwythe Manor, the home of Gilbert and Rosalind Murray. Frances Cornford had introduced them to Brooke during rehearsals for *Comus* and they had subsequently become friends. On his first day at Overstrand, he wrote to Noel about his possible plans; 'I spent most of yesterday talking to Frances. She's Ka's only decent real friend: she's good, &, not being a virgin, she understands things. She wants me to go abroad for a year – to Australia or somewhere, & work manually. It'd be better for Ka she thinks.' Rupert's only problem in going abroad for a period was his concern that Noel might succumb sexually to one of her other suitors, which now rather bizarrely included James Strachey. At the end of the month Noel drove the final nail into the coffin when she admitted, 'It was stupid of me even to have shared the little bit of love I had for you, and wicked of me to let you express your love for me . . . it was last November that I decided and you found out I didn't love you . . .'

Justin Brooke's home at Wotton in Surrey was also on Rupert's itinerary that August. From Beckwythe Manor he informed Noel, 'I go on Tuesday to c/o Justin, Leylands, Wotton, Dorking, Surrey, for a few days. You could say if we met what you thought about my retiring to California and how much you'd welcome the respite – yours as you left him, Rupert.'

Long associated with the Evelyn family since the days of the famous seventeenth-century English diarist, Wotton is undoubtedly still as much a piece of Old England as it was then, thanks to the arboricultural efforts of John Evelyn, whose passion for planting trees rapidly spread to the owners of other large country homes. During the Victorian era other eminent men brought their families to settle on the slopes of Leith Hill, with its stunning views across the Weald to the South Downs and its bracing 'Swiss' air, where the Evelyns live to this day.

In 1885 Arthur Brooke and his family acquired the expansive Leylands estate, having single-handedly built up his Manchester grocer's shop until they had become one of the largest tea merchants in Britain – Brooke Bond. Brooke and his wife Alice already had two daughters and five sons by the time they moved in, with a third daughter, Aline, arriving later. Their sixth youngest, Justin became close friends with Rupert Brooke at Cambridge, initially through the Cambridge Amateur Dramatic Club – both Brookes eventually becoming part of the group of friends that revelled in camping, swimming, walking and reading parties. As a good friend of Justin (who, coincidentally, had an older brother called Rupert), Rupert was always welcome at Leylands, where the walks, woods, views and tennis courts were major attractions.

A keen walker and lover of the English countryside, Rupert would surely have walked the short distance from the house, on the south-west corner of Leith Hill to Hull's Tower – at 965 feet the highest point in south-east England with its views to the South Downs and English Channel to the south and the entire London skyline and the Dunstable hills to the north. Built in 1765, the folly was erected by the altruistic Hull for his own pleasure, and for that of everyone else who wanted to take in the wonderful views. It is hard to believe that Brooke resisted the lure of the patchwork-quilt panorama, or the short walk to the secluded lake at Friday Street. Another draw in the area would have been Polesden Lacey, the playwright Sheridan's sometime home and then owned by the Hon. Ronald and Mrs Greville, she being one of the legendary Edwardian hostesses. Again commanding fine southerly views, the late classic house built in 1824 on the North Downs was sufficiently close to writer George Meredith's old home on Box Hill for Brooke to take them both in during his visits to Leylands. Although Meredith had died in 1909, just as Brooke came to know the area, he may still have gone, as he was one of the

Justin Brooke's family home, Leylands

young poet's influences and he had a high regard for his writing, except for his later work. Meredith had immortalised the forest near Wotton in 'The Woods of Westermain'.

> . . . Enter these enchanted woods
> You who dare
> Nothing harms beneath the leaves
> More than waves a swimmer cleaves
> Toss your heart up with the lark
> Fool at peace with mouse and worm
> Fair you fare
> Only at dread of dark
> Quaver, and they quit their form:
> Thousand eyeballs under hoods
> Have you by the hair
> Enter these enchanted woods
> You who dare

The tennis lawn at Leylands where Rupert, a keen player, would have spent many hours, is still there, only now the hard court close to it is used in preference; and the chimney stack on the north-east corner of the house, on the left of the photograph, has been demolished, but otherwise the house is much the same at it was, apart from occasional additions, and a fire damage which affected a section of the building in 1907–8. The ha-ha which still faces the house across what was the tennis lawn no longer has the floral display that greeted the house's occupants each morning with Alexander Pope's words from 'An Essay on Man I': 'Hope springs eternal.' There was obviously neither the space, nor a patient enough gardener, to continue with the rest of the quotation: 'in the human breast; Man never is, but always to be blest.' The house went out of the hands of Justin Brooke's family after the First World War, when his father Arthur retired, and it was bought by people called Hicks before being purchased by a Commander Whitworth. Whitworth eventually sold it to Justin's younger sister Aline (by then Arrowsmith-Brown) who moved back into her childhood home in her old age with her memories of the young poet Rupert Brooke and the days before the estate was split up in the 1930s.

Brooke's second cousin, Winifred Kinsman, whose grandmother Lucy Hoare was his mother's sister, also has a vivid recollection of Rupert, from the summer of 1912, even though she was not yet four years old:

> He came to my home in Rugby, with his mother, where my parents
> were having a party. There were some steps up to the drawing-room,

with a french window, and the party was going on inside. I was standing outside on the steps, and suddenly Rupert came out of the french windows and said 'I'll catch you', and I flew down the steps and into the garden, with Rupert chasing me. I remember quite clearly the excitement and the terror which I felt, and the real enjoyment as I was swept up into his arms and held above his head.

Another port of call was the house of the poet and novelist John Masefield and his wife Constance, which they took jointly with their friend Isabel Fry. Rectory Farm at Great Hampden in the Chilterns was described by Masefield in 1909 as 'a lovely little farm in Buckinghamshire, high up on a chalk hill surrounded by beechwoods and common land, a very fresh, pretty, but rather bare and cold country like most chalk hills'. Writing to Ka from there during a visit, Rupert wrote, 'I sit in front of the cottage writing . . . Mr Masefield is inside, singing sea shanties to the baby [their son Lewis].' Heaven knows what a two-year-old made of the 'sea shanties', as most of his nautical writings, like those in his 1902 collection, *Salt Water Ballads*, dealt with suffering and death, as in the last lines of 'The Turn of the Tide':

. . . An' the ship can have my blessing and the Lord can have my life
For it's time I quit the deck and went aloft.

The conversation between the two poets would probably have touched upon a problem with Masefield's newly published tragedy, *The Widow in the Bye Street*, a lengthy work of almost 500 verses. A strike had resulted in 2,000 of the 3,000 copies printed being held up for several weeks at London Docks, having arrived by sea from Edinburgh. The publishers were Sidgwick & Jackson, who had also published Brooke's poems. It would appear that Rupert was initially slightly jealous of Masefield's success, although the latter was his senior by almost a decade. Masefield, however, was never less than generous in his advice to Brooke and was happy to be counselled. Rupert asked him about a photographer called Murchisan, who wanted to take some photographs of him. Masefield duly gave him his advice, which ended with the telling words, 'Remember that if you become as famous as we all expect of you, he will be able to make a lot of money out of your portrait.' He was certainly right in terms of fame and longevity, as Brooke's likeness is still admired 85 years on.

At the end of August, Rupert was once again fraught with tension and in a state of collapse, when a fellow Apostle from Cambridge, Harry Norton, whisked him off to relax on a tour in Scotland. Among the places they stayed were the Annandale Arms Hotel at Moffat, near Galloway, and Sanquhar, in Dumfries, from where he wrote to Noel declaring his intentions once again of visiting Justin Brooke at Leylands and taking her to task over her admission to not loving him: 'You lie Noel. You may have persuaded yourself you don't love me, or engineered yourself into not loving me, now. But you lie when you say you never did – Penshurst & Grantchester & a thousand times. I know you did & you know it. And you could.' Noel replied:

> Wouldn't the best thing be for you to come to Limpsfield for two days, or three (as long as we needed to clear things up)? Inconveniently, there is no room in the Champions now – but perhaps you wouldn't have liked to be surrounded by the family. I've been thinking that you mightn't mind living in 'The Grasshopper' at Moorhouse Bank, about a mile and a half from here – thro' the woods and on the way to Westerham? If you thought that too remote there is the 'Carpenter's Arms' across the common, but it has no recommendations, or again you might just get a room & come here for meals.

Forever optimistic, Rupert agreed, but on meeting her at the Champions he realised it was all to no avail.

Avoiding Rugby, he visited Leonard and Virginia Woolf in London, and stayed at the National Liberal Club and then with Eddie Marsh at Raymond Buildings, where they hatched the idea of an anthology of verse, with contributions from contemporary poets. The seeds of the idea were sown on 12 September. While in bed there, Brooke hit upon a scheme of publishing a book of poetry that would include a selection of work from 12 different writers – six men and six women; he would write all the poems under pseudonyms. This led to Marsh and Brooke deciding they might just as well use the work of existing poets, and, fired by the idea, they invited Wilfred Gibson, John Drinkwater, Harold Monro and Arundel de Re (the latter two being editor and sub-editor of the *Poetry Review*) to 5 Raymond Buildings to discuss the plan, the following day, the consequence of which was to be the publication of *Georgian Poetry 1911–12*.

From his base at Raymond Buildings, Marsh introduced him to London society, Brooke becoming friendly with Asquith, the then Prime Minister, and his family, as well as meeting fellow writers Walter de la Mare, Drinkwater, Gibson and W.H. Davies, among others whose acquaintance he had already made including Henry James, John Masefield and W.B. Yeats.

Two days after conceiving the *Georgian Poets* scheme Brooke went to the first night of Shakespeare's *The Winter's Tale*, where he became rather taken with actress Cathleen Nesbitt, who was playing the part of Perdita; maybe it was possible to love again. A week later actor/manager Henry Ainley took her to a supper party given by Eddie Marsh at Raymond Buildings, where she was eager to meet the writer Gilbert Cannan, for whom she had great admiration. She found Cannan uncommunicative, but did strike up conversation with Rupert.

5 Raymond Buildings Grays Inn, Eddie Marsh's
home and Brooke's main base in London

I saw a very good looking, very shy young man, sitting in a corner and I do remember being struck by his extremely blue eyes, and I sat beside him and he said 'Do you know anybody here?' and I said 'No'. He said 'Neither do I' and then we vaguely started talking, and then we talked about Georgian Poetry, which was an anthology that Eddie Marsh had just brought out . . . I said there was an extraordinary poem called 'The Fish' in it, and I quoted quite a bit of it and he blushed very scarlet and said: 'You have very good taste – I wrote that . . .'

The meeting culminated in Brooke asking her to lunch, and the two of them becoming closer, although gradually, as they had both recently emerged from unhappy love affairs – Rupert with Ka, and Cathleen with Henry Ainley. She understood from Brooke that he was feeling 'neurotic, depressed and against love altogether'.

During September, Rupert was back seeking sanctuary under the chestnuts at Grantchester. 'Working for ten days alone at this beastly poetry. Working at poetry isn't like reading hard, it doesn't just tire and exhaust you. The only effect is that your nerves and your brain go. I was almost a mouthing idiot.' Rupert was to leave his beloved Old Vicarage later in 1912, and the days of the Grantchester summers would be over for ever.

*Cathleen Nesbitt – her close relationship with Brooke
lasted from early 1913 until his death*

The first book of *Georgian Poetry* was printed and ready to be published in December, with contributions from Brooke, Lascelles, Abercrombie, G.K. Chesterton, John Masefield and Wilfred Gibson. It would sell for 3s 6d.

The initial edition of *Georgian Poetry* included five of Brooke's poems: 'The Old Vicarage, Grantchester', 'Dust', 'The Fish', 'Dining Room Tea' and 'Town and Country'.

Town and Country

Here, where love's stuff is body, arm and side
Are stabbing-sweet 'gainst chair and lamp and wall.
In every touch more intimate meanings hide;
And flaming brains are the white heart of all.

164

Here, million pulses to one centre beat:
Closed in by men's vast friendless, alone,
Two can be drunk with solitude, and meet
On the sheer point where sense with knowing's one.

Here the green-purple clanging royal night,
And the straight lines and silent walls of town,
And roar, and glare, and dust, and myriad white
Undying passers, pinnacle and crown.

Intensest heavens between close-lying faces
By the lamp's airless fierce ecstatic fire;
And we've found love in little hidden places,
Under great shades, between the mist and mire.

Stay! though the woods are quiet, and you've heard
Night creep along the hedges. Never go
Where tangled foliage shrouds the crying bird,
And the remote winds sigh, and waters flow!

Lest-as our words fall dumb on windless noons,
Or hearts grow hushed and solitary, beneath
Unheeding stars and unfamiliar moons,
Or bough bend over, close and quiet as death, –

Unconscious and unpassionate and still,
Cloud-like we lean and stare as bright leaves stare,
And gradually along the stranger hill
Our unwalled loves thin out on vacuous air,

And suddenly there's no meaning in our kiss,
And your lit upward face grows, where we lie,
Lonelier and dreadfuller than sunlight is,
And dumb and mad and eyeless like the sky.

The year 1912 also saw Brooke's first poem being published in the United States, when 'Second Best' was included in Thomas Bird Mosher's *Amphoria, A Collection of Prose and Verse Chosen by the Editor of Bibelot.*

Early in October, Rupert was discussing more poetry, this time near Chichester. Between September and November 1912, 23-year-old John Middleton Murry, the editor of *Rhythm*, an avant-garde magazine of art literature and music, and his girlfriend of nine months, the 24-year-old New

Zealand-born writer Katherine Mansfield, rented Runcton Cottage at Runcton, West Sussex. A Queen Anne house, the dwelling was situated in the heart of a small hamlet that centred around the Manor and the Mill House, the latter being worked by the waters of Pagham Rife, which flowed from Vinnetrow, one of the dozen or so lakes to the north-east of the cluster of houses and past Runcton Cottage before emptying into the English Channel at Little Welbourne in Pagham harbour, two miles to the south. Brooke and Murry would walk for miles across the marshes; talking, discussing poetry and singing songs.

Rupert came to know Murry, a classical Oxford scholar, through Rhythm, which had first been mooted at Christmas 1910 by Murry and the painter J.D. Ferguson. The first issue appeared in June 1911. Murry's Oxford chum Frederick Goodyear wrote the manifesto and the publication attracted many illustrious contributors. During its two-year existence, before transmogrifying into The Blue Review, its pages were graced by the works of Wilfred Gibson, W.H. Davies, Frank Swinnerton, Frank Harris, John Drinkwater, Duncan Grant, Brooke and dozens of others from the world of art, literature and music. Brooke visited Murry and Katherine Mansfield on more than one occasion while they were living at Runcton Cottage, once arriving with Eddie Marsh, having affected the initial introduction between Marsh and Murry, and Frederick Goodyear.

Brooke was certainly at Runcton in early October 1912, writing a letter to Marsh on 4 October: 'I'm going to Runcton Cottage tomorrow for the weekend . . . I suppose the Tigers [as he called them] won't want me longer than till Monday . . .' Rupert stayed for several days with Murry and Katherine Mansfield at the house that could barely be described as a cottage, considering its size. Here they talked and discussed the future of Rhythm, blissfully unaware of the fact that 'Stephen Swift', the publisher of the organ was about to abscond, leaving a debt of £400, which Murry and Mansfield had to shoulder. During his stay at Runcton, Rupert shocked his host and hostess with a tale of an old woman who had sat motionless by her open window for so long that neighbours decided to force an entry, whereupon they discovered that all her lower half had been eaten by her cats! When Brooke left Runcton on Tuesday 8 October, he sent his love to 'the Tigers when you see them' in a letter to Eddie Marsh from Berlin the following month.

Brooke's enthusiasm for Rhythm was still very evident in a letter to E.J. Dent in February 1913, in which he tried (successfully) to enlist him as a music critic for the magazine: 'Rhythm, which is being reorganised on a fuller basis, but equally advanced, is having occasional articles on music – not so much reviews of concerts, as enlightenment on modern or ancient good things . . . They don't pay! But they're doing good work – if you're again in

London we might talk . . .' His friend from Rugby and Cambridge, Denis Browne, was the music critic for both *Rhythm* and *The Blue Review*, as well as the *New Statesman*. To Gwen Raverat, unconvinced about contributing, despite being a close friend, he wrote: '. . . it's by people who do good work and are under thirty-five. It shows there are such, and that they're different from and better than the Yellow Book or the Pre-Raphaelites or any other body . . .'

Murry and Katherine Mansfield left Runcton in November 1912 for Chancery Lane. Later they rented the Gables at Cholesbury in Buckinghamshire, with John commuting to London and often staying in Brooke's old room at Eddie Marsh's; Rupert eventually relinquished his keys to Murry in March. Brooke would write to Marsh on 10 March 1913, 'I grow Maudlin . . . I gave up my keys to Jack Tiger with a curse of jealousy . . .'

After a spell with Dudley and Anne Marie Ward in Berlin, he was back in Rugby for Christmas, from where he confessed to Eddie Marsh that his eyes were full of sleep and his heart was full of Cathleen Nesbitt.

CHAPTER X

From the Old World to the New World

O
n New Year's eve 1912, Brooke and Marsh went to the London
Hippodrome to see *Hello Ragtime* before seeing the New Year in on
the steps of St Paul's. The following day Rupert took a train to the
Lizard, this time staying with Francis and Frances Cornford, who were in
lodgings there. It proved to be a very productive 11 days for the young poet,
as he wrote two articles on H.J.C. Grierson's new edition of Donne's poems
published by the Clarendon Press, declaring that Donne was 'the one English
love poet . . . who was not afraid to acknowledge that he was composed of
body, soul, and mind'. A great lover and champion of the Elizabethan
metaphysical poet, he enthused that he was 'by far the greatest of our love
poets. 'It would seem that while fired up, Brooke also put the finishing
touches to his play *Lithuania*, and was also writing 'Funeral of Youth' amidst
the noise of the Cornford household – Frances recalled that he beavered away
quietly 'while people chatted and banged about the room'.

The Funeral of Youth: Threnody

The day that *Youth* had died,
Thee came to his grave-side,
In decent mourning, from the county's ends,
Those scatter'd friends
Who had liv'd the boon companions of his prime,
And laugh'd with him and sung with him and wasted,
In feast and wine and many-crown'd carouse,
The days and nights and dawnings of the time
When *Youth* kept open house,

Nor left untasted
Aught of his high emprise and ventures dear,
No quest of his unshar'd –
All these, with loitering feet and sad head bar'd,
Follow'd their old friend's bier.
Folly went first,
With muffled bells and coxcomb still revers'd;
And after trod the bearers, hat in hand –
Laughter, most hoarse, and Captain *Pride* with tann'd
And martial face all grim, and fussy *Joy*,
Who had to catch a train, and *Lust*, poor, snivelling boy;
These bore the dear departed.
Behind them, broken-hearted,
Came *Grief*, so noisy a widow, that all said,
'Had he but wed
Her elder sister *Sorrow*, in her stead!'
And by her, trying to soothe her all the time,
The fatherless children, *Colour*, *Tune*, and *Rhyme*
(The sweet lad *Rhyme*), ran all-uncomprehending.
Then, at the way's sad ending,
Round the raw grave they stay'd. Old *Wisdom* read,
In mumbling tone, the Service for the Dead.
There stood *Romance*,
The furrowing tears had mark'd her rouged cheek;
Poor old *Conceit*, his wonder unassuag'd;
Dead *Innocency's* daughter, *Ignorance*;
And shabby, ill'-dress'd *Generosity*;
And *Argument*, too full of woe to speak;
Passion, grown portly, something middle-aged;
And *Friendship* – not a minute older, she;
Impatience, ever taking out his watch;
Faith, who was deaf, and had to lean, to catch
Old *Wisdom's* endless drone.
Beauty was there,
Pale in her black; dry-ey'd; she stood alone.
Poor Maz'd *Imagination*: Fancy wild;
Ardour, the sunlight on his greying hair;
Contentment, who had known Youth as a child
And never seen him since. And *Spring* came too,
Dancing over the tombs, and brought him flowers –
She did not stay for long.
And *Truth*, and *Grace*, and all the merry crew,

The laughing *Winds* and *Rivers*, and lithe *Hours*;
And *Hope*, the dewy-ey'd; and sorrowing *Song*; –
Yes, with much woe and mourning general,
At dead *Youth's* funeral,
Even these were met once more together, all,
Who erst the fair and living *Youth* did know;
All, except only *Love*. *Love* had died long ago.

It is a fair supposition that 'Funeral of Youth' looked for its inspiration to an ode written in 1763 by the Cambridge-born Poet Laureate William Whitehead. Written for the double celebration of the end of the Seven Years War and the birth of George IV, it was written in the spirit of a patriotic poet who loved England. It is easy to see its influence on Brooke:

. . . Soft-smiling PEACE, whom *Venus* bore
When, tutor'd th' enchanting lore
Of *Maia's* blooming Son
She sooth'd the synod of the Gods
Drove *Discord* from the blest abodes
And *Jove* resum'd his throne
Th' attendant *Graces* gird her round
And sportive *Ease*, with locks unbound
And every Muse, to leisure born
And *Plenty*, with her twisted horn
While changeful *Commerce* spreads his lossen'd sails
Blow as ye list, ye winds, the reign of PEACE prevails!

And see, to grace that milder reign
And add fresh lustre to the year
Sweet *Innocence* adorns the train
In form, and features, Albion's heir!

During his stay with the Cornfords at the Lizard, Brooke wrote to Jacques Raverat: 'Cornwall's so nice, three hundred miles from anywhere . . .', and to Ka, who still carried a torch for Rupert, 'Love is being at a person's mercy. And it's a black look-out when the person's an irresponsible modern female virgin. There's no more to say . . .' The Lizard clearly proved inspirational for Brooke, as he confessed in a letter from there to Geoffrey Keynes: 'I have written nothing for months, till I came here . . .' Just over seven years before his visit to the Lizard, Marconi had transmitted the first-ever transatlantic radio message from the peninsular to Newfoundland – three dots, signifying the letter 'S'. Those three dots were to begin a new era in communication that was to revolutionise the entire world. A world Brooke would never see.

On 8 January 1913, Marsh attended the opening of Harold Monro's Poetry Bookshop just off Theobald's Road in London. The poet Henry Newbolt made an opening speech and Robert Frost, the American poet, was also present. Later that month he was to enjoy Brooke's first public reading there, although he felt that he tried to be a latter-day John Donne. At the opening Harold Monro introduced Marsh to W.H. Davies, the one-legged Welsh 'tramp' poet, who subsequently invited Marsh and Brooke to tea at the house where he boarded, in the then dormitory town of Sevenoaks, in Kent. His landlady was Wordsworth's niece. Davies's genuine fondness for children and his penchant for giving them sweets for halfpennies, aroused so much suspicion among the Sevenoaks parents that he was later forced to move.

Having admired the work of sculptor Eric Gill at the London Grafton Galleries the previous November, Brooke and Eddie Marsh went to visit him at Sopers, his home at Ditchling in Sussex, just before he moved from the village to Hopkins Crank, at Ditchling Common. Rupert had previously written to Geoffrey Keynes, 'I'm trying to buy a Gill. He's done an extraordinary good cast for a bronze – a Madonna. If he can only sell one cast he has to charge me an immense sum, which I can't pay. If more it gets cheaper. He can sell six at £8 or £10 each. If you're wanting a Gill, now's your chance!' Rupert did buy one, as a gift for Ka, although after their departure Gill referred to Brooke and Marsh as 'aesthetical beggars', presumably as the statue was desired more for its aesthetic beauty than its religious meaning.

During the last week of January and the first week of February 1913, Rupert was staying with Jacques and Gwen Raverat at Manor Farm, Croyden, in Cambridgeshire. He had his play *Lithuania* with him, meaning to copy it out but not finding the energy. He sent a letter to Ka from Manor Farm in which he jokingly refers to his host and hostess: 'I've been fairly comfortable with these people. I've even given them a few hints on sensible living – for they're apt to be too fidgety, and when Jacques' nerves are too bad for painting, he thinks it sensible to dig in the garden all day!' Jacques' nervous disorder, which flared up periodically for years, was eventually diagnosed as multiple sclerosis. Despite his condition, the Raverats also received Geoffrey Keynes and Justin Brooke during Rupert's visit there. Gwen was fast becoming an acknowledged wood engraver, and both of them were accomplished artists. While staying with the Raverats, Rupert wrote to Eddie Marsh asking him to try to include Cathleen Nesbitt in a theatre party he was organising, before adding the self-deprecating comment, 'But no doubt it's quite impossible – I suppose she dines with millionaires every night – I can see a thousand insuperable difficulties – it was scarcely worth mentioning it . . .' Cathleen turned out to be far more down-to-earth and approachable than Rupert imagined.

Croyden at the time rather confusingly had several alternative spellings including Croyden, Crawden and Croydon (the current spelling). In the past it had also been Croydon am Clapton and Croydon cum Clapton; the lost village of Clapton now lies beneath the fields above Croydon. The name is said to originate from Craw Dene, 'the valley of crows'. With the upper reaches of the Cam meandering below it, the village lies on the south slope of a low range of clay-covered chalk hills, about 15 miles south-west of Cambridge, overlooking southern Cambridgeshire and north Hertfordshire.

The 380 acres of Manor Farm was worked by Maurice Gribble in the Raverats' day, with the Gape Estate owning the whole. Jacques and Gwen Raverat had part of the farm converted into a studio by local builder W. King, who had the misfortune to walk in one day while Jacques was painting a picture of Gwen, posing in the nude. It must have created an impression, as the story is still told, along with yarns of the local peasants' revolt under the mythical Captain Swing, a would-be Ned Ludd, when they rioted against the new steam threshing machines by wrecking them, setting fire to hayricks and attacking stock. Manor Farm was worked by the Willinks after the First World War until the mid-1940s and from 1949 to 1990 by the Horsfords.

On 7 February, Dudley and Anne Marie Ward had a baby boy, Peter, so in a more buoyant mood Rupert headed off to Raymond Buildings to stay with Eddie, be thrown into the social whirl and hopefully to engineer a meeting with his favourite actress, Cathleen Nesbitt. To Noel he painted a gay picture: '. . . you, poor brown mouse, can't in the dizziest heights of murian imagination, picture the life of glitter and gaiety I lead. A young man about town Noel (I've had my hair cut *remarkably* short), dinners, boxes at the opera, literary lunch-parties, theatre supper-parties (the Carlton on Saturday next) – I know *several* actresses . . .'

By February, he was on first-name terms with Cathleen. The first time she had seen Brooke she confessed to being immensely 'taken by these looks', but was later attracted more by his 'vitality and his sense of fun and his fantastic enjoyment of life – rather sort of laughing at himself'. They went for outings to Kew Gardens and Hampton Court, Cathleen later recalling their blossoming romance with affection: 'I remember at the beginning – when we began to discover we'd been in love – and, as we'd both been in love with somebody else quite recently, we were both a little wary of whether this was real, and he wrote a little poem . . . he sent it to me on a postcard.'

There's Wisdom in Women

'Oh love is fair, and love is rare,' my dear one she said,
'But love goes lightly over.' I bowed her foolish head,

And kissed her hair and laughed at her. Such a child was she;
So new to love, so true to love, and she spoke so bitterly.

But there's wisdom in women, of more than they have known,
And thoughts go blowing through them, are wiser than their own,
Or how should my dear one, being ignorant and young,
Have cried on love so bitterly, with so true a tongue?

At Raymond Buildings Rupert entertained W.B. Yeats, Duncan Grant, Geoffrey Keynes, Denis Browne, Wilfred Gibson and Edward Thomas and read *Lithuania* aloud. John Masefield felt that he should place it on a music-hall bill, as it was only half an hour in duration and couldn't be billed as an evening's entertainment by itself, encouraging Rupert with a rather noncommittal, 'I hope that it will be produced and you will go on writing plays.'

When news reached Rupert at Gray's Inn that he had been elected a fellow of King's, Eddie hosted a supper party in Rupert's honour, where his protégé met Lady Cynthia Asquith, Winston Churchill's wife Clementine and the Prime Minister's daughter Violet Asquith, with whom he was to strike up a strong friendship. He thought her very witty; she in turn brought out the humour in him. The following month the two began a communication that was to gather momentum slowly. In March she sent a note inviting him to her birthday dinner at 10 Downing Street. Other guests included George Bernard Shaw, John Masefield, Edmund Gosse and J.M. Barrie. A fortnight later she accompanied Brooke and Marsh to the Hippodrome to see Chekhov's Uncle Vanya.

His fellowship eased the tension between Rupert and his mother as she felt he had at last achieved something worth while. His literary efforts were now centred on trying to find a home for his play. The Gaiety Theatre, Manchester, thought the theme hackneyed, and novelist and critic Gilbert Cannan gave it the thumbs down, although John Drinkwater guardedly admitted that it showed promise.

Rupert decided to heed the advice of Frances Cornford and other friends, that he should go abroad for a while, to clear his head and sort himself out; and so, having placated a mother riddled with condemnation for the scheme, he planned a journey abroad. Rupert had a sitting for photographs to be taken, but the session proved unsatisfactory, with the result that a second was set up with an American photographer based in Pimlico Square, Victoria, London. Sherril Schell was enthusiastic about photographing Brooke, who discussed the Russian Ballet, the London show *Hullo Ragtime* and asked questions about America, while Schell noted that Rupert had narrowly escaped being snub-nosed, that this hair was a golden-brown with

Brooke in April 1913, photographed by Sherril Schell at his flat in St Georges Square, Pimlico, London. Schell felt Brooke wore a 'spasmodic wistful expression'

sprinklings of red and that he had a well-shaped face that wore a spasmodic wistful expression. The twelfth and final shot, Schell admitted, was 'a pose that he himself suggested, his face in profile showing his bare neck and shoulders. For this he stripped to the waist, revealing a torso that recalled the young Heroes.' The photograph became widely known amongst his friends at Cambridge as 'your favourite actress'.

Clouds, George Wyndham's home at East Knoyle

He wrote of the sitting to Cathleen while staying as a house guest of Conservative politician George Wyndham at Clouds, his house in East Knoyle, near Salisbury, Wiltshire, the village in which Sir Christopher Wren was born. The imposing residence, with its fine commanding views to Salisbury Plain and across to Somerset and Dorset, had played host to several literary giants on 16 October 1910 when Henry James, G.K. Chesterton and Hilaire Belloc attended Percy Wyndham's golden wedding. George Wyndham, his son, succeeded him as 'lord of the manor' in 1911. At the time of Brooke's weekend visit in April 1913, the estate boasted 3,000 sheep, nine full-time shepherds, an army of servants, a team of laundresses and stable workers and ten gardeners under Mr Brown, who supplemented the food supply for guests from the three-acre kitchen garden. Brooke was clearly taken with George Wyndham's secretary, as he mentions her later that summer, in a letter to Eddie Marsh from Ottawa: 'The face (though not the name) of George Wyndham's secretary dwells in my mind, tenderly guarded.' Having spent some time in Germany, he would undoubtedly have talked to Fraulein Schneider ('Bun') during his stay, the godmother to Wyndham's niece Cynthia Asquith, whom he had met since the celebration party in Marsh's rooms and at a party given by Violet Asquith. Wyndham and Brooke discussed amongst other subjects, literature and poetry. One of George's sisters, Pamela Tennant, was a regular writer of poetry and prose, several of her poems having been published in a volume called *Windlestraw*, which contained verses written in 1908, 'Flowers and Weeds: a Garden Sequence'.

One wonders if this could have been an inspiration for 'The Old Vicarage, Grantchester'. Her poem begins

> Lilies and Pansies, and the Pink that grows
> In grey-leaved clusters by the garden's edge . . .

and later refers to

> . . . Poppies, hectic in their pride . . .

Brooke uses a similar arrangement as part of the start of his poem:

> . . . In my flower beds I think,
> Smile the carnation and the pink;
> And down the borders well I know,
> The poppy and the pansy blow . . .

Tennant writes of 'Red Roses' and 'Meadow-sweet', and Brooke of 'An English unofficial rose' and 'Thrilling-sweet'. Both gardens are set at a river's edge, and both describe the different atmospheres in them, by day and night. Tennant writes 'I know this garden at dawn' and 'When all the cobwebs drenched upon the lawn', while Brooke has a 'spectral dance before the dawn', with 'a hundred Vicars down the lawn'. Tennant knows her garden 'when night's sands have run, And yet no daylight shows upon the skies', in Brooke's garden 'black and white, creep whispers through the grass all night'. They both eulogise over their respective meadows, Tennant confessing 'I love these meadows', and Brooke writing of his 'deep meadows'. Early birds, too, feature in both, the fifth verse of Tennant's poem containing the line 'Before the birds awake, before the sun', Brooke's 'Old Vicarage' using 'grey heavens the first bird's drowsy calls'. In her last verse Tennant writes of her garden 'That it should be encompassed by no hedge', while Brooke wrote, 'Unkempt about those hedges blow'. Tennant has leaves 'listening, waiting for the little breeze', as there is no moment there 'in the quiet trees'; Brooke, however, longs to 'hear the breeze sobbing in the little trees'. 'Rout', it must be agreed, is an unusual word to use in a poem about gardens, but it is found in both: in 'Flowers and Weeds' 'our places in the motley rout', and in 'The Old Vicarage' 'The prim ecclesiastic rout'. In her revision of the poem, also in 1908, Tennant set her garden in the month of May: 'the scent of May in flower round fields'; Brooke extolling the virtues of the same month: 'How the May fields all golden show'. Is it pushing the proposed influence of Pamela Tennant's poem too far to suggest that the cluster of words in the sixth verse might well have suggested, and been incorporated into, another of

Brooke's classic poems, 'Dining Room Tea'? Tennant writes of 'flower-cups', 'the air a-stream' and 'glittering', within three lines and, albeit in a different context, Brooke also uses within three lines 'marble-cup', 'hung on the air, an amber stream' and 'glittering'. Both poems also refer to petals dropping.

At the time of writing her poem, Pamela was the wife of Sir Edward Tennant (later to become Lord Glenconner). In 1922 she married former Foreign Secretary Sir Edward Grey.

On the Saturday night of his weekend with George Wyndham at Clouds, Rupert wrote from his bed, to Cathleen:

> Dear child
>
> Champagne and port and whisky make one too sleepy to write. Nor is there anything frightfully important to write about – except the fact that you are incomparably the most loveable and lovely and glorious person in the world, and I've a dim, sleepy idea I may have mentioned that before. I've been discussing literature and politics with my host all night, and to send myself to sleep I'm going to continue making up a poem that's in my head. In this interval I write . . . Outside the wind's howling like anything (this place is 700 feet above the sea). It's been raining . . . My American photographer has sent a photograph of me – Eddie says it's very good. I think it's rather silly . . . My literary labours haven't been progressing very well. The only complete poem I've produced lately is –
>
> There was once a lovely Cathleen
> I don't think she can ever have been
> It's not *likely* you know
> Perhaps I dreamt it so
> There aren't *really* such things as Cathleen
>
> It rather expresses my occasional state of mind. The champagne was good. The port was very good. But I'm thirsty for you.
> Dearest child, goodnight.
>
> Rupert

Only weeks after Brooke's visit on 9 June, George Wyndham died in Paris. Rupert wrote to Eddie Marsh from America: 'But I was shocked last night to hear about Wyndham. It seemed abrupt.' Even in November when he wrote to Marsh from Fiji, a fondness for the man he knew only briefly is clearly still there: 'Talking of affairs at home (of which I think continually, to the exclusion of romance) there's nice things in the Cornhill article on Wyndham. I wish he hadn't died!'

Among the functions Rupert attended in London were the Ballets Russes performing *Les Sylphides* at Covent Garden, the Fabian Society debate with George Bernard Shaw and Hilaire Belloc, and Richard Strauss's opera *Elektra*, conducted by Thomas Beecham. His favourite London show was *Hullo Ragtime*, which had opened at the Hippodrome in December; Brooke thoroughly embraced the new 'ragtime' craze, which the older generation saw as rather subversive and modern. Cathleen Nesbitt, who thought Brooke 'such tremendous fun', often accompanied him: '. . . we went to see *Hullo Ragtime*, and he saw it ten times I'm told, altogether, seven of which I was with him. But sometimes I'd get a letter saying "I cheated – I took someone else to see it – because it's so wonderful everybody should see it." He adored the excitement and sort of panache of it . . .' The revue had been devised by Max Pemberton and Albert de Courville with music by Louis Hirsch and additional songs by various songwriters including Irving Berlin. The cast comprised Bonita, Jamieson Dodds, Lew Hearn, Shirley Kellog, Gerald Kirby, Eric Roper, Maud Tiffany and Brooke's favourite, Ethel Levey, with Hirsch conducting the Ragtime quintet. The show opened at London's Hippodrome on 23 December 1912, and contained such songs as 'How Do You Do Miss Ragtime', 'Hitchy Koo', 'You're My Baby', and two Irving Berlin songs, 'Ragtime Soldier Man' and 'Snooky Ookums'. Brooke made countless references to the show, which enticed him back time and time again, in his letters to Cathleen Nesbitt: 'I see we shall scarcely know *Hullo Ragtime* when we see it again: for Ethel Levey has introduced "Waiting For The Robert E. Lee", in her own version, and some new performers have appeared . . .' In another missive, he bemoans the temporary demise of his favourite singer: 'Ethel Levey is out of *Hullo Ragtime* all this week – I expect you know. I thought it worth while preventing your disappointment, in case you didn't know.' It was another part of his life shared more with his new London friends than with the old guard of neo-pagans. In a letter to Ka he informed her that the latest London news was 'A new American review (It's funny to think that Rag-time perhaps means nothing to you) . . .'

While *Hullo Ragtime* was his favourite show, the Pink and Lily was his favourite watering hole. The pub sits high in the hills above Princes Risborough, just over two miles out of town on the Lacey Green-to-Hampden road and was discovered, presumably, during one of his frequent walking tours of the Chilterns or perhaps on his visits to John Masefield's cottage. Rupert adored the Chilterns, frequently walking from Wendover to the Pink and Lily to take in the deep cool woods and the splendid north-westerly views over the Thames valley. The Chilterns form the central section of a great chalk belt that runs from the coast of Dorset to the Wash, the hills running in a virtually straight line like vertebrae south-west to north-east, and over 50 miles in length. The range has its beginnings in Berkshire, before running

Landlord Tom Wheatley's door is open . . . maybe Brooke is already sitting in his favourite room reliving the walk from Wendover . . .

into Oxfordshire and through Checkendon, Nettlebed and Stonor, then over the border into Buckinghamshire and eventually Hertfordshire and Bedfordshire; its chalk escarpment towns include Princes Risborough, Wendover, Tring and Markyate, up to Lilley Hoo, north-east of Luton. This is where the Chilterns are accepted as ending, although the hills continue north-east to Baldock and beyond. A section of the Icknield Way, a pre-Roman route, runs to the north of the Chilterns, for a majority of their course; it is the oldest known road in Britain, dating from the Bronze Age or earlier, although improved in parts by the Romans, and the route eventually runs up to Norfolk. Brooke wrote of the Icknield Way:

> I'll take the road . . .
> The Roman road to Wendover
> By Tring and Lilley Hoo
> As a free man may do . . .

Rupert's much loved Pink and Lily made the transition from a private house around 1800, when Mr Pink, a butler from nearby Hampden House, moved there, followed a little later by Miss Lillie, a chambermaid from the same residence. The former employees of the Hampden family set up home together, and, although unmarried, had a son, Richard, who took his mother's name and succeeded them in the hostelry, becoming the registered licensee there in 1833 when he amended the name 'Lillie' to 'Lily'. By the time Rupert was frequenting the Pink and Lily, the landlord and landlady were Mr and Mrs Tom Wheatley, who had taken over the pub around 1900. Mrs Wheatley ran it until it was sold by auction on 5 September 1929, up until when the rent was £12 per annum.

Rupert frequented the hostelry many times with both Cathleen and Jacques Raverat. On one occasion when Brooke was at the Pink and Lily with Jacques he wrote the following lines:

> Never came there to the Pink
> Two men such as we, I think.

The following couplet came from the mind of Raverat:

> Never came there to the Lily
> Two men quite so richly silly.

Before Brooke continued:

> So broad, so supple, and so tall
> So modest and so brave withal
> With hearts so clear, such noble eyes
> Filled with such safe philosophies
> Thirsty for good secure, secure for truth
> Fired by a purer flame than youth
> Secure as age, but not so dirty,
> Old, young, mature, being under thirty
> Were ever two so fierce and strong
> Who drank so deep and laughed so long
> So proudly meek, so humbly proud
> Who walked so far, and sang so loud?

After a lunch at the inn the pair left some food by the roadside with this note pinned to it:

> Two men left this bread and cake
> For whomsoever finds to take
> He and they will soon be dead
> Pray for them that left this bread.

The pub was the subject of a second piece of light-hearted verse by Brooke.

Ah Pink ah Pub of my desire
Ah lily for my meandering feet!
I am the ash that once was fire.
I would forget that youth was fleet
I wander on till I can greet
At the way's end so dark and hilly
Firelight & rest a snack to eat
And bitter at the Pink and Lily.

Courage! (I said) my soul respire!
Fate has rewards for the discreet
Thirst will be thirst, till you expire
The tale of love is not complete.
One buys such beer in many a street
And love as good in Piccadilly
And always there is bread and meat
And bitter, at the Pink and Lily.

That Disillusionment's a liar
Locality a damned deceit
he has no pity on a crier
She rambles on, Youth's still a cheat,
And beer is still a minor treat
And thoughts of love are just as silly
And just as frequent, just as sweet
And bitter at the Pink and Lily.

Prince, I have spoken in some heat
Being tired of love, that's damp and chilly
Sick of my bloody self conceit
And bitter at the Pink and Lily.

In March 1913, he sat in the small corner room that he usually frequented and scribbled a note to Cathleen: 'I write in the Pink and Lily. The hill drops a few hundred feet in front, and beyond is half Buckinghamshire, Berkshire and Oxfordshire. In this little room is the publican, asleep rather tipsy . . .' Cathleen and Rupert loved to spend time in the local countryside: 'I do remember once when we were walking – we used to go for walking tours in the Chilterns – and we sort of lay down in a bank and held hands . . . he never kissed me or anything like that,' just held hands, and we felt our souls communing in the air, and we both turned round to each other and said Donne's "Exstasie" – this is it; we had a kind of excitement in the mere touch and look of each other. Donne's "Exstasie" is no exaggeration of the feeling we had, and we could often come back, you know, from a day in the country, . . . quite drunk with each other.'

The Exstasie

Where, like a pillow on a bed,
A Pregnant banke swel'd up, to rest
The violets reclining head,
Sat we two, one anothers best.
Outer hands were firmely cimented
With a fast balme, which thence did spring,
Our eye-beames twisted, and did thred
Our eyes, upon one double string;
So to entergraft our hands, as yet
Was all the meanes to make us one,
And pictures in our eyes to get
Was all our propagation . . .

On 21 March, Rupert dropped a line to Geoffrey Fry asking him to subscribe to *Rhythm*, as Brooke's poems were being published in it: 'I wrote in January on a puff-puff. *Rhythm* is being reorganised and permanently draws, hereafter, on Gilbert Cannan, L. Abercrombie, W.W. Gibson, me, W.H. Davies, Walter de la Mare, Hugh Walpole, Dent, A. Rothenstein, Duncan Grant, D. Lees and a hundred more artists . . .' Rupert's poems, which he dismissively describes as being 'on a puff-puff', was 'The Night Journey', which had been inspired by the overhead steam railway in Berlin near Dudley Ward's flat, and tipped its hat to Brooke's love of the dramatist Strindberg.

The Night Journey

Hands and lit faces eddy to a line;
The dazed last minutes click; the clamour dies.
Beyond the great-swung arc o' the roof, divine,
Night, smoky-scarv'd, with thousand coloured eyes
Glares the imperious mystery of the way.
Thirsty for dark, you feel the long-limbed train
Throb, stretch, thrill motion, slide, pull out and sway,
Strain for the far, pause, draw to strength again . . .

As a man, caught by some great hour, will rise,
Slow-limbed, to meet the light or find his love;
And, breathing long, with staring sightless eyes,
Hands out, head back, agape and silent, move

Sure as a flood, smooth as a vast wind blowing;
And, gathering power and purpose as he goes,
Unstumbling, unreluctant, strong, unknowing,
Borne by a will not his, that lifts, that grows,

Sweep out to darkness, triumphing in his goal,
Out of the fire, out of the little room . . .
There is an end appointed, O my soul!
Crimson and green the signals burn; the gloom

Is hung with steam's far-blowing livid streamers.
Lost into God, as lights in light, we fly,
Grown one with will, end-drunken huddled dreamers.
The white lights roar. The sounds of the world die.

And lips and laughter are forgotten things.
Speed sharpens; grows. Into the night, and on,
The strength and splendour of our purpose swings.
The lamps fade; and the stars. We are alone.

When *Rhythm* was reconstituted as *The Blue Review*, in May 1913, Albert Rothenstein was assistant editor, Brooke was on the committee and Murry was still at the helm. Unfortunately it closed down after just three issues; despite financial help from Eddie Marsh, Murry would declare bankruptcy in 1914, unable to keep up payments of the debt incurred by the absconding publisher.

During March, Brooke was living at 5 Thurloe Square in Kensington, London, at the apartment of Albert Rothenstein. They discussed the new discoveries and revelations by the wireless pioneer Marconi, as well as seeing Arnold Bennett's play *The Great Adventure*, a dramatisation of his novel *Buried Alive*. An enthusiast for Bennett's work, Rupert had also read and enjoyed *The Old Wives Tale*, *Hilda Lessways*, and seen *What the Public Wants* on the London stage; and later he wrote to his mother from New Zealand enthusiastically quoting *Clayhanger*.

In a letter to Walter de la Mare from Kensington Square, Rupert reveals a day's eating habits – at least three square meals. 'I shall be lunching at Treviglio's (in Church Street) at 1.30–3.00 . . . & dining at the *Pall Mall*,

Haymarket at 6.45 (on the balcony) . . . If you don't come up for lunch, drink coffee with me. Or come to tea at Gallina's, opposite the Royalty Theatre.' He wrote from Rothenstein's to Cathleen, pledging his love yet determined to leave England for a while to clear his head: 'I've got to wander a bit. You chain one to England horribly.' His other close friends received pre-departure letters from the Kensington Square address. To Jacques and Gwen: 'We may meet again in this world – I brown and bearded, you mere red round farmers. When that'll be, I know not . . . My literary agent is Eddie. My heart is yours.' To Francis Cornford he poured out his concern for Ka, still recovering from being let down by him: 'Ka is still in a bad way . . . Ka has no one – her family know nothing of her real life, and she won't see much of them. So her friends have to look after her . . .' On a final postcard to Cathleen, he wrote a poem that was to take the title 'The Ways That Lovers Use'. He asked her to give it a name and rather obviously she chose the first line.

The Ways That Lovers Use

The way that lovers use is this:
They bow, catch hands, with never a word,
And their lips meet, and they do kiss,
– So I have heard.

They queerly find some healing so,
And strange attainment in the touch;
There is a secret lovers know,
– I have read as much.

And theirs no longer joy nor smart,
Changing or ending, day or night;
But mouth to mouth, and heart on heart,
– So lovers say.

Cathleen understood Rupert's reasons for his decision to travel to America, even with no specific time limit attached. But safe in the knowledge that all was on an even keel with her, he seemed more concerned about leaving Noel to her other suitors. He worried that she might submit herself to one of them during his time abroad.

Edward Thomas received a letter excusing Rupert from not coming down to see him before he went: 'I could leave the muses of England in your keeping – I do that anyhow . . .' He went to take his leave from the Ranee, with whom he discussed the merits of poets Lascelles Abercrombie, John Drinkwater and Wilfred Gibson. W. Denis Browne, his musician friend from Cambridge, and long-time chum Geoffrey Keynes received a few lines of farewell. A day or so before departing, he dined with Noel at Treviglio's in London's Soho.

His trip was to be subsidised by *The Westminster Gazette*, the periodical's literary editor Naomi Royde Smith having suggested that he should be paid four guineas an article for his impressions of the United States and Canada. Just two days before sailing he was officially engaged as a correspondent for the newspaper.

Two weeks before Brooke's departure, Eddie Marsh hosted a farewell supper at Raymond Buildings, the guests including Violet Asquith, Cathleen Nesbitt, Wilfred Gibson and Gilbert Cannan. Marsh gave Rupert a full set of Jane Austen novels as a parting gift the following day. Eddie was also journeying abroad on 9 May, aboard the *Enchantress*, in the company of the Prime Minister, Mrs Asquith, Violet Asquith and the Churchills. There was another 'last supper' on the evening before he was due to sail. A gathering in London's Regent Street under Gambrinus, between 10.00 p.m. and midnight, saw the likes of Wilfred Gibson, Geoffrey Keynes and John Middleton Murry in attendance. Murry wrote to his wife Katherine Mansfield about the evening; 'I'm going to supper with Rupert tonight because he's going off to America in the morning; it's all very silly but a free meal is fascinating.'

Although Eddie Marsh was a generous benefactor of the *Georgian Poets*, who, of course, included Brooke, those he did not publish in the book rebelled. Murry certainly did: 'They are spreading a miasma of sickening falsity. Page after page of the Georgian book is not merely bad poetry – that would be a relief – but sham naive, sham everything . . .'

Despite Murry's criticism *Georgian Poets* ran for many years. None of the poets involved, or Marsh himself, would have dreamt that the next edition would carry an 'In Memoriam' to Brooke.

CHAPTER XI

Ships – Ocean-going, Laureate and Friend

On 22 May, the train carrying Rupert pulled out of London's Euston station with its stunning, now long-demolished booking hall. At Liverpool Docks he boarded the SS *Cedric*, where he gave a local ragamuffin named William sixpence to wave him goodbye. Ensconced in Cabin 50, selected because that was his phone number at Rugby, he set off on a voyage that was to be of an indeterminable length and produce far more than a series of articles. Angry that he had left all his letters of introduction at Thurloe Square, he had time to dwell upon the conversation he had had the previous day with Denis Browne about the possibility of collaborating on a musical show the following year. He set out to explore the ship and study his fellow passengers.

On board, he wrote a long rambling missive to Cathleen, which included a reference to Ka: 'O child, it's hard work cutting off from people one's been intimate with. (I told you I'd been with a girl I loved – and you'll not ever tell anyone about it, child: for it's not wholly my secret.) I've got, I feel, to stop even writing to her, for her sake, to give her a chance to get free . . .' He mentioned the presence on board of the Liverpudlian poet Richard le Gallienne – a topic he also raised in a letter written from the SS *Cedric* to Eddie Marsh:

> One of my fellow passengers is Richard le Gallienne. Oh Eddie, he *is* a nasty man. He mouches about with grizzled hair and a bleary eye: and Mrs le G., an ex-Golden Girl, follows him with a rug. And Miss le G. plays deck-tennis with the American girls. He eyes me suspiciously – he scents a rival, I think. We've not spoken yet. His shoulders are bent. His mouth is ugly and small and mean. His eyes are glazed. His manner is furtive . . . Is it to that we come . . . I think

I will drown myself at thirty . . . I do not care for the fate of a poet
. . . I have started a ballade, in imitation of Villon: but it may not be
printed . . .

Brooke and le Gallienne weren't acquainted, but were undoubtedly aware
of each other's presence and would almost certainly have met on the journey.
His disparaging comments about le Gallienne to Marsh didn't touch on the
ever-present urn containing the ashes of his great love and first wife Mildred,
which le Gallienne took with him everywhere. Brooke's keen eye would not
have failed to notice this bizarre behaviour by the Liverpool poet; and it was
clearly the inspiration for what could be construed as Rupert's cruellest piece
of satire. But was it a deliberate attempt at satire? The poem certainly reads
as if Brooke were writing with genuine compassion, but his reference to 'a
ballade, an imitation of Villon' is a possible clue to the style of poem that was
really in Brooke's mind. The fifteenth-century French poet was not only
famous for his satiric humour, but also gifted in the field of lyrical pathos. It
seems that 'For Mildred's Urn' was one of a batch of poems that Rupert was
to mislay while travelling through Canada, and has remained unpublished
until now.

For Mildred's Urn

Precious the box that Mary brake
Of spikenard for her Master's sake,
But ah! It held nought half so dear
As the sweet dust that whitens here.
The greater wonder who shall say,
To make so white a soul of day
From clay, to win a face so fair.
Those strange real eyes, that sunlit hair

A ripple o'er her witty brain, –
Or turn all back to dust again.

Who knows but in some happy hour
The God, whose strange alchemic power
Wrought her of dust, again may turn
To woman, this immortal urn;
May take this dust and breathe thereon,
And give me back my little one.

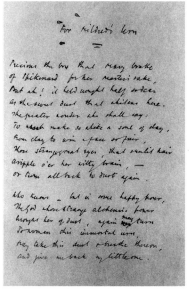

*For Mildred's Urn – one of Brooke's
lost poems*

On docking he checked into New York's Broadway Central Hotel, and, feeling sorry for himself, was overwhelmed by feelings of loneliness and homesickness:

> . . . It's a beastly hotel: and I'm in a beastly room over a cobbled street where there's the Hell of a noise; and I've been tramping this damned city all day, and riding its cars (when they weren't too full); and it's hot; and I'm very tired and cross; and my pyjamas haven't come; and my letters of introduction, which I left behind *en masse*, haven't come; and nothing's come; and I don't know a soul in New York; and I'm *very* tired; and I don't like the food; and I don't like the people's faces; and I don't like the newspapers; and I haven't a friend in the world; and nobody loves me; and I'm going to be extraordinarily miserable these six months; and I want to die . . .

Subsequently, though, he began to perk up a little and to look to his task of committing his observations to paper and arranging them into digestible parcels for *The Westminster Gazette*. His second article began: 'In fine things America excels modern England – fish, architecture, jokes, drinks and children's clothes . . .' He also noticed that '. . . the American by race walks better than we; more freely, with a taking swing, and almost with grace. How much of this is due to living in a democracy, and how much to wearing no braces, it is very difficult to determine.' Another interesting observation was the scope of educational facilities, much broader than the British system, not academically, but in terms of opportunity. 'As a child, he [the American] gets education, then evening-classes, continuation-schools, gymnasia, military training, swimming-baths, orchestra, facilities for the study of anything under the sun, from palaeography to cherokee, libraries, holiday-camps, hospitals, ever-present medical attendance . . .'

During much of his time in New York, he was looked after by Russell H. Loines, a New York lawyer, through an introduction from his former tutor Lowes Dickinson. Loines showed Brooke the sights and took him canoeing in the rapids on the Delaware river. Loines made many young Englishmen welcome at his house on Staten Island. Rupert took time out to write to Ka: '. . . you must get clear of me, cease to love me, love and marry somebody – and somebody worthy of you . . .'

To Cathleen his tone was decidedly warmer and more descriptive: 'The little white wisps of mist are creeping and curling along the face of the great wide river . . .'

Back in work mode, Brooke also captured the noise and bustle of the city. 'Theatres and "movies" are aglare. Cars shriek down the street; the elevated train clangs and curves perilously overhead; newsboys wail the baseball news; wits cry their obscure challenges to one another, "I should worry!" or "She's some daisy!" or "Goodnight nurse!".' He wrote to Marsh on different topics, including the candidates in the running for the Poet Laureateship following the death of Alfred Austin: 'All the papers have immense articles, with pictures of Masefield and Noyes. They mention everybody except me and Wilfred. Even Will Davies . . .'

From New York he travelled to Boston, where a middle-aged lady told him, 'What is wrong with America, is this democracy. They ought to take the votes away from these people, who don't know how to use them, and give them only to us, the educated.'

After Boston he attended the Harvard–Yale baseball match across the river in Cambridge, where he witnessed cheerleaders raising the crowd to new heights. At Harvard he noted a march by graduates from the class of 1912 stretching back to the veterans of the 1850s: 'It seems to bring the passage of time very presently and vividly to the mind. To see, with such emphatic regularity, one's coevals changing in figure, and diminishing in number, summer after summer!' At Harvard one octogenarian asked Rupert, 'So you come from Rugby, tell me do you know that curious creature Matthew Arnold?' Brooke noted, 'I couldn't bring myself to tell him that even in Rugby, we had forgiven that brilliant youth his iconoclastic tendencies some time since, and that, as a matter of fact, he had died when I was eight months old.'

But it was time to put the United States behind him.

> My American friends were full of kindly scorn when I announced that I was going to Canada. 'A country without soul' they cried and pressed books upon me to befriend me through the Philistine bleakness . . . I was taken in a motor car some twenty miles or more over the execrable roads round here, to a lovely little lake in the hills, north-west of Ottawa. We went to little French villages and fields at first and then through rocky, tangled woods of birch and poplar, rich with milk-weed and blue cornflowers, and the aromatic thimbleberry blossom and that romantic light, purple-red flowers which is called fireweed, because it is the first vegetation to spring up in the prairie after a fire has passed over and so might be adapted as the emblematic flower of a sense of humour.

Brooke took leave of Harvard and headed north to Canada on the Montreal Express, from where he wrote to Eddie Marsh, '. . . now I'm shut up in my upper half of the sleeping-berth, I'm empty but a little easier. Beneath me sleeps – oh, a mattress and a plank between us – a fat old lady. Every other berth in the car is shared between married people, so it is – naturally – the prevalent opinion that the fat woman is my wife.' Marsh's mischievous reply included a newspaper cutting stuck on to the letter: 'BROOKE – On the 9th July, at Ashford Hill, Newbury the wife of R.C. Brooke, of a daughter' adding, 'Evidently the fat lady seen in the train has nipped over to England and is foisting her bastard on you – so beware.'

The American and Canadian magazines were still full of talk of an imminent appointment of a Poet Laureate. In a letter to Marsh, Brooke wrote: 'Laureateship is discussed ardently and continually. They think le Gallienne is in the running otherwise they're fairly sane. Except that everybody here thinks Noyes a *big* poet; bigger than Yeats or Bridges for instance . . . why not Bridges? . . . Kipling'd be fine too . . .' Masefield, however, seemed to be quite candid about his chances: 'I haven't got a ghost of a chance, and never had. I can't possibly be in the six most likely names. As far as one can see, the appointment lies between the following: Robert Bridges, Edmund Gosse, Henry Newbolt, Austin Dobson, Thomas Hardy and Sir Quiller Couch . . .' Masefield would become Laureate, but not for another 17 years after the death of the man who would be named as Laureate, Robert Bridges.

The younger poets were able to make their voices heard in several literary organs including John Middleton Murry's *Rhythm* which became *The Blue Review* in the spring of 1913. The magazine also encompassed articles on other aspects of the arts as well as featuring literary contributions from such writers and poets as Lascelles Abercrombie, Gilbert Cannan, Wilfred Wilson Gibson, W.H. Davies and Brooke. Vol. 1 no. 3, which was eventually published in July 1913, contained two of Brooke's poems, 'Love' and 'The Busy Heart'.

The Busy Heart

Now that we've done our best and worst, and parted,
I would fill my mind with thoughts that will not rend.
(O heart, I do not dare go empty-hearted)
I'll think of Love in books, Love without end;
Women with child, content; and old men sleeping;
And wet strong ploughlands, scarred for certain grain;
And babes that weep, and so forget their weeping;
And the young heavens, forgetful after rain;
And evening hush, broken by homing wings;
And Song's nobility, and Wisdom holy,
That live, we dead. I would think of a thousand things,
Love and durable, and taste them slowly,
One after one, lie tasting a sweet food.
I have need to busy my heart with quietude.

Of all the contributors to that edition, Rupert seemed most impressed with the work of Katherine Mansfield: 'She *can* write, damn her.' *The Blue Review* collapsed after that particular edition, with Murry moving to Paris in an attempt to escape his creditors. His problems had begun when the publisher of *Rhythm* absconded in October 1912 leaving a printing debt of £400. Murry would be made bankrupt in February 1914, and another outlet for Brooke's poems was sealed off.

Occasional bursts of homesickness saw Brooke making up 'minor painful songs':

Would God were eating plover's eggs
And drinking dry champagne
With the Bernard Shaws, Mr & Mrs Masefield
Lady Horner, Neil Primrose, Raleigh, The Right
Honourable Augustine Birrell, Eddie, six or
Seven Asquiths, & Felicity Tree, in Downing Street again.

In Canada, Brooke visited Quebec, from where he sailed up the St Lawrence Seaway, 18 miles across at the point where his boat turned up the Saguenay, which flows beneath massive cliffs of black granite, to Chicotimi.

In Montreal he noted how the British sector was dominated by the Scots; and after its 'strain and lightness' considered Ottawa a relief. 'The streets of Ottawa are very quiet, and shaded with trees. The houses are mostly of that cool, homely, wooden kind. With verandahs, on which, or on the steps, the whole family may sit in the evening and observe the passers-by.' In Ottawa he stayed with the poet Duncan Campbell Scott and his family. He wrote to Wilfred Gibson about Scott, 'Poor devil, he's so lonely and dried there: no one to talk to. They had a child – daughter – who died in 1908 or so. And it knocked them out . . . Their house is queerily desolate, it rather went to my heart . . .' Scott had been an introduction from John Masefield.

During Brooke's Canadian travels, Wilfred Gibson and Lascelles Abercrombie had come up with a bright publishing idea for publishing their poems from the Gallows, the Abercrombies' house in Dymock, Gloucestershire. Gibson wrote to Rupert about it in a letter that caught up with him on the banks of Lake Ontario. Rupert passed the exciting information on to his mother in a letter from the King Edward Hotel, Toronto, dated 21 July 1913.

Gibson has been staying with Abercrombie and has got a great idea that he, Abercrombie, Drinkwater, and I should combine our publics and publish from the Abercrombies (Mrs A does the work) a Volume four times a year. A. has done it with some of his own stuff, and finds he makes most money that way. The other three seem to be keen on

Brooke with fellow poet Duncan Campbell Scott in Ottawa

the idea. Rather a score for me, as my 'public' is smaller than any of theirs! But it's a secret at present.

The working title was to be 'Gallows Garlands'.

The first of the literary circle that was to become known as the 'Dymock Poets' to move to the area 'did a Dymoke' (a phrase meaning to have extricated oneself from a tricky situation or accomplished a difficult task) was Lascelles Abercrombie. Abercrombie had successfully liberated himself from being a trainee quantity surveyor to enter the world of literature on a full-time basis, as a reviewer for various newspapers in Manchester and Liverpool. In 1910 he came temporarily to Much Marcle, Herefordshire, where his married sister had settled, before moving to the Gallows, a pair of cottages on Lord Beauchamp's estate, just to the south-east of Much Marcle, at Ryton. His writing flourished and he published 'Emblems of Love', 'The Sale of St Thomas' and 'Ryton Firs':

. . . From Marcle Way
From Dymock, Kimpley, Newent, Bromesbarrow,
Redmarley, all the meadowland daffodils seem
Running in gold tides to Ryton Firs . . .

Wilfed Gibson moved to the area in 1913, taking the Old Nailshop at Greenway Cross, the former house of the Sadlers, the local nailmakers, having initially stayed close by with the Abercrombies. Some three years older than Lascelles, Gibson turned 35 in 1913 and Abercrombie 32. The former's reputation was rapidly growing via his volume of verses *Daily Bread*, by then in its third edition, and *The Stonefolds*. Gibson, like Abercrombie, was also moved by the beauty of this remote part of England, as he expressed in poems such as 'In the Meadow', 'The Elm' and 'Trees'.

Rupert and Wilfred Gibson, whom Brooke nicknamed 'Wibson', had been introduced by Eddie Marsh in London in September 1912, when they had gone to watch a fire blazing at King's Cross. The two became friends, and Gibson visited Rupert at the Old Vicarage, Grantchester, and attended the farewell gathering in May 1913 in London's Regent Street.

A year younger than Abercrombie and five years older than Brooke, John Drinkwater was a professional actor with the Birmingham Company, the Pilgrim Players, becoming the first manager of the newly built Birmingham Repertory Theatre in February 1913, directing countless production and increasing his reputation as a dramatist. Brooke was excited about the scheme, without doubt being delighted at the prospect of working with Gibson, to whom he would refer in August 1913 as 'the most loveable and simple person in the world'.

From Toronto, Rupert was scribbling snatches of nostalgic verse, to his friends in England:

> My heart is sick for several things
> Only to be found in King's.
> I do recall those haunts with tears
> The Backs, the Chapel, and the Rears . . .

and

> . . . Dear Home of my Rememberings!
> O Kings! O Kings! O Kings! O Kings!
> Spot where I cheered the college bumps!
> Place where I read the first Less'n in pumps!
> Founded in New Jerusalem!
> And breakfasted at 3pm!

At the Niagara Falls, Brooke saw the commercial and vulgar face of tourism.

> Hotels, power-houses, bridges, trams, picture postcards, sham legends, stills, books, rifle-galleries and side-shows . . . Niagara is the central home and breeding place for all the touts on earth . . . Touts insinuating, and touts raucous, greasy touts, brazen touts, and upper-class refined, gentlemanly, take-you-by-the-arm touts: touts who wheedle; touts who would photograph you with your arm around a young lady against a faked background . . . touts who would bully you into cars, char-a-bancs, elevators or tunnels . . . touts who would sell you picture postcards, moccasins, sham Indian bead-work, blankets, tee-pees and crockery . . .

From the Niagara Falls and Toronto he went to Sarnia, at the southern tip of Lake Huron, taking a boat north through its waters to Lake Superior, before travelling overland to Winnipeg, Manitoba. He found the local architecture displeasing. 'It is hideous, of course, even more hideous than Toronto or Montreal; but cheerily and windily so. There is no scheme in the city, and no beauty, but it is at least preferable to Birmingham, less dingy, less directly depressing.'

He wrote to Cathleen on 3 August: 'Today, O my heart, I am twenty-six years old. And I've done so little. I'm very much ashamed. By God I'm going to make things hum, though. – But that's all so far away. I'm lying quite naked on a beach of golden sand . . .' He wrote again from Edmonton, a town that had ballooned from a population of 200 in 1901 to 50,000 by 1913. Rupert was not only communicating with Cathleen; he had had a disturbing letter from Noel, in which she revealed that one of her other suitors, either Ferenc Bekassy or James Strachey, had told her that Brooke had complained that he was becoming bored with her. The tone of her letter hints at her feeling sorry for herself as well as being cynical. He replied: 'You're a devil. By God you're a DEVIL. What a bloody letter to write to me! . . . Bekassy and James, who you say, tell you I'm bored, lie, on the whole. Certainly they can't know.' Then came the flash of the dagger as he plunged in with bravado: 'I'm practically engaged to a girl you don't know to whom I'm devoted & who is in love with me. And if I don't marry her, I shall very swiftly marry one of two or three others, & be very happy.' She didn't rise to his taunts but did admit that it was Rupert's unpleasant sense of humour that finally killed off any love she had for him.

From Winnipeg he crossed the Prairies, visited Regina, Edmonton, Calgary and the Rockies and mourned the passing of the days of the old west; 'Hordes of people – who mostly seem to come from the great neighbouring

Commonwealth, and are inspired with the National hunger for getting rich quickly without deserving it – prey on the community by their dealings in what they call "Real Estate". For them our fathers died.'

At Calgary, photographs arrived from Duncan Campbell Scott, taken during his stay with him. In his thank-you letter Rupert commented, 'I don't know why the one of me alone should have caught me at a moment when I was trying to look like Arnold Bennett.' He wrote to Eddie Marsh from Calgary, about the number of interviews he was undertaking and how various towns saw him differently. Some considered him an expert politician, others a poet and others a thinker. 'When I come back, though, I shall demand a knighthood from Winston. I've been delivering immense speeches on his naval policy.'

At Lake Louise, 100 miles north-west of Calgary, Brooke met a young American widow, the Marchesa Mannucci Capponi. They were obviously attracted to one another and were to keep in touch. Rupert was captivated by the scenery: 'Lake Louise is of another world . . . Imagine a little round lake 6,000 feet up, a mile across, closed in by great cliffs of brown rock, round the shoulders of which are thrown mantles of close dark pine. At one end the lake is fed by a vast glacier, and its milky tumbling stream; and the glacier climbs to snow fields of one of the highest and loveliest peaks in the Rockies, which keeps perpetual guard over the scene.'

From Vancouver he dashed off many missives, including one to his mother, before visiting Victoria and Vancouver Island. Having completed the cross-Canada route through Quebec, Ontario, Manitoba, Saskatchewan, Alberta and British Columbia, Brooke took a train to San Francisco, from where he bemoaned to the Marchesa Capponi the loss of his work: 'That notebook which contained 2 months' notes on my travels, and unfinished sonnets, and all sorts of wealth I lost in British Columbia – yessir isn't it too bloody. I've been prostrated with grief ever since. And God knows how I shall get through my articles on Canada.' He reported to Eddie Marsh that the Californians were friendly people and that mention of the name of Masefield opened many doors, and that he was upset to learn that the series of articles for *The Westminster Gazette* would probably be limited to six and that there was little hope for a second series.

CHAPTER XII

Goe, and Catch a Falling Starre

(John Donne)

Rupert boarded the SS *Sterra* bound for Honolulu. To the backdrop of a happy atmosphere on the boat provided by a crowd of young men with mandolins, he wrote in October 1913 the poem 'Clouds', imagining the clouds to be spirits of the dead, scudding across the moon and observing the living beneath them.

Clouds

Down the blue night the unending columns press
In noiseless tumult, break and wave and flow,
Now tread the far South, or lift rounds of snow
Up to the white moon's hidden loveliness.
Some pause in their grave wandering comradeless,
And turn with profound gesture vague and slow,
As who would pray good for the world, but know
Their benediction empty as they bless.

They say that the Dead die not, but remain
Near to the rich heirs of their grief and mirth.
I think they ride the calm mid-heaven, as these,
In wise majestic melancholy train,
And watch the moon, and the still-raging seas,
And men, coming and going on the earth.

The poem was to become a favourite of both his mother and Cathleen Nesbitt.

On the same journey he began 'A Memory', a cathartic poem about Noel Olivier, born out of a letter written to Cathleen relating the story of his relationship with Noel.

A Memory

Some while before the dawn I rose, and stept
Softly along the dim way to your room,
And found you sleeping in the quiet gloom,
And holiness about you as you slept.
I knelt there; till your waking fingers crept
About my head, and held it. I had a rest
Unhoped this side of Heaven, beneath your breast.
I knelt a long time, still; nor even wept.

It was great wrong you did me; and for gain
Of that poor moment's kindliness, and ease,
And sleepy mother-comfort!
Child, you know
How easily love leaps out to dreams like these,
Who has seen them true. And love that's wakened so
Takes all too long to lay asleep again.

To Cathleen he wrote, 'I would like to make a litany of all the things that bind me to the memory of holiness – of peaks. It would mean – "The Chilterns" – "Hampton Court" – "*Hullo Ragtime*" – "Raymond Buildings" and a few more names. And it would begin and end with Cathleen.' He was also beginning to come to terms with his guilt over the Ka situation and being able to think of her without discomfort. Being able to regard it from a distance, he put his feelings into another poem.

Waikiki

Warm perfumes like a breath from vine and tree
Drift down the darkness. Plangent, hidden from eyes,
Some where an *eukaleli* thrills and cries
And stabs with pain the night's brown savagery;
And dark scents whisper; and dim waves creep to me,

Glean like a woman's hair, stretch out, and rise;
And new stars burn into the ancient skies,
Over the murmurous soft Hawaiian sea.

And I recall, lose, grasp, forget again,
And still remember, a tale I have heard, or known,
An empty tale, of idleness and pain,
Of two that loved – or did not love – and one
Whose perplexed heart did evil, foolishly,
A long while since, and by some other sea.

He took a boat to Kanai before returning to Honolulu and catching the SS *Ventura* on 27 October. The *Ventura* put into Samoa on 2 November. He described the scene to Cathleen. 'In the evening the wharf was covered with

Brooke in Samoa

torches, lamps and a mass of Samoans, all with some "curios" or other on little stalls . . . great bronze men, with gilded hair, and Godlike limbs lay about on the grass . . . The whole was lit up by these flaming lights against the tropical nights and the palms and the stars, so that it looked like a Rembrandt picture . . .' He wrote to Eddie Marsh, 'I lived in a Samoan house (the coolest in the world) with a man and his wife, nine children, ranging from a proud beauty of 18 to a round object of 1 year, a dog, a cat, a proud hysterical hen, and a gaudy scarlet and green parrot . . .'

He dispatched poems to Wilfred Gibson for possible inclusion in the new project. The name for the anthology of verse was for a while to be The New Shilling Garland, after Laurence Binyon's The Shilling Garland, before the idea of naming it The Gallows Garland was mooted. By the time the plans were finalised, the title of New Numbers had been settled upon. The publication would contain the work of Brooke, Gibson, Abercrombie and Drinkwater.

After a visit to Apia, Rupert took the SS Torfua to Fiji. There he entertained the fascinated locals with his prehensile toes, journeyed to the island of Kandarra, played Fijian cricket, took in Suva and sailed to the island of Taviuni. He wrote many letters home, factual to his mother, romantic to Cathleen, general to Eddie Marsh and others to the likes of Edmund Gosse, Dudley Ward and Denis Browne. 'Denis! . . . it is mere heaven. One passes from Paradise to Paradise. The natives are incredibly beautiful, & very kindly. Life is one long picnic. I have been living in native villages and roaming from place to place . . . These people are nearer to Earth & the joy of things than we snivelling city-dwellers.' England, though, was still in his heart, as he informed Jacques Raverat: 'Oh I shall return. The South Seas are Paradise. But I prefer England . . .' To Violet Asquith he joked from 'Somewhere in the mountains of Fiji', 'It's twenty years since they've eaten anybody in this part of Fiji, and four more since they've done what I particularly and reasonably detest – fastened the victim down, cut pieces off him one by one, and cooked and eaten them before his eyes . . .'

In mid-December he took the RMS Niagara from Fiji. From the Grand Hotel in Auckland he gave vent to his frustration to Cathleen. 'Why precisely I'm here, I don't know. I seem to have missed a boat somewhere; and I can't get on to Tahiti till the beginning of January. Damn. And I hear that a man got to Tahiti two months ahead of me, and found – and carried off – some Gauguin paintings on glass. Damn! Damn! Damn!' He described New Zealand as 'a sort of Fabian England, very upper middle class and gentle and happy (after Canada), no poor and the government owning hotels and running charabancs. All the women smile and dress very badly, and nobody drinks.' He stayed for a while with one of the early New Zealand families, the Studholmes, at Ruanni in the middle of the North Island, as well as seeing Warapei and Wellington where, at the Wellington Club, he read several of his

Westminster Gazette articles and a complimentary write-up of Cathleen's performance in the play *Quality Street*. He saw a specialist in Wellington about some poisoning in his foot, before sailing a week or two behind schedule to Tahiti. On board was the statuesque contralto Clara Butt and her family. They got on so well that they dined together on arriving at Tahiti in early February.

Rupert described his new surroundings to his mother.

> I have found a fine place here, about thirty miles from Papeete, the chief town in Tahiti. It is a native village, with one fairly large European house in it, possessed by the chief, and inhabited by a 3/4 white man . . . it is the coolest place I've struck in the South Seas (Papeete was very hot), with a large veranda, the sea just in front, and the hills behind . . . there's a little wooden pier out into the sea (which is thirty yards away in front of the house). With a dive into deep water . . . P.S. They call me *Pupure* here – it means 'fair' in Tahitian – because I have fair hair!

Brooke immediately fell in love with the island, deciding to stay for at least a month, fishing, swimming, canoeing, exploring and eating 'the most wonderful food in the world, strange fishes and vegetables, perfectly cooked'.

When the original settlers, the Polynesians, first came here in the seventh or eighth century, the vegetation was limited to seeds and spores, forcing them to bring taro, yams, coconuts, bananas and breadfruit; missionaries later introduced corn, citrus fruits, tamerinds, pineapples, guavas, figs and

A photograph from Brooke's camera of the house in Mataia where he lived during the early part of 1914

other vegetables. The first European to set foot on Tahiti, the most famous of French Polynesia's 130 islands, was Captain Wallis of the HMS *Dolphin* in 1767; Captain Cook arrived there two years later, and HMS *Bounty* under Captain Bligh in 1788.

One hundred and twenty-five years on, no mutiny was necessary for Brooke to enjoy the Tahitian way of life for as long as he pleased. Within a day or two of arriving he met a local girl, Taatamata, who symbolically gave him a flower. Wearing a flower over the right ear meant you were looking for a sweetheart; over the left ear, that you had found a sweetheart; and behind both ears, that you had found one sweetheart and were looking for another. To Cathleen he wrote: 'A white flower over each ear, my dear, is dreadfully the most fashionable way of adorning yourself in Tahiti. Tonight we will put scarlet flowers in our hair and sing strange slumberous South Seas songs to the concertina and drink red wine and dance obscure native dances and bathe in a soft lagoon by moonlight and eat great squelchy tropical fruits – custard apples, papia, pomegranate, mango, guava, and the rest . . .'

From Eddie Marsh he heard news of Wilfred Gibson's impending marriage, and Marsh's delight at receiving Brooke's poem 'Heaven'.

Taatamata photographed by Brooke in the early spring of 1914

Heaven

Fish (fly-replete, in depth of June,
Dawdling away their watery noon)
Ponder deep wisdom, dark or clear,
Each secret fishy hope or fear.
Fish say, they have their Stream or Pond;
But is there anything Beyond?
This life cannot be All, they swear,
For how unpleasant, if it were!
One may not doubt that, somehow, Good
Shall come of Water and of Mud;
And, sure the reverent eye must see
A Purpose in Liquidity.
We darkly know, by faith we cry,
The future is not Wholly Dry.
Mud unto Mud! – Death eddies near –
Not here the appointed End, not here!
But somehow, beyond Space and Time,
Is wetter water, slimier slime!
And there (they trust) there swimmeth One
Who swam ere rivers were begun,
Immense, of fishy form and mind,
Squamous, omnipotent, and kind;
And under that Almight Fin,
The littlest fish may enter in.
Oh! never fly conceals a hook,
Fish say, in the Eternal Brook,
But more than mundane weeds are there,
And mud, celestially fair;
Fat caterpillars drift around,
And Paradisal grubs are found;
Unfading moths, immortal flies,
And the worm that never dies.
And in that Heaven of all their wish,
There shall be no more land, say fish.

Marsh confessed to Rupert, 'I do long to see you. Every now and then it comes over me, how much more I should be enjoying everything if you were here.' He also mentioned the impending publication of the first edition of the Brooke/Abercrombie/Gibson/Drinkwater co-operative publication *New Numbers*. The volume published in February 1914 contained three of

Rupert's sonnets, 'A Memory', 'Sonnet (Suggested by some of the Proceedings of the Society for Psychical Research)' and 'One Day' written in the Pacific.

One Day

Today I have been happy. All the day
I held the memory of you, and wove
Its laughter with the dancing light o' the spray,
And sowed the sky with tiny clouds of love,
And sent you following the white waves of sea,
And crowned your head with fancies, nothing worth,
Stray buds from that old dust of misery,
Being glad with a new foolish quiet mirth.

So lightly I played with those dark memories,
Just as a child, beneath the summer skies,
Plays hour by hour with a strange shining stone,
For which (he knows not) towns were fire of old,
And love has been betrayed, and murder done,
And great kings turned to a little bitter mould.

During his time in the South Seas, the quality and depth of Rupert's poetry reached a new maturity, while at home his reputation was growing. Wilfred Gibson was a little peeved that he had not been offered 'Heaven' for *New Numbers*, and the English Association wanted to include 'The Old Vicarage, Grantchester' in an anthology of modern poetry for use in secondary schools. The editor of a new series of *Body and Modern Development of Modern Thought* was keen for Brooke to contribute, having been impressed by his review of *Poems of John Donne*. Eddie Marsh suggested he might manage 40,000 words on somebody like the Stockholm playwright Johan August Strindberg, a subject close to Brooke's heart. There was a splendid review of *New Numbers* in *The Times*, which quoted his 'Sonnet (Suggested by some of the Proceedings of the Society for Psychical Research)'.

Sonnet

Not with vain tears, when we're beyond the sun,
We'll beat on the substantial doors, nor tread
Those dusty high-roads of the aimless dead
Plaintive for Earth; but rather turn and run

Down some close-covered by-way of the air,
Some low sweet alley between wind and wind,
Stoop under faint gleams, thread the shadows, find
Some whispering ghost-forgotten nook, and there

Spend in pure converse our eternal day;
Think each in each, immediately wise;
Learn all we lacked before; hear, know, and say
What this tumultuous body now denies;
And feel, who have laid our groping hands away;
And see, no longer blinded by our eyes.

New Numbers was being printed by the Crypt House Press at Gloucester and stamped and dispatched by the local postmaster Mr Griffiths with the help of Dymock postmen Charlie Westen and Jack Brooke. The first edition was oversubscribed, to the extent that the project was deemed to be a veritable success, Eddie Marsh writing to Rupert, 'N.N. is out. It's very good, the shape, print and appearance quite excellent.'

As Brooke's reputation was spreading, via Eddie he had had a direct entrée to the right social, literary and political circles; so why did he tread water in Tahiti rather than race home to embrace success and capitalise on it? The answer was Taatamata, and a *laissez-faire* way of life that appealed to his neo-paganism. From Paaeete Rupert was to declare to Marsh: 'All I want in life is a cottage & the leisure to write supreme poems & plays . . .'

Five of Rupert's South Seas poems would appear in the third volume of *New Numbers* in July 1914, one of them, 'Tiare Tahiti', making reference to Taatamata, whom he called Mamua. Although he affords her only the odd allusion in his letters home, they enjoyed a full physical relationship and she nursed him back to health when he was feverish with coral poisoning. On the face of it, it was a dalliance that suited them both, and he waxed lyrical about her: 'I have been nursed & waited on by a girl with wonderful eyes, the walk of a Goddess, & the heart of an angel, who is, luckily, devoted to me. She gives her time to ministering me, I mine to probing her queer mind. I think I shall write a book about her – only I fear I'm too fond of her . . .'

The idyllic life could not continue: he had run out of money and the call of England was too great. Homesickness tore him from the arms of Taatamata, and from the Pacific he wrote, 'Call me home, I pray you, Cathleen. I have been away long enough. I am older than I was. I have left bits of me about – some of my hair in Canada, and one skin in Honolulu, and another in Fiji, and a bit of a third in Tahiti, and half a tooth in Samoa, and bits of my heart all over the place.'

The *Tahiti*, with Brooke aboard, left in early April. He described his sadness at leaving in a letter to Cathleen, understandably omitting his prolonged and personal farewell to Mamua.

> I was sad at heart to leave Tahiti but I resigned myself to the vessel, and watched the green shores and rocky peaks fade with hardly a pang. I've told so many of those that loved me, so often, Oh yes, I'll come back . . . next year perhaps: or the year after . . . I suddenly realised that I'd left behind those lovely places and lovely people perhaps for ever. I reflected that there was surely nothing else like them in this world, and very probably nothing in the next . . .

His final South Seas poem was 'Hauntings'.

Hauntings

In the grey tumult of these after-years
Oft silence falls; the incessant wranglers part;
And less-than-echoes of remembered tears
Hush all the loud confusion of the heart;
And a shade, through the toss'd ranks of mirth and crying,
Hungers, and pains, and each dull passionate mood –
Quite lost, and all but all forgot, undying,
Comes back the ecstasy of your quietude.

So a poor ghost, beside his misty streams,
Is haunted by strange doubts, evasive dreams,
Hints of a pre-Lethean life, of men,
Stars, rocks, and flesh, things unintelligible,
And light on waving grass, he knows not when,
And feet that ran, but where, he cannot tell.

Still in the Pacific on board the Tahiti, he wrote to Frances Cornford, addressing the contents to her six-month-old daughter Helena: '. . . lately, I have been having English thoughts – thoughts certainly of England – and even, faintly, yes, English thoughts – grey, quiet, misty, rather mad, slightly moral, shy & lovely thoughts . . .'

On the way back home, Brooke went back to the United States travelling through Arizona to San Francisco, where he already started to yearn for Tahiti: 'How I hate civilisation & houses & towns & collars . . .' And miss Mamua: '. . . waiting there to welcome me with wide arms . . . under the constellation the Southern Cross'

CHAPTER XIII

The 'Brussels-Before-Waterloo Feeling'

Rupert described the Grand Canyon as '. . . very large and very untidy, like my soul. But unlike my soul, it has peace in it.' From the brick-red desert of Arizona, he dispatched several other 'Grand Canyon' letters to Jacques Raverat, Mrs Brooke, the Marchesa Capponi and Russell Loines. He described the place to his mother: 'The Canyon itself is gigantic, a mile from the edge where you stand to the river at the bottom. For we're 7,000 feet, and the river is 2,000 above sea level. The opposite rim of the Canyon is 13 miles away, and one can see up and down it for some thirty miles in each direction . . .' He implored Cathleen not to let anybody know the exact date of his return: 'It's my fancy to blow in on them unexpected. Just wander into Raymond Buildings, and hear Eddie squeal "Oh my dear! I thought you were in Tahiti" . . .'

On 29 April Rupert climbed off the train at Chicago and checked in at the Auditorium Hotel on Michigan Avenue, next door to the Fine Arts building where the Chicago Little Theatre had its premises on the fourth floor. The theatre was the brainchild of Maurice Browne and his wife, the actress Ellen Van Volkenburg. It had opened on 12 November 1912, to produce classical and modern plays, both tragedy and comedy at affordable prices. It was supported by some 400 people, who paid an annual subscription of ten dollars, and by the sale of seats to the public. The theatre was run by 35 staff and players, and had for its object 'the creation of a new plastic and rhythmic drama in America'.

Rupert went to the theatre to meet Browne and his wife with a letter of introduction from Harold Monro, who was married to Browne's sister. They got on like a house on fire, Brooke reading his South Seas poems and he also read his play *Lithuania*, which impressed Browne and Ellen sufficiently for them to stage it the following year. The husband and wife would respectively direct and act it. It would have a three-week run in Chicago after Brooke's death, without being an overwhelming success. Brooke's ten days with them was, according to Browne, 'a riotous blur of all-night talks, club-sandwiches, dawns over Lake Michigan, and innumerable "steins"'. Rupert gave Ellen several chains of South Seas shells and a copy of Hilaire Belloc's Four Men, which by then he knew virtually off by heart. They insisted that he read all his South Seas poems, and invited others, including a Davenport attorney Arthur Davison Ficke, who, according to Browne, 'came, saw and fell', and Llewellyn Jones, the literary editor of the *Chicago Evening Post*. Ficke would later celebrate the meeting in his 1917 poem 'Portrait of Rupert Brooke', published in New York as part of 'An April Elegy'.

Portrait of Rupert Brooke

One night – the last we were to have you –
High up above the city's giant roar
We sat around you on the studio floor –
Since chairs were lame and stony or too few –
And as you read, and the low music grew,
In exquisite tendrils twining the heart's core,
All the conjecture we had felt before
Flashed into torch-flame, and at last we knew.

And Maurice, who in silence long has hidden
A voice like yours, became a wreck of joy,
To inarticulate ecstasies beguiled.
And you, as from some secret world now hidden
To make return, stared up, and like a boy
Blushed suddenly, and looked at us, and smiled.

Browne noted that 'Brooke read well – much better of course than the average professional reader or actor reads poetry – quietly and shyly, with little tone-variation, dwelling slightly on significant vowel sounds and emphasising rhyme and rhythm: reading in fact, as a good lyric poet always reads good lyric poetry, taking care of the sound and letting the sense take care of itself.'

According to Browne, Rupert dazzled the people of Chicago in their windy city: '. . . every woman who passes – and every other man – stops, turns round, to look at that lithe and radiant figure . . . his hair longish, wavy, the colour of his skin: a sort of bleached gold . . .' Rupert had more photographs taken in Chicago, this time by Eugene Hutchinson, who had been present at several of Brooke's readings:

I found myself confronted by an unbelievably beautiful young man. There was nothing effeminate about that beauty. He was man-size and masculine, from his rough tweeds to his thick-soled English boots. He gave me the impression of being water-loving and well washed. Perhaps this was due to the freshness of his sun-tanned face and the odd smoothness of his skin, a smoothness you see more in women than in men . . . He seemed like a Norse myth in modern clothes – yet there was no vanity in the man . . .

April saw the second publication of *New Numbers*, which carried only one of Rupert's poems, 'Heaven', the work that Wilfred Gibson had wanted to include in the first book. A short time later *The Little Review* carried a quote

The Gallows Cottage, home of New Numbers. *The part of the house nearest the gate was linked by a wooden passageway to the thatched part of the property – long since demolished*

from W.B. Yeats that underlined Hutchinson's observations: he declared Brooke 'the most beautiful young man in England'.

Rupert spent a night in Pittsburgh, before moving on to Washington, where he renewed his friendship with the Marchesa Capponi, whose heart he had clearly captured the previous summer in Canada. In the interim period she had visited England, and actually made her way to Rugby, where she called on Brooke's mother. The Ranee found her charming, and was delighted to hear a complimentary account of her son.

The newspapers were increasingly reporting the delicate state of relations between some of the European countries. The previous year Bulgaria, Greece, Serbia and Montenegro had argued over Macedonia, the Ottoman Empire having surrendered it after its defeat, on the understanding that it would become the new independent state of Albania. Despite the treaty, there was still unease in Europe. Brooke was able to follow developments in the American press. '[President Woodrow] Wilson gets forced more and more into war. The newspapers are wicked. But there's nothing like the popular excitement a war generally causes. It'll be a "sort of war" – dragging on and on . . .'

By mid-May, Rupert was in Boston, before heading to New York to board the SS *Philadelphia*, which would sail on 29 May, taking him to Plymouth. He booked on to the same boat as Maurice Browne and Ellen Van Volkenburg as he felt that their company would make the journey more pleasurable. A telegram from the Marchesa Capponi, which he received on boarding, was an unexpected and pleasant surprise. Ellen wrote several letters from the boat to her parents, containing constant references to 'Mr Brooke'. Among their fellow passengers were many French, Germans, an Indian chief, 30 members of the University of California Glee Club, a Roman Catholic priest and the printer Ronald Hargreave. Teaming up with the latter, Browne, Ellen and Rupert intrigued many of the other passengers, several of whom took photographs of Brooke as he and his party kept themselves to themselves, playing bridge and having a sonnet-writing competition, in which the lines had predetermined end words. Hargreave, Brooke and Browne allowed themselves between 5.00 p.m. and 6.15 p.m. on 3 June to compose a sonnet each, to be read then to the others. An unsatisfied Hargreave threw his overboard, but Rupert considered his good enough to later rework it. This is the original.

The True Beatitude

They say, when the Great Prompter's hand shall ring
Down the Last Curtain upon earth and sea,
All the Good Puppets have Eternity
To praise their God, worship and love and sing,

Or, to the walls of Heaven wandering,
Look down on those damned for some fretful d –,
Mock them (all theologians agree
On this reward for virtue), laugh, and fling

New sulphur on the sin-incarnadined . . .
– Ah, Love! Still temporal, and still atmospheric,
Teleologically unperturbed,
We share a peace by no divines divined,
An earthly garden hidden from any cleric,
Untrodden of God, by no Eternal curbed.

This was Browne's contribution:

Plato was Right

When Wagner, drunk with music, belched the *Ring*,
He had not the excuse the emetic sea;
Time did not lengthen to eternity,
Nor drive him, like us wretched men, to sing
Endless rhymed-endings. (Rupert, wandering,
Stares seaward; Ronald growls an angry d –,
Both scratch their heads, and hiccough; and I agree:
Villainous verse, and wine, not fit to fling
Even to the fishes). He wasn't incarnadined
With shipboard claret; he sat by atmospheric
And philadelphic victuals unperturbed;
He could walk dry land, and chuckle; he wasn't divined
By a fat divine, nor scowled on by a thin cleric . . .
And yet he sang. Pegasus should be curbed.

Brooke and Browne were treated to an experiment of Hargreave's '. . . in projecting scenery, by painting a landscape on glass, putting it in a kodak in place of the film, then setting an electric bulb [at the] back of it and throwing the reflection on a big piece of paper some distance ahead . . .'

As they approached England, Ellen recorded, 'We're almost in . . . land was sighted a long time ago, and we can smell new-mown hay! Mr Brooke is leaning over the taff rail, sniffing ecstatically.'

Rupert was met at the station in London by Cathleen, Eddie Marsh and Denis Browne, before going on to Rugby to see his mother and write to the Marchesa Capponi: 'I was so happy all the voyage. We had splendid weather,

Dymock goes to Birmingham – to see one of John Drinkwater's plays, only Brooke is absent. (Left to right) John Drinkwater, Wilfred Gibson, Eddie Marsh, Lascelles Abercrombie, Geraldine Gibson, Catherine Abercrombie

and there were nice people on board. I thought of you and rejoiced. You give me great quietness and peace . . . you are very good to me . . .'

After Rugby, he spent a few days at Manor Farm with the Raverats and their fellow guest, the French writer André Gide, a close friend of Oscar Wilde from late 1891 until the latter's death in 1900. Back in London, Rupert went to the ballet to see *Les Papillons* and *Petrushka* with Marsh and the Brownes. Queen Alexandra, George Moore, Arnold Bennett and the Bernard Shaws were also in attendance, Ellen thinking that Shaw 'looked like a very solemn English clergyman'. After the ballet, they retired to Raymond Buildings, where they were joined by friends of Marsh's, whom Maurice thought 'the loveliest people in London'. The party went on till dawn, with Mrs Elgy serving iced coffee and Rupert, usually a resolute non-dancer, performing a South Seas island dance with a flame-haired girl called Jane, on the lawns of Gray's Inn.

On another occasion in Marsh's room Brooke, Gibson, Abercrombie and Monro talked metaphysics long into the night, whilst being observed by Maurice Browne, also present, who noted, 'Brooke's grasp and handling of intellectual abstractions was much more than usual, he was a child in the philosophical hands of Abercrombie, perhaps the most compelling, conversationally of contemporary British metaphysicians . . .' With Violet Asquith he visited the Masefields at their new home in south Oxfordshire, Collingdon Farm near Wallingford. Constance Masefield recorded the visit in her diary: 'The two days

A cheque from Brooke for six copies of New Numbers

were full of charm and friendship and happiness . . .' They walked over Collingdon Hill and the Berkshire Downs, with a disbelieving Rupert and Violet laughing at Masefield's suggestion that the Austro–Serbian conflict might at some point involve Britain. Within a short while he was proved right, and their new home was temporarily requisitioned for the Cavalry.

Rupert was busy picking up all his old threads: Cathleen, Eddie Marsh, the London social scene, Dudley Ward, Hugh Dalton, the Chiltern Hills and the Pink and Lily.

On 20 June 1914, he extolled the virtues of his beloved Chilterns to Cathleen in a letter from the Pink and Lily whilst he was there with Eddie Marsh, Ben Keeling and Dudley Ward:

> . . . we dissected and discussed and adjudged all the poets with infinite perspicacity and responsibility, and then we walked by those glorious woods to Wendover (you know the walk from Wendover, my dear) and drank much beer there, and ate, and started back, and slept in the heather, and walked on through arcades of mysterious beechen gloom and picked flowers and told stories and got back to roast beef, and more beer and poems. I wish you had been there.

A second volume of *Georgian Poetry* was being planned, but more imminent was the third *New Numbers*, due out in a few weeks, which would lead with five of Rupert's poems: 'Tiare Tahiti', 'Retrospect', 'Waikiki', 'Hauntings' and 'The Great Lover'.

The Great Lover

I have been so great a lover: filled my days
So proudly with the splendour of Love's praise,

The pain, the calm, and the astonishment,
Desire illimitable, and still content,
And all dear names men use, to cheat despair,
For the perplexed and viewless streams that bear
Our hearts at random down the dark of life.
Now, ere the unthinking silence on that strife
Steals down, I would cheat drowsy Death so far,
My night shall be remembered for a star
That outshone all the suns of all men's days.
Shall I not crown them with immortal praise
Whom I have loved, who have given me, dared with me
High secrets, and in darkness knelt to see
The inenarrable godhead of delight?
Love is a flame: – we have beaconed the world's night.
A city: – and we have built it, these and I.
An emperor: – we have taught the world to die.
So, for their sakes I loved, ere I go hence,
And the high cause of Love's magnificence,
And to keep loyalties young, I'll write those names
Golden for ever, eagles, crying flames,
And set them as a banner, that men may know,
To dare the generations, burn, and blow
Out on the wind of Time, shining and streaming . . .

These I have loved:
            White plates and cups, clean-gleaming,
Ringed with blue lines; and feathery, faery dust;
Wet roofs, beneath the lamp-light; the strong crust
Of friendly bread; and many tasting food;
Rainbows; and the blue bitter smoke of wood;
And radiant raindrops couching in cool flowers;
And flowers themselves, that sway through sunny hours,
Dreaming of moths that drink them under the moon;
Then, the cool kindliness of sheets, that soon
Smooth away trouble; and the rough male kiss
Of blankets; grainy wood; live hair that is
Shining and free; blue-massing clouds; the keen
Unpassioned beauty of a great machine;
The benison of hot water; furs to touch;
The good smell of old clothes; and other such –
The comfortable smell of friendly fingers,
Hair's fragrance, and the musty reek that lingers

About dead leaves and last year's ferns . . .
                                    Dear names,
And thousand other throng to me! Royal flames;
Sweet water's dimpling laugh from tap or spring;
Holes in the ground; and voices that do sing;
Voices in laughter, too; and body's pain,
Soon turned to peace; and the deep-panting train;
Firm sands; the little dulling edge of foam
That browns and dwindles as the wave goes home;
And washen stones, gay for a hour; the cold
Graveness of iron; moist black earthen mould;
Sleep; and high places; footprints in the dew;
And oaks; and brown horse-chestnuts, glossy-new;
And new-peeled sticks; and shining pools on grass; –
All these have been my loves. And these shall pass,
Whatever passes not, in the great hour,
Not all my passion, all my prayers, have power
To hold them with me through the gate of Death.
They'll play deserter, turn with the traitor breath,
Break the high bond we made, and sell Love's trust
And sacramented covenant to the dust.
– Oh, never a doubt but, somewhere, I shall wake,
And give what's left of love again, and make
New friends, now strangers . . .
                                    But the best I've known
Stays here, and changes, breaks, grows old, is blown
About the winds of the world, and fades from brains
Of living men, and dies.
                        Nothing remains.

O dear my loves, O faithless, once again
This one last gift I give: that after men
Shall know, and later lovers, far-removed,
Praise you, 'All these were lovely'; say, 'He loved.'

He had written this in Mataiea, in the South Seas, as he had 'Retrospect',
during January 1914.

Retrospect

In your arms was still delight,
Quiet as a street at night;
And thoughts of you, I do remember,
Were green leaves in a darkened chamber,
Were dark clouds in a moonless sky.
Love, in you, went passing by,
Penetrative, remote, and rare,
Like a bird in the wide air,
And, as the bird, it left no trace
In the heaven of your face.
In your stupidity I found
The sweet hush after a sweet sound.
All about you was the light
That dims the greying end of night;
Desire was the unrisen sun,
Joy the day not yet begun,
With tree whispering to tree,
Without wind, quietly.
Wisdom slept within your hair,
And Long-Suffering was there,
And, in the flowing of your dress,
Undiscerning Tenderness.
And when you thought, it seemed to me,
Infinitely, and like the sea,
About the slight world you had known
Your vast unconsciousness was thrown . . .
O haven without wave or tide!
Silence, in which all songs have died!
Holy book, where hearts are still!
And home at length under the hill!
O mother-quiet, breasts of peace,
Where love itself would faint and cease
O finite deep I never knew,
I would come back, come back to you,
Find you, as a pool unstirred,
Kneel down by you, and never a word,
Lay my head, and nothing said,
In your hands, ungarlanded;
And a long watch you would keep;
And I should sleep, and I should sleep!

215

The metre of 'Retrospect' closely followed that of Robert Louis Stevenson's 'Requiem', a poem that had been written in the year of Brooke's birth. It also incorporated several ideas from the Stevenson poem:

Under the wide and starry sky,
Dig the grave and let me die.
Glad did I live and gladly die,
And I laid me down with a will.

This be the verse you grave for me;
Here he lies where he longed to be;
Home is the sailor, home from sea,
And the hunter home from the hill.

In Robert Bridges's 1915 anthology *The Spirit of Man*, he juxtaposes Brooke's 'Soldier' and Stevenson's 'Requiem', as the latter continues the sentiments of the former.

During June, prior to the publication of the third edition of *New Numbers*, Rupert went to stay at the Old Nailshop, Greenway, near Dymock, with Geraldine and Wilfred Gibson. From there he wrote to Russell Loines:

Dear Loines

You will have received from Wilfred Gibson a parcel of *New Numbers*, as you demanded. The thing is going pretty well: about seven or eight hundred of each number, which pays expenses very easily and leaves a good bit for division. It goes on selling steadily and I suppose it always will – I mean that back numbers will continue to go off. I hope so, for the more it's sold the more poetry and less reviews Abercrombie and Gibson can write, and the better for the world . . .

He continued, '. . . I've stayed two days with Gibson. He is still a Heaven of delight. I'm going down there again in August . . .', and was moved to comment on Abercrombie's residence, 'You didn't see his cottage did you? Only the Gibsons? Abercrombie's is the most beautiful you can imagine: black-beamed and rose-covered. And a porch where one drinks great mugs of cider and looks at fields of poppies in the corn. A life that makes London a very foolish affair . . .'

By the summer of 1914 the American poet Robert Frost had come to stay with the Abercrombies before taking Little Iddens at Leddington, a mile or two away. His friend Edward Thomas came to the Dymock area for a while in the late summer, renting Oldfields, two meadows away from Frost. Brooke, of course, already knew Thomas, having stayed with him at Froxfield Green in Hampshire.

Having read D.H. Lawrence's *Sons and Lovers* while journeying back through the United States, Rupert had been urging Eddie Marsh to effect an introduction to the author, but Marsh wrote to him at the Old Nailshop admitting to having no luck in tracking him down. In London, though – where there was a reunion for the Cambridge Apostles at the Connaught Rooms, which Brooke attended, the assembled company including James Strachey, Maynard Keynes, G.E. Moore, Harry Norton (with whom he had travelled to Scotland) and Gerald Shove – he had an excellent day with D.H. Lawrence at last. He also went to 10 Downing Street, and had supper at the Savoy Hotel with, among others J.M. Barrie, who had been made a baronet the year before, George Bernard Shaw, Herbert Asquith, G.K. Chesterton, Mrs Patrick Campbell, W.B. Yeats, Marie Tempest, Eddie Marsh and Charles Ricketts, yet to write his *Recollections of Oscar Wilde*. A cinematographer with a biograph appeared in the room and proceeded to take a moving film of the assembled company. Could this historic piece of footage be sitting, unmarked, in somebody's archive?

Brooke then breakfasted with W.H. Davies and Siegfried Sassoon, a would-be poet a year older than himself, at Raymond Buildings. Sassoon recalled:

> Davies departed, and I was alone with Rupert Brooke for about half an hour. Some way removed from me, he sat by a window serenely observing the trees of Gray's Inn Gardens. From time to time his eyes met mine with a clouded though direct regard. I was conscious that his even-toned voice was tolerant rather than communicative, and that his manner had become gravely submissive to the continuing presence of strength. He may have been shy, but I am afraid he was also a little bored with me. We agreed that Davies was an excellent poet and a most likeable man.

They discussed the pros and cons of Kipling's poetry, and Sassoon fought shy of declaring his admiration for Rupert's work, especially 'The Old Vicarage, Grantchester'. *Eumenides* was talked about, as Sassoon had seen the production in which Brooke had performed in his first term at Cambridge.

> It came back to me vividly now. For the Herald had been such a striking figure that everybody in Cambridge had talked about him . . . I was only one in the procession of people who were more interested in him than he was in them . . . to him I was merely an amateur poet who had scarcely arrived at publication, strongly favoured with the philistinism of the hunting field. His intellectual development was years ahead of me, and his character was much more fully formed than mine . . . I felt rather like a lower fifth form boy talking to the Head of the school! During that singular encounter it was his kindness, I think, which impressed me, and the almost mediative deliberation of his voice. His

movements so restful, so controlled, and so unaffected. But beyond that was my assured perception that I was in the presence of one on whom had been conferred all the invisible attributes of a poet. To this his radiant good looks seemed subsidiary . . . There is no need to explain that our one brief meeting had a quite unpredictable significance . . .

Encouraged as a poet by Eddie Marsh, and subsequently taking a three-year lease on his own rooms at Raymond Buildings, Sassoon may have thought that he and Rupert would meet again. They did not, but history was to bind them together as two of the First World War poets whose names, along with those of Wilfred Owen and Robert Graves, would still be the first on people's lips 80 years on. Perhaps Rupert's apparent indifference to Sassoon was because his mind was on matters of the heart. In an anguished letter to Jacques he wailed, 'I *must* marry soon. And I can't find anyone to marry – oh, I suppose one *could* marry anyone; but, I mean, I can't decide whom to marry. It seems such an important step. Perhaps there's a better choice in Samoa.'

In July, Eddie Marsh took Rupert and Denis Browne to dine with the Duchess of Leeds, where he met the Duke of Wellington's daughter, Lady Eileen Wellesley. Later that evening, Rupert met Sir Ian Hamilton, who was soon to be his commander-in-chief, before Marsh, Browne and Rupert saw

Lady Eileen Wellesley

218

Eileen back to Apsley House at Hyde Park Corner, the building with the illustrious address of No. 1, London. He was immediately taken with Eileen, but then he was inclined to eulogise over the spiritual attributes he attached to the women he idealised. He had placed Noel on a pedestal, then Ka (briefly) and then Cathleen, all of whom were women who needed a normal relationship. Cathleen confessed, '. . . he had a great belief that I was very good, and I don't know why. I don't think I was good particularly, but that was one of the little icons he made, and he had to put it inside a body to worship. It was important to him I think, in a sense.' Of the three of them Cathleen probably understood him the best:

> I think like all artists who have a neurotic strain, that he would always have needed – I knew in the South Seas that he'd had a lovely girl there, and somewhere in Canada I always suspected their was a red-haired girl that he'd had an affair with. When he wrote I could sort of read between the lines – and I always felt that there might, although I didn't feel possessive about him then, I felt if I were married to him, I probably would and that I would probably suffer a great deal, because I thought there was no chance of his ever being a one woman man.

At the end of July, Brooke and D.H. Lawrence were waiting for Eddie at the Ship restaurant in London, when Marsh arrived to tell them that Sir Edward Grey, the Foreign Secretary, had just succeeded in averting war with Germany. Europe had been in a dangerous state since the assassination of Archduke Franz Ferdinand, the heir to the Austro–Hungarian Empire, by a Serbian nationalist, Gavril Princip, who had triggered a time-bomb that would be the catalyst for millions of deaths.

The result was Austria declaring war on Serbia, followed by Austria and Germany declaring war on Russia. In a letter to Jacques Raverat, Rupert confided:

> Everyone in the governing classes seems to think we shall be at war . . . *I* want Germany to smash Russia to fragments, and then France to break Germany. Instead of which I'm afraid Germany will badly smash France and then be wiped out by Russia. France and England are the only countries that ought to have any power. Prussia is a devil. And Russia means the end of Europe and any decency. I suppose the future is a Slav Empire, world-wide, despotic, and insane . . .

Also from Bilton Road, Rugby, he wrote of his love of his country to Eileen from his bed on Sunday, 2 August 1914.

> I'm a Warwickshire man. Don't talk to me of Dartmoor or Snowdon or

the Thames or the Lakes. I know the *heart* of England. It has a hedgy, warm bountiful dimpled air. Baby fields run up & down the little hills & all the roads wriggle with pleasure. There's a spirit of rare homeliness about the houses and the countryside, earthy, uneccentric yet elusive, fresh, meadowy, gaily gentle. It is perpetually June in Warwickshire and always six o'clock of a warm afternoon . . . Here the flowers smell of heaven; there are no such larks as ours, and no such nightingales . . . In Warwickshire there are butterflies all the year round and a full moon every night, every man can sing 'John Peel'. Shakespeare and I are Warwickshire yokels. What a county!

With typical perversity, Brooke follows this flowery prose with: 'This is nonsense; and I will grant you that Richmond Park is lovelier than all the Midlands and certainly better inhabited.' He ended, 'Eileen there's something solid & real & wonderful about you, in a world of shadows. Do you know how real you are? The time with you is the only waking hours in a life of dreams. All that's another way of saying I adore you.' He also described a trip he and his brother Alfred took in Mrs Brooke's motor car to Hampden-in-Arden. Within a fortnight the England in which they had grown up would be changed for ever.

Rupert in the meantime had travelled to the north Norfolk coast, at the invitation of Frances and Francis Cornford, to Cley-next-the-Sea, where they were staying at Umtata, a house facing the 400 or so acres of Cley Marsh. Rupert was to stay at the cottage next door, Umgeni. Completing the row of unusually named dwellings was Umvolosi. The origins all three were names of ships of the Rennie Line, which sailed to Natal, called after towns and rivers in South Africa – the names being Zulu in origin. The names arrived in Cley with a Captain Lewis, who had sailed with the fleet, and built and bought properties in the village. To Brooke, the house names seemed magical. He wrote to Frances from Rugby on 31 July, 'I'm sure I shall love Umgeni. It sounds far more romantic than Fiji . . . I'd be happy with anyone – except three or four persons, I feel you somehow aren't likely to have staying with you . . .' It is a reasonable assumption that one of these would be Lytton Strachey, who still *persona non grata* with Brooke, who continued to nurse a grudge over the role he assumed Lytton had played in the Ka Cox/Henry Lamb affair at Lulworth, which had precipitated Rupert's nervous breakdown. Only recently, he had cut Strachey dead at a London theatre.

Three days later, Brooke sent his temporary address to Eddie Marsh: 'I'm going (D.V.) on Tuesday to c/o F.M. Cornford, Umtata, Cley, Norfolk, for at least a week.' The day before he wrote to Marsh, Germany had declared war against France, having declared war against Russia the previous day. He prophetically included the following words in his letter to Marsh: 'Do you have a Brussels-before-Waterloo feeling? That we'll all – or some – meet with other eyes in 1915?' He knew in his head, as did millions of others, that war was imminent. He was right. On the following day, Germany invaded Belgium, compelling Britain to declare war on Germany. On the same day, Rupert turned 27. Writing from Cley on Thursday, 6 August, Rupert tried to placate Jacques Raverat, who had obviously reacted violently to the war.

> My dear Jacques
> You mustn't get excited. I asked Eddie about interpreters' jobs. He didn't seem to think anyone was wanted just now. He promised to keep you in mind . . . One can't 'go and fight' in England. Volunteers are admitted neither to the navy nor the army. If we join the Territorials now, they give you six months' training, and then let you garrison the chief ports and sea towns, *if* the Expeditionary Force leaves England – It *might* be worth doing . . .

The village from which Brooke was writing was a major English sea port in the thirteenth and fourteenth centuries, but by 1914 had not been 'next-to-the-sea' for nearly 300 years. Rupert's stay at Cley was, of course, dominated by the unnerving uncertainty of the future. To Frances he confessed, 'The best possible thing that could happen for her [Ka] is that I should be blown to bits by a shell. Then she should marry someone else and be happy.' In the evenings at Umgeni and Umtata, Rupert talked of the South Seas, his concern for Dudley Ward, who was living in Berlin, and Walter de la Mare, whom he declared was probably the best of his contemporaries. By day, he swam in the cold waters of the North Sea, which was a brisk walk over the reed marshes from where he was staying, and entertained the Cornfords' infant daughter Helena with his humorous antics.

Rupert was still at Cley the following weekend, writing to Cathleen Nesbitt on Saturday, 8 August, '. . . the papers report that Dudley Ward had rather a bad time in Berlin. He nearly got mobbed . . . Oh, my dear, I wish I were with you . . . I feel dazed and troubled these days. The general uneasiness and tension of minds seems to take all the strength out of me.' On 10 May, his restlessness roused him into returning to London, where Eddie would have his finger on the pulse of the latest war news.

At the little Norfolk village, things were much the same. Frances admitted in a letter to Brooke that she couldn't believe that Britain was actually at war, as '. . . the sea and the pebbles are so exactly the same'.

Today, Umgeni and Umtata remain the first port of call for the biting Siberian winds coming off the North Sea, and are among the first houses in the firing line when the ocean breaches the sea defences and races across the reed marshes. And here, coincidentally, lives Peter Ward, son of Brooke's great friend Dudley: a Cley resident now for over 40 years.

CHAPTER XIV

I Can't Fly or Drive a Car or Ride a Horse

B y 12 August Rupert was back in London at Raymond Buildings with Eddie Marsh. From there he met and communicated with Eileen Wellesley:

> I find myself in two natures – not necessarily conflicting, but – different. There's half of my heart which is normal & English . . . what's the word, not quite 'good' or 'honourable' – '*straight*' I think . . . but the other half is a wanderer and a solitary, selfish, unbound and doubtful. Half of my heart is of England, the rest is looking for some home I haven't found yet. So when this war broke out, there was some part of my nature and desires that said let me alone – what's all this bother? I want to work. I've got ends I desire to reach. If I'd wanted to be a soldier I should have been one. But I've found myself other dreams . . . I feel so damnably incapable. I can't fly or drive a car or ride a horse sufficiently well . . .

Before heading back to Rugby to break it to his mother that he felt it was his duty to go and fight, he gave a reading of his poems at Harold Monro's bookshop in London. Perhaps it put him back in the poetic mood, moving him to write a poem from Bilton Road, which he intended to call 'Unpacking', 'Contemplation' or 'The Shore'. In the end it would become 'The Treasure', published in *1914 and Other Poems*.

Treasure

When colour goes home into the eyes,
And lights that shine are shut again,
With dancing girls and sweet birds' cries
Behind the gateways of the brain;
And that no-place which gave them birth, shall close
The rainbow and the rose –

Still may Time hold some golden space
Where I'll unpack that scented store
Of song and flower and sky and face,
And count, and touch, and turn them o'er,
Musing upon them; as a mother, who
Has watched her children all the rich day through,
Sits, quiet-handed, in the fading light,
When children sleep, ere night.

During the third week of August, Rupert was ill and in bed at 10 Downing Street, being looked after by the Asquiths, and getting up only to meet Henry James and Eileen Wellesley. After recovering, he caught a train to Great Yarmouth to see Cathleen, who was on tour, before retreating to London, where he went to the first night of *Outcasts* at Wyndham's Theatre with Eddie. His favourite from *Hullo Ragtime*, Ethel Levey, was in it, but Rupert thought the play foolish, apart from the fact that *New Numbers* was used as a prop on stage, much to his delight. He turned down an invitation from Ka to go and stay for the weekend: '. . . through me you have been greatly hurt, and two or three years of your life – which can be so wonderful – have been changed and damaged. And I'm terrible ashamed before you . . .' He was still in touch with Noel, but there, at least, there was no broken heart, or so it would seem.

Eddie Marsh recommended Rupert and Denis Browne for a new unit that was being formed, the Royal Naval Division. The Division would comprise Royal Marines, the Naval Reserve and other seamen. Through his position at the Admiralty Marsh was able to organise things so that no interview or official forms would be necessary. Brooke and Browne were enrolled as sublieutenants of the Royal Naval Volunteer Reserve attached to His Majesty's ship *Victory*. By mid-September, Rupert was preparing for life at camp, which would be nothing new to him – and in a way he was looking forward to it. He wrote a self-deprecating letter to Eileen: 'Oh I'm rather a horror. A vagabond, drifting from one imbecility to another. You don't know how pointless and undependable and rather rotten a thing you've got hold of. Don't laugh. I know it's funny. But it's all true. Well, child, if you're happy with me; that's something isn't it? I'm certainly happy with you . . .' Similar sentiments were expressed in a letter to Cathleen, written at the same time: 'Cathleen, if you *knew* how much I adore you, and fight towards you. I want to cut away all the evil in me, and be wholly a thing worthy of you . . .' He also confided some of Churchill's war strategy: 'Winston was very cheerful at lunch, and said one thing which is exciting, but a *dead* secret. You mustn't *breathe* it. That is, that it's his game to hold the Northern Ports – Dunkirk to Havre – at all costs . . . so we may go to camp on Saturday, and be under fire in France on Monday!'

Cathleen later recalled:

> I don't think it was, in a sense, so much an escape, as an odd fulfilment that he didn't have to think about what he was doing with his life, because I think he took very seriously what one ought to do. He was a great believer in goodness and solidity, and he felt he hadn't been either a good or solid person. He exaggerated of course when he wrote, but so many of the letters I got from the South Seas in which he said 'I need something to hold on to' and 'I don't live up to myself' and 'I'm only half a person' . . . strange things like that, which allowing for 50% exaggeration, was still I think, a kind of not quite certain of where he was going.

On his penultimate day as a civilian, Rupert had lunch with Eddie and the new Poet Laureate Robert Bridges before departing from Charing Cross with Denis Browne, Eddie seeing off the two new recruits to the Anson Battalion, 2nd Naval Brigade. At the camp at Betteshanger Park, about three miles inland from Deal on the Kent coast, Brooke became sub-lieutenant in command of the 15th Platoon, D Company, with 35 men under him. Rupert's brother Alfred was also an officer, in the Active Service Battalion of the Post Office Rifles. Suddenly socialising, life, plans and romance were put on hold for everyone. Eddie was now at Winston's side for 16 hours a day, all thoughts of a new edition of *Georgian Poetry* set aside indefinitely. At camp, probably as a little occupational therapy, Rupert worked on two sonnets that would subsequently be lost in Belgium, and wrote to Cathleen and Eileen. To the latter he described '. . . rows of naked, superb men, bathing in a September sun or in the camp at night under a full moon, front lights burning through the ghostly tents, & a distant bugler blowing *lights out* – if only I were sensitive. But I am not. I'm a warrior . . .'

The call to action came on Sunday, 4 October. The Battalion marched the seven or eight miles south to Dover, being cheered by the locals and singing the platoon's theme song 'Hello, Who's Your Lady Friend?'. They were to relieve the Belgians at Antwerp. He captured the atmosphere in a letter to Cathleen on his return.

After dark the senior officers rushed round and informed us that we were to be going to Antwerp, that our train was sure to be attacked, and that if we got through we'd have to sit in trenches till we were wiped out. So we all sat under lights writing last letters: a very tragic and amusing affair. My dear it *did* bring it home to me how very futile and unfinished life was. I felt so angry. I had to imagine, supposing I was killed. There was nothing but a vague gesture of goodbye to you and my mother and a friend or two . . . we stopped in the town square in Vieux Dieu; five or six thousand British troops, a lot of Belgians, guns going through, transport wagons, motor-cyclists, orderlies on horses, staff-officers, and the rest. An extraordinary and thrilling confusion . . .

He and his troops bedded down in an ornamental garden, while shells burst around them and over their heads, before being ordered to relieve the Belgians in trenches at Fort Seven. The sat in the trenches waiting for orders, but eventually, the German bombardment having caused so much destruction, the order came to retreat. Rupert had to retreat without his kit bag containing field glasses given him by E.M. Forster, and draft manuscripts, as the local station at Wylrich had been destroyed, with his and most of the brigade's belongings. He was later to describe the retreat in a letter to Leonard Bacon, whom he had met in San Francisco:

Hundreds of thousands of refugees, their goods on barrows and handcarts and perambulators and wagons, moving with infinite slowness out of the night, two unending lines of them, the old men mostly weeping, the women with white, hard drawn faces, the children playing or crying or sleeping. That's what Belgium is now: the country where three civilians have been killed to every one soldier . . . half a million people preferred homelessness and the chance of starvation, to the certainty of German rule. It's queer to think one has been a witness to one of the greatest crimes of history . . . It's a bloody thing, half of the youth of Europe blown through pain to nothingness, in the incessant mechanical slaughter of these modern battles . . .

To Maurice Browne and Ellen Van Volkenburg he wrote, 'There's nothing to say, except that the tragedy of Belgium is the greatest and worst of any country for centuries. It's ghastly for anyone who liked Germany as well as I did. Their guilt can never be washed away. I'm afraid fifty years won't give them the continuity and loveliness of life back again.' He also asked Browne to try and send him a new pair of field glasses, as none were to be had in England. Browne himself did not have the money to help, but assistance came from the Marchesa Capponi, who forwarded a pair of her own to Rupert.

Back in London, Rupert, and Arthur 'Oc' Asquith, the Prime Minister's son, were taken by Eddie Marsh to report on the fall of Antwerp. Before returning to camp, he saw J. Hartley Manners' play *Peg o' My Heart* at the Comedy Theatre and attended a play . . . reading at the home of Bryn Olivier and her husband Hugh Popham. It was his last known meeting with Noel. He then travelled to the east coast to see Cathleen:

> The last time I saw him was before he went abroad, and I was touring and I was in Yarmouth, the theatre called the Aquarium, and we went back to my lodgings and there was a fire of logs, sea logs, and we just sat there and talked for a while and he said, 'Read me something quite beautiful', and I read Donne's 'Anniversarie', and then there's that lovely thing:
>
> > Here upon earth, we'are Kings, and none but wee
> > Can be such Kings, nor of such subjects bee . . .
> > Who is so safe as we? Where none can doe
> > Treason to us, except one of us two.
>
> So I read it right through to the end. Then about three days later, he sent me the first copy of the sonnets, and one of them was called 'Safety', and he said 'You don't mind my printing ours, because it's private, nobody knows it's ours', and then he said: 'I'm a little ashamed of writing poetry in a soldier's uniform. I feel it isn't right somehow, but Philip Sidney did it', and then he sent me the galley sheet, with one or two corrections on it . . .

In 'Safety', he incorporated the 'Who is so safe as we?' line that Donne had written in the 1590s.

Safety

> Dear! of all happy in the hour, most blest
> He who has found our hid security,
> Assured in the dark tides of the world at rest,
> And heard our word, 'Who is so safe as we?'
> We have found safety with all things undying,
> The winds, and morning, tears of men and mirth,
> The deep night, and birds singing, and clouds flying,

And sleep, and freedom, and the autumnal earth.
We have built a house that is not for Time's throwing.
We have gained a peace unshaken by pain for ever.
War knows no power. Safe shall be my going,
Secretly armed against all death's endeavour,
Safe through all safety's lost, safe where men fall;
And if these poor limbs die, safest of all.

Back at Betteshanger Camp, he heard a whisper from Denis Browne that the Old Vicarage was to be pulled down, prompting him to put pen to paper and write to Francis Cornford to see if the rumour were true, and, if so, if anything could be done to save it. He made noises about the possibility of buying the land, or at least getting someone to paint a picture of it or a local photographer to capture it for posterity. He wrote to Ka, asking her to send toilet paper, a tin mug with a handle and some sweet scented soap, among other things. A few days later, the battalion was moved to Chatham Barracks, where he heard the good news that the Old Vicarage would be spared, and vowed to buy it after the war. By the end of May 1914, however, the freehold of the Old Vicarage, the Orchard and other property belonging to the family of the late Samuel Page Widnall had been sold. The Stephensons, until then the tenants of the Orchard, had bought it outright, along with the Old Vicarage, with the Neeve family staying on there as tenants until after the First World War. Possibly the new owners' idea had been to demolish the house next door, in order to extend the tea garden down to the bank of the Granta.

He wrote from Chatham to E.J. Dent, 'In the room where I write are some twenty men. All but one or two have risked their lives a dozen times in the last month. More than half have gone down in torpedoed ships and have been saved sans their best friends. They're waiting for another ship. I feel very small among them . . .' In another letter to Leonard Bacon he commented:

All my friends but a few, are training or serving. One or two have been killed. Others wounded and are going back. The best great scholar of the younger generation at Cambridge, Cornford, is a musketry instructor at Aldershot. Among my fellow officers are one of the best young English pianists, and a brilliant composer. Gilbert Murry gets up every morning to line a hedgerow, gun in hand, before dawn. What a world! Yet I'm still half ashamed of England, when I hear of the holocaust of the young poets, painters and scholars of France and Belgium – and Germany . . .

Reports were gradually coming in of his own friends being killed or wounded; he informed Eileen Wellesley that his best friend at Rugby had been reported wounded and missing. He began brooding over the fact that if he were killed there was no one to carry on his name: no immortality; no sons; no grandsons; no descendants.

His emotions were poured into a third sonnet 'The Dead'. Peculiarly, two of Brooke's five war sonnets bear this title. The first borrows a little from a poem he knew well by W.E. Henley, which ran:

> What have I done for you,
> England, my England?
> What is there I would not do.
> England, my own?
> With your glorious eyes austere,
> As the Lord were walking near,
> Whispering terrible things and dear
> As the Song on your bugles blown,
> England –
> Round the world on your bugles blown!
>
> Where shall the watchful Sun,
> England, my England,
> Match the master-work you've done,
> England, my own?
> When shall he rejoice agen
> Such a breed of mighty men
> As come forward, one to ten,
> To the Song on your bugles blown,
> England –
> Down the years on your bugles blown?
>
> Ever the faith endures,
> England, my England: –
> 'Take and break us: we are yours,
> 'England, my own!
> 'Life is good, and joy runs high
> 'Between English earth and sky:
> 'Death is death; but shall we die
> 'To the Song on your bugles blown,
> 'England –
> 'To the stars on your bugles blown!'
>
> They call you proud and hard,
> England, my England:

You with worlds to watch and ward,
England, my own!
You whose mailed hand keeps the keys
Of such teeming destinies
You could know nor dread nor ease
Were the Song on your bugles blown,
England,
Round the Pit on your bugles blown!

Mother of Ships whose might,
England, my England,
Is the fierce old Sea's delight,
England, my own,
Chosen daughter of the Lord,
Spouse-in-Chief of the ancient sword,
There's the menace of the Word
In the Song on your bugles blown,
England –
Out of heaven on your bugles blown!

Brooke's poem was originally entitled 'The Slain'.

The Dead

Blow out, you bugles, over the rich Dead!
There's none of these so lonely and poor of old,
But, dying, has made us rarer gifts than gold.
These laid the world away; poured out the red
Sweet wine of youth; gave up the years to be
Of work and joy, and that unhoped serene,
That men call age; and those who would have been,
Their sons, they gave, their immortality.

Blow, bugles, blow! They brought us, for our dearth,
Holiness, lacked so long, and Love, and Pain.
Honour has come back, as a king, to earth,
And paid his subjects with a royal wage;
And Nobleness walks in our ways again;
And we have come into our heritage.

After a brief transfer to the Nelson Battalion at Portsmouth he moved, with

Sub-Lieutenant Brooke at Blandford Camp

Eddie Marsh's influence, to Blandford Camp in Dorset, as sub-lieutenant in charge of No. 5 Platoon, A Company, Hood Battalion, commanded by Colonel Quilter. The company commander was Colonel Bernard Freyberg, a former Cambridge man, who had accompanied Captain R.F. Scott on his South Pole expedition as a biologist. At the camp he lived in a wooden hut measuring 15 feet by eight, with seven other men, home comforts being provided by the likes of Brooke's mother and Ka Cox. His fellow officers included Denis Browne, Oc Asquith and Oxford man Patrick Shaw-Stewart, from Barings Bank, whom Brooke knew from Raymond Buildings. At Blandford, Rupert crafted his second sonnet called 'The Dead' – his favourite of the five war sonnets.

The Dead

These hearts were woven of human joys and cares,
Washed marvellously with sorrow, swift to mirth.
The years had given them kindness. Dawn was theirs,
And sunset, and the colours of the earth.

These had seen movement, and heard music; known
Slumber and waking; loved; gone proudly friended;
Felt the quick stir of wonder; sat alone;
Touched flowers and furs and cheeks. All this is ended.

There are waters blown by changing winds to laughter
And lit by the rich skies, all day. And after,
Frost, with a gesture, stays the waves that dance
And wandering loveliness. He leaves a white
Unbroken glory, a gathered radiance,
A width, a shining peace, under the night.

The December edition of *New Numbers* was delayed, which gave Brooke time to work on another sonnet. With his equipment in Antwerp he had lost a poem about Mataia, the little township on Tahiti, which he had been working on and just before Christmas had had a disturbing dream about Taatamata, in which he was told she was dead by her own hand. She was not, and in mid-January he would have the first news of her for nine months.

At the beginning of January, Brooke stayed, at Violet Asquith's behest, at Walmer Castle in Kent, where he worked on what was to become his most famous sonnet, initially called 'The Recruit', before he changed it to 'The Soldier'.

The Soldier

If I should die, think only this of me:
That there's some corner of a foreign field
That is forever England. There shall be
In that rich earth a richer dust concealed;
A dust whom England bore, shaped, made aware,
Gave, once more, her flowers to love, her ways to roam,
A body of England's, breathing English air,
Washed by rivers, blest by suns of home.

And think this heart, all evil shed away,
A pulse in the eternal mind, no less
Gives somewhere back the thoughts by England given;
Her sights and sounds; dreams happy as her day;
And laughter learnt of friends; and gentleness,
In hearts at peace, under an English heaven.

The seeds of the idea for 'The Soldier' were undoubtedly sown by Hilaire

Belloc's *The Four Men* which Brooke read in 1912. Belloc himself, as the main narrator, recounts a journey across his beloved Sussex, with three companions: Grizzlebeard, the Sailor, and the Poet – a fictional tale based on geographical actuality. It was the first verse of a poem at the end of the farrago that was the inspiration for 'The Soldier'.

> He does not die that can bequeath
> Some influence to the land he knows
> Or dares, persistent, interwreath
> Love permanent with the wild hedgerows;
> He does not die, but still remains
> Substantiate with his darling plains.

After Walmer, Rupert lunched with Denis Browne, the Churchills and Herbert Asquith at the Admiralty. On 5 January, he heard that his friend the poet James Elroy Flecker had died in Switzerland and he was asked to write his obituary. This he did at the table at Raymond Buildings where the two of them had last sat together. To Eileen he wrote, 'He was my friend. Who'll do The Times for me, I wonder? Damn them.'

On his return to Blandford, a letter was waiting from Taatamata, dated 2 May 1914. It had been forwarded from Ottawa, having been recovered by divers from the *Empress of India*, the wreck he had heard about on his arrival from New York the previous spring. It seems that she had given it to someone to post, which was duly done in Vancouver, the letter being sent eventually on the *Empress*, which had gone down in the St Lawrence Seaway. The letter lay at the bottom until December, and was rather washed out and frayed by the time it reached him.

> My dear Love darling
>
> I just wrote you some lines to let you know about Tahiti to day whe have plainty people Argentin Espagniole, and whe all very busy for four days. Whe have good times all girls in Papeete have good times whit Argentin boys. I think they might go away to day to Honolulu Lovina are giving a ball last night for them. beg ball. they 2 o'clock this morning.
>
> I hope to see you here to last night, Lovina make plainty Gold Money. now. About Mrs Rosentale she is went to [indecipherable]. whit crower by Comodore before they go away to whe been drive the car to Lage place. Enton and I. Mrs Rosental Crower Williams Banbridge to whe got 12 Beers Bred Sardines only whe tout come right away to lage the car Break and whe work down the beach. have drinking beer. Music and whe come away 5 o'clock morning . . . pas dormir.

I wish you here that night I get fat all time Sweetheart you know I always thinking about you that time when you left me I been sorry for long time. whe have good time when you was here I always remember about you forget me all readly oh! Mon cher bien aime je l'aimerai toujours.

Le voila Cela partir pour San Francisco je lui ais donne quel cadeau pour lui he told me to send you his regards je me rappeler toujour votre petite etroite figure et la petite bouche qui me baise bien tu m'a percea mon coeur et je aime toujours ne m'oubli pas mon cher maintenant je vais finir mon lettre. parceque je me suis tres occupee le bateau par a l'instant. 5 heurs excuse me write you shot letter. hope you good health and good time.

I send my kiss to you my darling
xxxxxxxxxxxxxx mlle kiss

Taatamata

Brooke was already aware that he was not sterile, following his relationship with Ka, so what chance had Taatamata had of not falling pregnant after two months of unprotected sexual relations with Rupert? The clue is there in her letter; 'I get fat all time sweetheart'. Was he genuinely oblivious to the comment, or did he deem it best to ignore it and bury the guilt within himself? After all, what would have been the Ranee's reaction to a half-Tahitian grandson or granddaughter? Later developments would suggest that if he did have concerns, he confided only in Dudley Ward.

By mid-January he and the platoon were informed that a major campaign was afoot, but in the meantime he would be able to submit his five sonnets for *New Numbers*: 'Safety', 'The Dead', 'The Dead', 'The Soldier' and 'Peace'.

Peace

Now, God be thanked Who has matched us with His hour,
And caught our youth, and wakened us from sleeping,
With hand made sure, clear eye, and sharpened power,
To turn, as swimmers into cleanness leaping,
Glad from a world grown old and cold and weary,
Leave the sick hearts that honour could not move,
And half-men, and their dirty songs and dreary,
And all the little emptiness of love!

Oh! We, who have known shame, we have found release there,
Where there's no ill, no grief, but sleep has mending.

Naught broken save this body, lost but breath;
Nothing to shake the laughing heart's long peace there
But only agony, and that has ending;
And the worst friend and enemy is but Death.

He tried to persuade John Drinkwater to enlist: 'Come and die – it'll be great fun. And there's great health in the preparation. The theatre's no place now. If you stay there you'll not be able to start afresh with us all when we come back . . .' He also confessed that he felt it was 'Not a bad place to die, Belgium, 1915? I want to kill my Prussian first. Better than coughing out a civilian soul amid bedclothes and discomfort and gulping medicines in 1950 . . . I had hopes that England'ld get on her legs again, achieve youth and merriment, and slough the things I loathe – capitalism and feminism and hermaphroditism and the rest . . .' He also tried to get Browne to enlist: 'Come over and fight when you get bored with the theatre. England's slowly waking, and purging herself of evil things.' He wrote of Blandford, 'The camp lies between Eastbury House, where George Bubb Doddington lived, and Badbury Rings, where Arthur defended the Saxons. And on the chalk down where our huts are, was a Roman camp once, and a Celtic before that, and before that, an Iberian. – And we march through thousand year old English villages. England! England! I'm very happy . . .'

In Rupert's semi-autobiographical prose piece, 'An Unusual Young Man', which represents his own feelings on the declaration of war in 1914, his thoughts turn to his favourite English views. 'He seemed to be raised high, looking down on a landscape compounded of the western view of the Cotswolds, and the Weald, and the high land in Wiltshire, and the Midlands seen from the hills above Princes Risborough.'

The Chilterns

Your hands, my dear, adorable,
Your lips of tenderness
– Oh, I've loved you faithfully and well,
Three years, or a bit less.
It wasn't a success.

Thank God, that's done! and I'll take the road,
Quit of my youth and you,
The Roman road to Wendover
By Tring and Lilley Hoo,
As a free man may do.

For youth goes over, the joys that fly
The tears that follow fast;
And the dirtiest things we do must lie
Forgotten at the last;
Even Love goes past.

What's left behind I shall not find,
The splendour and the pain;
The splash of sun, the shouting wind,
And the brave sting of rain,
I may not meet again.

But the years that take the best away,
Give something in the end;
And a better friend than love have they,
For none to mar or mend,
That have themselves to friend.

I shall desire and I shall find
The best of my desires;
The autumn road, the mellow wind
That soothes the darkening shires,
And laughter, and inn-fires.

White mist about the black hedgerows,
The slumbering Midland plain,
The silence where the clover grows,
And the dead leaves in the lane,
Certainly, these remain.

And I shall find some girl perhaps
And a better one than you,
With eyes as wise, but kindlier,
And lips as soft, but true.
And I dare say she will do.

From Blandford Camp he was putting feelers out as to who might produce and perform in *Lithuania*, and was mentally gearing himself to writing a play about Antwerp during his sick leave. He communicated with Violet Asquith, his mother and Dudley Ward. After the Division being inspected by King George V and Rupert dining with Winston Churchill and Eddie Marsh at Admiralty House, he informed his mother:

. . . we are going to be part of a landing force to help the fleet break through the Hellespont and the Bosphorus and take Constantinople, and open up the Black Sea. It's going to be one of the important things of the war, if it comes off. We take 14–16 days to get there. We shall be fighting for anything from 2–6 weeks. And back (they reckon) in May . . . we are only taking 5 days' provisions (. . . beyond what we have on the boats); so we obviously aren't expected to have a long campaign!

CHAPTER XV

'Some Corner of a Foreign Field'

On 27 February, Brooke's battalion moved to Shillingstone, some ten miles away, before catching a train to Avonmouth, and boarding the SS *Grantully Castle*. On 1 March 1915, Rupert, Denis Browne, Oc Asquith, Patrick Shaw-Stewart, F.S. 'Cleg' Kelly and Co. slipped away from the shore. Violet Asquith saw them off.

Browne and Kelly, both gifted musicians, used the ship's piano to lead community singing. Browne, who Rupert had known through their years at Rugby and Cambridge, was a great fan of the composer Scriabin, and no doubt would have gone on to greater things. He collaborated with Clive Carey and set some of Brooke's poems to music. Kelly's musical genius was overshadowed during his time at Eton and Oxford by his extraordinary prowess as an oarsman. The triple Diamond Sculls winner was not only regarded as a sporting hero, but his talents on the piano were such that he performed at both Queen's Hall and Aeolian Hall, both major London venues; he was also a friend of such eminent composers as Percy Grainger and Edward Elgar. However, he was not above playing the popular songs of the day for his fellow officers and their men.

On board the crew exercised and wrote letters home, as did Brooke, who wore around his neck, along with his identification disc, an amulet that had been sent to him anonymously, via Eddie Marsh, to bring him luck. He knew who it was from, but even in thanking her in a letter to Eddie, he couched his gratitude in the anonymous manner in which it had been given. It was almost certainly a gesture from either Cathleen, Lady Eileen Wellesley or Violet Asquith.

Rupert had taken Sir Charles Eliot's book *Turkey in Europe* with him to familiarise himself with the territory, customs and people he would be likely to encounter. Published in 1908, it included chapters on the Turks, Greeks,

Bulgarians and Serbs, Albanians and Armenians. On board ship, north of Tunis, he wrote to Eddie Marsh, 'I've read most of *Turkey in Europe*. But what with parades and the reading of military books I've not written anything . . .' The contents of the book, with its simple cover of the crescent moon and five-point star, inspired him to admit in a letter to Dudley Ward, 'I think of joining the Orthodox Church . . .'

By 9 March the SS *Grantully Castle* was off Greece and the reality of the situation started to set in. He began to put his literary and personal effects into order. To Marsh he wrote:

On board SS Grantully Castle *en route to Gallipoli. Brooke is standing left foreground*

I suppose I must imagine my non-existence, & make a few arrangements. You are to be my literary executor. But I'd like my mother to have my MSS till she dies – the actual paper & ink I mean – then you – save one or two might let Alfred [his brother] & Katherine Cox have, if they care.

If you want to go through my papers, Dudley Ward'll give you a hand. But you won't find much there. There may be some old stuff at Grantchester.

You must decide everything about publication. Don't print much bad stuff.

Give my love to the *New Numbers* folk, & Violet & Masefield & a few who'd like it. I've tried to arrange that some money should go to Wilfred & Lascelles & de la Mare (John is childless) to help them write good stuff, instead of me.

There's nothing much to say, you'll be able to help the Ranee with one or two arrangements. You've been very good to me. I wish I'd written more. I've been such a failure.

Best love & goodbye

Rupert

Get Cathleen anything she wants.

Before going abroad he discussed with Cathleen the fact that he ought to make a will. 'He said: "Would you like me to leave it to you?" – and I said: "Leave what to me?" – and he said: "The proceeds of my poems", and we both laughed, and he said: "Oh, it might be twenty pounds a year, you never know".'

With a sense of impending doom he also wrote to Ka.

I suppose you're about the best I can do in the way of a widow. I'm telling the Ranee that after she's dead you're to have my papers. They *may* want to write a biography! How am I to know if I shan't be eminent? And take any MSS you want. Say what you take to the Ranee. But you'd probably better not tell her much, Let her be. Let her think we might have married. Perhaps it's true.

My dear, my dear, you did me wrong; but I have done you a very great wrong. Every day I see it greater.

You were the best thing I found in life. If I have memory, I shall remember. You know what I want from you. I hope you will be happy, and marry and have children.

It's a good thing I die.

239

SS Grantully Castle

Rupert clearly felt that Eddie should be his literary executor, with the manuscripts only going to his mother and then to Ka on her death. An element of panic might well have been setting in, with regard to certain correspondence which would be among his papers, and which he would not have wished anyone else to see. To the faithful Dudley Ward he wrote:

> I want you, now – I've told my mother – to go through my letters (they're mostly together but some scattered) and *destroy* all those from (a) Elizabeth Van Rysselbergh. These are signed E.V.R. and in a handwriting you'll pick out easily once you've seen it. They'll begin in the beginning of 1909–1910, my first visit to Munich, and be rather rare except in one or two bundles. (b) Lady Eileen Wellesley: also in a handwriting you'll recognise quickly, and generally signed Eileen. They date from last July on . . . Indeed, why keep anything? Well I *might* turn out to be eminent and biographable. If so, let them know the poor truths . . . Try to inform Taata of my death. Mlle Taata, Hotel Tiarre, Papeete, Tahiti. It might find her. Give her my love . . . You'll have to give the Ranee a hand about me: because she knows so little about great parts of my life . . .

And to Jacques Raverat: 'I turn to you. Keep innumerable flags flying. I've only two reasons for being sorry for dying – (several against) – I want to destroy some evils, and to cherish some goods. Do it for me. You understand. I doubt if anyone else does – almost . . .'

By the beginning of April, he was laid up at the Casino Palace Hotel at Port

Said, Egypt, with what he thought was sunstroke. Patrick Shaw-Stewart had the same symptoms – headache, sickness and diarrhoea – but he was soon up and about while Rupert was still laid low. On the first day of his illness, the new Commander-in-Chief, General Sir Ian Hamilton, offered Brooke a staff job, but he turned it down, preferring to stick it out with his men and see the war through.

The fourth edition of *New Numbers* had now been published, far later than the December 1914 date that the cover bore. It included 'The Treasure', and all five of Rupert's war sonnets. He complained to Abercrombie, 'A saw a notice of *NN* in *The Times*; by a laudatory half-wit. He didn't seem to realise that it was "goodbye".'

By the time the SS *Grantully* had gained Lemnos, Rupert had begun to feel he had shaken off his illness, but he still undertook only light duties. His heart was not really in an impromptu fancy dress ball held on the ship on 5 April, and he had an early night. Two days later a party from the ship landed on, and explored, the Greek island of Skyros, the vessel being anchored in Trebuki Bay.

Skyros is divided into two nearly equal parts by a low-lying isthmus, with Trebuki, or Tris Boukes Bay (bay of the three mouths), being one of its natural harbours. The north half of the island is the more fertile, and contains the capital, Skyros, and Mount Olympus. Beyond the forests of oak, pines and beeches are numerous herds of sheep and goats, the latter descendants of the animals that were once highly prized. As a classical scholar, Brooke would have been well aware of the importance of the island in Greek mythology. Skyros was the refuge of Achilles, who, disguised as a girl, was sent by his mother Thetis to the court of Lykomedes, King of Skyros, to prevent his going to the Trojan War. Her precaution was in vain, for Ulysses lured him to Troy, where he was killed before it fell. It was in Skyros that Lykomedes treacherously killed Theseus, King of Athens, who had sought asylum with him.

In the mail came a letter from Eddie Marsh, containing a cutting from *The Times* of 5 April reporting on Dean Inge's sermon at St Paul's in which he had read 'The Soldier' to the congregation: '. . . a sonnet by a young writer who would, he ventured to think, take rank with our great poets . . .' The report also commented on a glowing review of *New Numbers* in *The Times Literary Supplement* of 11 March:

> It is impossible to shred up this beauty for the purpose of criticism. These sonnets are personal. Never were sonnets more personal since Sidney died – and yet the very blood and youth of England seemed to find expression in them . . . They speak not for one heart only, but for all to whom her call has come in the hour of need and found instantly

ready . . . no passion for glory here, no bitterness, no gloom, only a
happy, clear sighted, all-surrendering love.

His hour had arrived, his poetry was being acclaimed and his name was on
people's lips. For Rupert, though, it was too late.

He was not feeling in particularly good spirits when he took his platoon on
an exercise on the island of Skyros, and he was glad of a brief rest with Shaw-
Stewart and fellow officer Charles Lister, in a small olive grove. After
operations, the others decided to swim the mile back to the ship, but Rupert,
usually the keenest of swimmers, declined; he returned in a small fishing
boat. During a part on board that evening, he retired early as he could feel
his lip swelling. The following day the swelling had increased and was
accompanied by back and head pains, which he attributed to general
exhaustion. The battalion surgeon noted a temperature of 101°F. By the
following day, 21 April, his temperature had risen to 103°F, and his
resistance, never good at the best of times, was very low. His condition was
now considered grave enough to send for the fleet surgeon and the battalion
medical officer. They discussed the situation with the battalion surgeon and
agreed that the swelling had emanated from a mosquito bite on the lip and it
was agreed that they should make an incision to determine the type of
poison. Brooke's condition worsened and he was moved to a French hospital
ship, the *Duguay-Trouin*, anchored near by. He was laid in a little white cabin
in the round-house, and the whole of the ship's medical staff was mobilised
to monitor his condition and cope with any complications. Brooke stirred
just enough to say 'hello' to Denis Browne and later ask for water. Denis went
to the lead ship, the *Franconia*, where he wrote out marconigrams to Sir Ian

Denis Browne

Hamilton and Winston Churchill in case the worst happened: 'Condition very grave. Please inform parents and send me instructions re. disposal of body in case he dies and duplicate them to *Duguay-Trouin*.' Denis and Patrick felt sure Rupert would rather be buried on the island he'd been so taken with as opposed to being buried at sea. Cleg Kelly in his journal wrote, 'I have a foreboding that he is one of those like Keats, Shelley, and Schubert, who are not suffered to deliver their full message . . .' Churchill passed on the grave news to Eddie Marsh, who telegrammed Mrs Brooke. She replied, 'If message of love can be sent send it please at once waiting anxiously for the news Brooke.'

Early on 23 April 1915, French surgeons began an operation to cauterise the infection, and although he briefly regained consciousness at lunchtime he was not able to speak. His condition worsened and at 2.00 p.m. Denis Browne returned to Brooke's side with the chaplain from the *Franconia*. Browne was with him when he died at 4.46 p.m. of septicaemia.

While a coffin was being prepared, news came in that the fleet was to sail that night, so the simple wooden box was hurriedly covered with an English flag and 16 palms. On it the French officers laid a bunch of flowers collected from the island and tied with the French colours. Asquith seared the words 'Rupert Brooke' into the oak. A launch put out with the coffin. J. Perdriel-Vaissieres described the atmosphere: '. . . other boats put off from the warships. There are many of them, and they glide over the water like a holiday procession . . . music sounds as they pass; the huge ships one after another send them gusts of harmony, but the air is solemn and low. The night is soft with a sheen of moon, bestarred. The perfume of the Isle drifts throughout the night, becoming stronger and stronger.'

His fellow officers had decided to bury him in the olive grove on Skyros, where he had sat with Lister and Shaw-Stewart a few days before. Denis marked out a spot for the grave, on the western slope of Mount Kokhilas, and 12 bearers carried the coffin some one and a half miles up the hill, to where the digging party had been at work. Twelve large Australians in their broad-brimmed felt hats carried Brooke's coffin.

> The Australians made slow headway. A meagre light is spread about them by lanterns and torches which illume one step and leave the next in darkness. Sometimes they slip, half stumble, and cannot help their jolting burden. The marble pebbles turn under their feet. The brambles hide pitfalls. Their heavy laced boots press the aromatic shrubs. A bewitching odour, a mingling of pepper and musk rises like incense. The wan moonlight lingers on the end of the procession where the torches flicker no more . . . not a village, not a house, not a road . . .

Patrick Shaw-Stewart commanded a guard of honour and a rough wooden cross was hastily put together. The chaplain performed the service; three volleys were fired into the air and Malachi William Davey, the 18-year-old bugler, sounded the Last Post. The rifle shots rolled

> . . . through the mountains rending the air with abrupt claps which are tossed from one elevation to another, echoing. Thereupon the silent night becomes mysteriously alive. The owls cry out scarred, and little bells, any number of little bells, tinkle all around. They come from the drowsy flocks which are frightened, from the sheep and goats suddenly awakened in terror and rushing away headlong through the sweet-scented brushwood . . . and then it is silence; and it shall always be silence.

The cross bore an inscription in Greek, which translates as

> Here lies
> the servant of God
> Sub-lieutenant in the
> English navy
> who died for the
> deliverance of Constantinople from
> the Turks

Rupert's grave on Skyros

Just hours before the Hood Battalion sailed to Gallipoli, Kelly wrote in his journal, 'It was as though one were involved in the origin of some classical myth.' He began to work on a musical elegy to Rupert, as well as penning this poetic eulogy:

> . . . He wears
> The ungathered blossom of quiet; stiller he
> Than a deep well at noon, or lovers met;
> Than sleep, or the heart after wrath. He is
> The silence following great words of peace.

Kelly would not survive the war, nor would colonel Quilter, Denis Browne, Charles Lister or Patrick Shaw-Stewart. Rupert's brother Alfred would be killed the following month.

Browne wrote a long explanatory letter to Eddie Marsh, describing Rupert's burial place: '. . . one of the loveliest places on earth, with grey-green olives around him, one weeping above his head; the ground covered with flowering sage . . . think of it all under a clouded moon, with the three mountains around & behind us . . . he actually said in chance talk some time ago that he would like to be buried on a Greek island . . . he will not miss his immortality . . .'

CHAPTER XVI

He Does Not Die That Can Bequeath Some Influence To The Land He Knows

On 26 April 1915 *The Times* published a short obituary, soon followed by a valediction, to which Winston Churchill, First Lord of the Admiralty, put his name:

> Rupert Brooke is dead. A telegram from the Admiralty at Lemnos tells us that this life has closed at the moment when it seemed to have reached its springtime. A voice had become audible, a note had been struck, more true, more thrilling, more able to do justice to the nobility of our youth in arms engaged in this present war, than any other – more able to express their thoughts of self-surrender, and with a power to carry comfort to those who watched them so intently from afar. The voice has been swiftly stilled. Only the echoes and the memory remains; but they will linger.
>
> During the last few months of his life, months of preparation in gallant comradeship and open air, the poet-soldier told with all the simple force of genius the sorrow of youth about to die, and the sure triumphant consolations of a sincere and valiant spirit. He expected to die; he was willing to die for the dear England whose beauty and majesty he knew; and he advanced towards the brink in perfect serenity, with absolute conviction of the rightness of his country's cause, and a heart devoid of hate for fellow-men.
>
> The thoughts to which he gave expression in the very few incomparable war sonnets which he has left behind will be shared by many thousands of young men moving resolutely and blithely forward into this, the hardest, the cruellest, and the least-rewarded of all the wars that men have fought. They are a whole history and revelation of Rupert

Brooke himself. Joyous, fearless, versatile, deeply instructed, with classic symmetry of mind and body, he was all that one would wish England's noblest sons to be in days when no sacrifice but the most precious is acceptable, and the most precious is that which is most freely proffered.

As the tributes poured in, Brooke was swiftly elevated to a state of legendary proportion:

Gilbert Murray: 'I cannot help thinking that Rupert Brooke will live in fame almost as a mythical figure.'

The Sphere: 'the only English poet of any consideration who has given his life in his country's wars since Philip Sidney . . . in 1586'

Daily News: 'To look at he was a part of the youth of the world.'

D.H. Lawrence: 'I first heard of him as a Greek God under a sunshade, reading poetry in his pyjamas at Grantchester . . .'

Frieda Lawrence: 'He was so good-looking, he took your breath away.'

The Star: 'He is the youth of our race in symbol . . .'

Nation: 'I should be afraid to say how many poems commemorative of R.B. I have received since his untimely death.'

Walter de la Mare: 'But once in a way Nature is as jealous of the individual as of the type. She gave Rupert Brooke youth, and may be, in these hyper-enlightened days, in doing so grafted a legend.'

Edward Thomas: 'He was eloquent. Men never spoke ill of him.'

Wilfred Gibson was moved to write on 23 April:

The Going

He's gone.
I do not understand.
I only know
That as he turned to go

And waved his hand
In his young eyes a sudden glory shone:
And I was dazzled by a sunset glow,
And he was gone.

The glorification of Brooke brought swift verbal and written rejoinders from several people, including E.J. Dent and Harold Monro, who tried to maintain a balanced view by hoping that his new-found celebrity status would not reach idiotic proportions or result in him being used as a tool for recruitment. The attempted balance was temporarily maintained:

> New Statesman: 'A myth has been created but it has grown round an imaginary figure very different from the real man.'

> Gwen Raverat: '. . . they never get the faintest feeling of his being a human being at all.'

His friends and the iconoclasts, though, could not stem the surging tide of popularity.

> The Academy: 'It may well be, as more than one writer has suggested, that in the future he will live as a mythical figure, a legend almost . . .'

> Maurice Browne: 'The beauty of the outer man was as the beauty of a young god; the beauty of the inner man outshone the beauty of the outer by so much as the glory of the sun is outshone by the glory of the human heart.'

The news of Brooke's death also made an impact on his four-year-old second cousin Winifred Kinsman: 'I remember going out with my mother for a walk, and she told me that Rupert had died, and I remember feeling that he couldn't have. It was just impossible. I said, "What will Aunt May [Rupert's mother] do?", and my mother said, "She will be very brave, but she's now only got Alfred left".'

Within a week or so of Brooke's death, Frances Cornford was moved to write:

Rupert Brooke

Can it be possible when we grow old
And Time destroys us, that your image now
Clearer than day to us – the image of you

248

Who brought to all serenely like a gift
The eternal beauty of youth – as tho' you'd lain
A moment since in English grass by the river
Thinking & dreaming under the fresh sky
When may was in the hedges. Can it be
That is, – your hair flung back – your smile which kept
A kind of sweetness like a child's
Tho' you might be most sad – the whole of you –
Must when we die in the vast air of time
Be swallowed like a candle? Nothing left
To the enamelled hard revolving world
(Full, full forever of fresh births & deaths
And busyness) of all you were?
                    Perhaps
A thousand years ago some Greek boy died,
So lovely-bodied, so adored, so young,
Like us they grieved & treasured little things
(And laughed with tears remembering his laughter),
And there was friendship in the very sound
Of his forgotten name to them. But now?
Now we know nothing, nothing is richer now
Because of all he was. O friend we have loved
Must it be thus with you? – and if it must be
How can men bear laboriously to live?

All his friends remembered him, in their own ways, which included verse
and music. One of his many Cambridge colleagues, Raglan H.E.H. Somerset,
recalled:

> I used to wake him on Sunday mornings to bathe in the dam above
> Byron's Pool. His bedroom was always littered with books, English,
> French, and German, in wild disorder . . . we used to go back and feed,
> sometimes in the Orchard and sometimes in the Old Vicarage garden
> on eggs and that particular brand of honey referred to in the
> 'Grantchester' poem. In those days he always dressed in the same way:
> cricket shirt and trousers and no stockings . . .

The Old Vicarage Grantchester inspired Sub-lieutenant Jeffrey Day to write
his poem 'An Airman's Dream'. He wrote 'I had sent myself to sleep and
endured dull sermons by thinking of my house and its surroundings.' Day
was shot down and went missing in February 1918.

Fellow poet John Drinkwater grieved for him:

> There can have been no man of his years in England who had at once
> so impressive a personality and so inevitable an appeal to the affection
> of everyone who knew him, while there has not been, I think, so
> grievous a loss to poetry since Shelley. Some of us who knew him may
> live to be old men, but life is not likely to give us any richer memory
> than his; and the passion and shapely zest that are his work will pass
> safely to the memory of posterity.

While the tributes poured in, the war was gathering momentum and many
of his friends would also die. Hugh Russell-Smith was killed a year after
Brooke's own death, by which time his old home Watersgreen House, where
Brooke had spent many a happy hour lazing in the hammock in the garden,
had become a nurses' home, caring for wounded Indians, before becoming a
centre for the wounded soldiers of New Zealand.

Cynthia Asquith wrote in her diary on 27 April, 'So very sorry to hear
[about] Rupert Brooke . . . I have only met him once or twice, never got to
know him, but always looked forward to doing so some day, and it does stab
one to think of this beautiful young poet's face with that cornfield head. He
had the most lovely *regard* I have ever seen I think. Poor Eddie will be broken
hearted – I think he was his favourite protégé.' Eddie Marsh was indeed
broken-hearted, as he expressed in his letter of condolence to Mrs Brooke: 'It
is the great sorrow I could have, and I dare not think what it must be to you
– I have never known or heard of anyone like him – his genius and his beauty,
his wisdom, honour, gentleness and humour made him such a man as
seldom lived. Everybody loved him, there was no one who had so many
devoted friends and so many charmed acquaintances.'

With those words Marsh set the tone for his memoir of Rupert, which
appeared to glorify Brooke and therefore be condemned by his mother. Initially
she was grateful to Marsh for his support and devotion to Rupert, and asked
him to use his influence to obtain special leave for Alfred, adding a comment
about Rupert: 'the many painful attacks of illness which he had as a boy would
fill a book . . . All my life and surroundings are so bound up in him, my sitting
room is full of his books and things waiting for his return as my heart is.'
Gradually, however, areas of Rupert's life of which she had no knowledge
emerged, arousing in her, one suspects, a not unnatural jealousy of a world that
Rupert had shared more with Eddie and his circle than with her. Cathleen
Nesbitt's name came up, and not for the last time she had to write to Eddie for
a wider picture, a scenario she undoubtedly came to increasingly resent.

Late in May, Marsh's grief was still as fresh as he poured out his heart to
Violet Asquith.

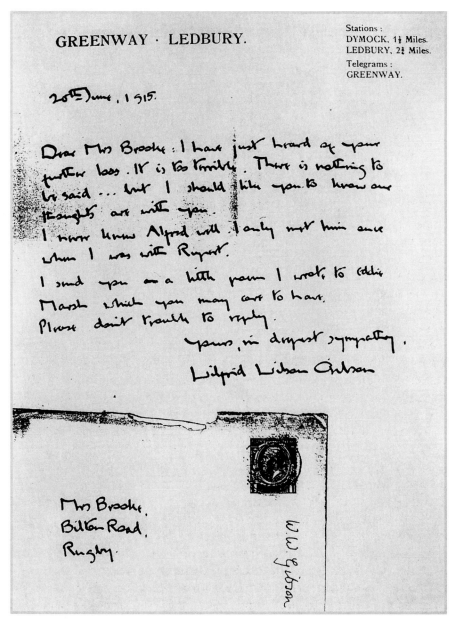

Wilfred Gibson's letter of condolence to Rupert's mother

It was sad and sweet to see the places he had loved so much . . . every ray and ever leaf and flower seemed to cry out for him – the elm-clumps greatly standing, the mayfields all golden showing, the sleepy grass and the collapse of hours – all his lovely phrases came back to me, and most of all 'Her sights and sounds, dreams happy as her day'

... dear old Winston, at dinner last night, had suddenly broken out, a propos nothing, in the midst of discussing his own troubles, that nothing had grieved him, or went on grieving him, so much as Rupert's death . . .

THE GALLOWS,
RYTON, DYMOCK,
GLOUCESTER.

July 2nd 1915

My Dear Mrs Brooke,

I did not dare to intrude before on the terrible privacy of your grief; and I only do so now to assure you of my most deep sympathy. I pray you may find comfort in the splendour of your sacrifice. There is nothing nobler in England today than your sorrow. But words must seem mere impertinence to you. I wish I could let you know the truth of what I feel for you.

Believe me
Yours in all humility

Lascelles Abercrombie

Lancelles Abercrombie adds his sympathy to the grieving Mrs Brooke

Mrs Brooke, strong as she was, was becoming morbidly inconsolable as the reality of her son's death hit her. Dudley Ward and Jacques Raverat went to the Old Vicarage to sort out papers, letters and books, with the worried Mrs Neeve not certain that she was doing the right thing by consenting to it, without Mrs Brooke's knowledge. The Ranee, in accordance with Rupert's wishes, was happy for Eddie to be the literary executor, but she felt that his personal letters should perhaps go to her at Rugby. She was unaware of Rupert's plea to Dudley to destroy some of them. Always a loyal friend, he made sure that they went to Raymond Buildings for sorting. Meanwhile the tributes continued.

One of Rupert's peers at Cambridge wrote this short but colourful cameo of him: 'Suddenly a freshman, with long and not unhyacinthine locks, was seen to tear through the muddy scrum. It was Rupert Brooke, and we paused in our game to observe this semblance of a Greek god in a football shirt.' Another friend, although more a contemporary of Rupert's younger brother Alfred, poured out his feelings in a letter to Mrs Brooke in June 1915: 'Cambridge and King's particularly are full of ghosts for me, and I fear they will soon be so full that I shall feel more at home among the ghosts than I do among the living.'

June saw the publication of Rupert's *1914 and Other Poems*, and the death in action of Denis Browne. The following week, Marsh and Henry James spent an evening together, Marsh reading Browne's letter relating the details of Rupert's last moments. James was deeply affected: '. . . the ghost telling of the ghost moved me more than I could find words for.'

Bereavement was making Mrs Brooke edgy, and she felt that Marsh was organising Rupert's letters, books and photographs without consulting her. He was undoubtedly more able to deal with Rupert's literary legacy than she was, but what the Ranee saw was it all happening with indecent haste. Marsh was shaken even more by the deposing of Churchill as First Sea Lord, and he was as faithful to him as he had been to Rupert. Mrs Brooke's life was shattered on receiving news that her only surviving son, Alfred, had been killed by a mortar bomb at Vermelles, France, while serving as a reserve machine-gun officer in the Post Office Rifles. Within a fortnight, Eddie took Rupert's belongings from the SS *Grantully* to her at Rugby; '. . . and when we got upstairs and I opened the boxes she broke down – I have never seen such suffering . . .' The items included clothing and a lock of Rupert's hair.

From Rugby, Marsh went to Wilfred Gibson's house, the Old Nailshop, where he began his memoir of Brooke. During his stay, on 10 June Gibson wrote a poem commemorating the first time Eddie had introduced him to Rupert and they had gone to King's Cross to watch a timber yard on fire.

The Old Nailshop – home of Wilfred Gibson, where Brooke stayed, and where Eddie Marsh wrote his memoir of Brooke

To E.M.
(In memory of R.B.)

The night we saw the stacks of timber blaze
To terrible golden fury, young and strong
He watched between us with dream-dazzled gaze
Aflame, and burning like a god of song,
As we together stood against the throng
Drawn from the midnight of the city ways.

To-night the world about us is ablaze
And he is dead, is dead . . . Yet, young and strong
He watches with us still with deathless gaze
Aflame, and burning like a god of song,
As we together stand against the throng
Drawn from the bottomless midnight of hell's ways.

Marsh finished his memoir in eight days, in a little room at the top of the house, before suggesting to Henry James that he write a preface to Brooke's *Westminster Gazette* articles that Marsh was also preparing for publication. Ironically, Marsh's fear that Mrs Brooke might not like the memoir and his paving the way with unnecessarily mollifying notes made her worry far more than she would have otherwise. He glossed over love affairs, referred to Cathleen Nesbitt as 'X' and insisted that he wanted only to do justice and honour to Rupert and to use only material with which Mrs Brooke would be happy. She hated feeling that the Rupert publicity machine was happening in spite of her feelings, and feared that a memoir at that moment, while so many were still dying, was not in the best taste. Marsh felt it important that the memoir should appeal to the youth of the country. She blocked it, insisted that it be postponed for at least a year, as well as being reworked: 'It is too evidently written by someone who knew him for a comparatively short time and even for that time quite a small part of him.' She was right, but even as his mother, she knew very little of major parts of his life. So who would be best qualified to write a memoir? The simple answer was no one person. There were so many different aspects to his make-up that friends and acquaintances were shown different faces, moods, character traits and displays of temperament, and any truly well-balanced account of him would have to include contributions from everyone who knew him. Whilst Mrs Brooke acknowledged that Marsh meant well, she must have felt that the memoir turned the son she had known into a son she did not know, with even the intimacy of his memory was being taken away from her.

However, there *was* much she did not know. Rupert's romance with Eileen Wellesley had been conducted with a high degree of discretion. There were two main clues to its actual depths. Several months earlier, Marsh's housekeeper, Mrs Elgy, had discovered Eileen's hairpins in Rupert's bed at Raymond Buildings, and an entry in Cynthia Asquith's diary for 3 July 1915 added fuel to the fire: 'Mary Herbert [a close friend of Eileen Wellesley] disobeyed her mother and came to see me in the afternoon. She told me Eileen Wellesley claims very serious love affair with Rupert Brooke saying that quite unsuspected of everyone else they used to meet in Richmond Park and Eddie's flat. No doubt Rupert Brooke had the thoroughly polygamous instincts of most poets.'

John Masefield, who was now undertaking a lot of work for the British Red Cross, was working with its motor boat ambulance service, which involved, among other things, taking small craft out to the Dardenelles. It was his intention, *en route*, to land on Skyros and visit Rupert's grave, but by early September heavy weather had set in, making it impossible to go ashore. Instead he painted three small watercolours of the island from different angles, and later presented them to Eddie Marsh. On returning home, he wrote his vivid and moving impression of the island, and his memory of Rupert.

The Island of Skyros

Here, we stood together, we three men,
Before the war had swept us to the East
Three thousand miles away, I stand again
And hear the bells, and breathe, and go to feast.
We trod the same path, to the selfsame place,
Yet here I stand, having beheld their graves,
Skyros whose shadows the great seas erase,
And Seddul Bahr that ever more blood craves.
So, since we communed here, our bones have been
Nearer, perhaps, than they again will be,
Earth and the worldwide battle lie between,
Death lies between, and friend-destroying sea.
Yet here, a year ago, we talked and stood
As I stand now, with pulses beating blood.

I saw her like a shadow on the sky
In the last light, a blur upon the sea,
Then the gale's darkness put the shadow by,
But from one grave that island talked to me;
And, in the midnight, in the breaking storm,
I saw its blackness and a blinking light,
And thought, 'So death obscures your gentle form,
So memory strives to make the darkness bright;
And, in that heap of rocks, your body lies,
Part of this crag this bitter surge offends,
While I, who pass, a little obscure thing,
War with this force, and breathe, and am its king.'

In Rupert's last letter to Noel Olivier dated 10 January 1915 he commented on the fact that another of her suitors, and fellow King's man, Ferenc Bekassy, had also enlisted: 'Dreadful if you lost all your lovers at once,' adding rather cryptically – 'Ah, but you won't lose all!' Bekassy was killed not long after Rupert. Noel was distraught at both deaths, declaring that there was no chance now that she'd ever marry for love. She did marry though. In 1919, two years after qualifying as a doctor, she married a Welsh colleague, Arthur Richards, and bore him a son and four daughters. Bizarrely, in 1932 she began a ten-year love affair with James Strachey. James's overtures to Rupert having been rejected as had Rupert's to Noel, the irony would surely have affected Brooke's delicate nervous system had he lived.

In October 1915, six months after Brooke's death, his American friends at

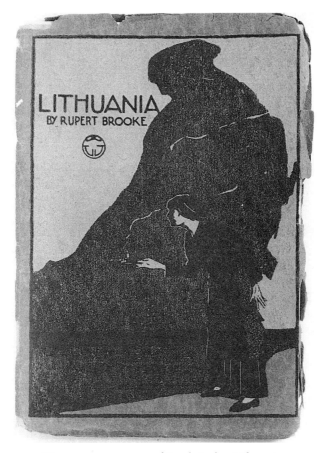

The programme cover of Brooke's play Lithuania

the Chicago Little Theatre, Maurice Browne and Ellen Van Volkenburg, produced his play *Lithuania*, in conjunction with Andreyev's *Pretty Sabine Women*. In Rupert's play, Ellen portrayed the daughter, the father being played by Browne, who also directed the piece. In having his play performed at the Little Theatre, Brooke's name was added to the list of illustrious playwrights whose works had been performed there, among them Ibsen, Strindberg, Wilde, Shaw and Yeats. The cover for the slim volume of the published play was designed by C. Raymond Johnson, who also staged the play. The production ran for three weeks, but was a financial disaster, failing to appeal to its rapidly dwindling audiences. Notwithstanding the work's lack of success, Brooke's increasing popularity in the States caused a rapid escalation of the price of the published play. Initially selling for 35 cents, it soon became so sought after that the Chicago *cognoscenti* were paying $20 for a single copy within the decade.

Rupert's play would be performed again two years later at the Social

Theatre, by the Varsity Players, with Van Volkenburg again taking the role of the daughter and Adolph Axelrad playing the father. The programme notes talk up what is really quite an ordinary play; 'A small edition of the play was printed and published by the Chicago Little Theatre: this edition has long been out of print and is now one of the rarities of modern literature. The play itself is extraordinarily grim and powerful, avoiding melodrama only by the skill with which it's handled; its terrible intensity recalls the murder scene in *Macbeth* and indicates the dramatic heights to which Rupert Brooke might have risen.'

In Wilfred Gibson's 1916 collection of poetry entitled Friends, the opening poem was called simply 'Rupert Brooke'.

Rupert Brooke

I

Your face was lifted to the golden sky
Ablaze beyond the black roofs of the square,
As flame on flame leapt, flourishing in air
Its tumult of red stars exultantly,
To the cold constellations dim and high;
And as we neared, the roaring ruddy flare
Kindled to gold your throat and brow and hair
Until you burned, a flame of ecstasy.

The golden head goes down into the night
Quenched in cold gloom – and yet again you stand
Beside me now with lifted face alight,
As, flame to flame, and fire to fire you burn . . .
Then, recollecting, laughingly you turn,
And look into my eyes and take my hand.

II

Once in my garret – you being far away
Tramping the hills and breathing upland air,
Or so I fancied – brooding in my chair,
I watched the London sunshine feeble and grey
Dapple my desk, too tired to labour more,
When, looking up, I saw you standing there,
Although I'd caught no footstep on the stair,
Like sudden April at my open door.

Though now beyond earth's farthest hills your fare,
Song-crowded, immortal, sometimes it seems to me
That, if I listen very quietly,
Perhaps I'll hear a light foot on the stair,
And see you, standing with your angel air,
Fresh from the uplands of eternity.

III
Your eyes rejoiced in colour's ecstasy
Fulfilling even their uttermost desire,
When, over a great sunlit field afire
With windy poppies, streaming like a sea
Of scarlet flame that flaunted riotously
Among green orchards of that western shire,
You gazed as though your heart could never tire
Of life's red flood in summer revelry.

And as I watched you little thought had I
How soon beneath the dim low-drifting sky
Your soul should wander down the darkling way,
With eyes that peer a little wistfully,
half-glad, half-sad, remembering, as they see
Lethean poppies, shrivelling ashen grey.

IV
October chestnuts showered their perishing gold
Over us as beside the stream we lay
In the Old Vicarage garden that blue day,
Talking of verse and all the manifold
Delights a little net of words may hold,
While in the sunlight water-voles at play
Dived under a trailing crimson bramble-spray,
And walnuts thudded ripe on soft black mould.

Your soul goes down unto a darker stream
Alone, O friend, yet even in death's deep night
Your eyes may grow accustomed to the dark,
And Styx for you may have the ripple and gleam
Of your familiar river, and Charon's bark
Tarry by that old garden of your delight.

In February 1916, Eddie Marsh submitted a revised version of his memoir, which met with Mrs Brooke's approval. It carried with it a proposal that others such as Dudley Ward, Geoffrey Keynes and Brooke's godfather Robert Whitlaw should contribute to the Cambridge section. They declined, with the result that Mrs Brooke promptly withdrew her permission to publish, as Keynes was not involved. She had a point. Geoffrey had known Rupert throughout his schooldays at Rugby and then Cambridge. In later years he was to prove as jealous a guardian of Brooke's memory as Marsh.

Rupert's articles for *The Westminster Gazette* were published on 8 March as *Letters from America*, with a lengthy preface by Henry James. Within weeks, the American novelist suffered a stroke and was unable to write again. His introduction mentioned Marsh's impending memoir, which succeeded only in antagonising Mrs Brooke even more, as she felt she was being pushed into its publication. To Marsh she wrote, 'You couldn't bear me taking my stand as his mother . . . you have never recognised my position in it all.' One of the first women to be made a magistrate, she was not only capable of making clear and balanced judgements, but was also known for her concern for those she tried. Her great-niece Winifred spoke of Mrs Brooke's 'remarkable courage', and of her being a 'remarkable woman'. She was clearly not someone to be crossed, as Marsh discovered. The rift between them was now great. Brooke himself would have been distraught at the thought of two people for whom he cared so much arguing so vehemently over his memory. The preface to *Letters of America* was Henry James's last work, for he died soon after its publication.

In April, Brooke was posthumously awarded the Howland Prize from Yale University, Charles Howland himself being a subscriber to *New Numbers*. Despite Rupert's growing reputation, Eddie became resigned to putting the memoir on hold indefinitely.

On 9 May, under the direction of John Drinkwater, Brooke's *Lithuania*, starring Martin Harvey, was performed at His Majesty's Theatre in London, on a bill with Wilfred Gibson's *Hoops* and the main item, *King Lear's Wife*, with Viola Tree in the title role. Edward Thomas was in the audience and commented favourably to Robert Frost about the play.

Brooke's royalties were being distributed, as he had directed, to de la Mare, Abercrombie and Gibson, and were making a substantial difference to their lives. Even Robert Graves, who had never met Brooke, was affected by him. Lying in hospital at Rouen, wounded, he dreamed of Brooke: 'this afternoon I had a sort of waking dream about meeting and making friends with Rupert: it was absolutely vivid and I feel I know him ten times better than before. We talked poetry most of the time and he said among other things that it wasn't so bad being dead as you got such splendid opportunities of watching what was happening.'

In a letter to Robert Frost, Edward Thomas put down some of his thoughts on Rupert: 'I think he succeeded in being youthful and yet intelligible and interesting (not only pathologically) more than most poets since Shelley . . . Radically, I think he lacked power of expression. He was a rhetorician, dressing things up better than they needed.'

It was not only his friends who sang his praises in verse. Eden Phillpotts, the novelist, poet and sometime collaborator with one of Brooke's favourite writers, Arnold Bennett, included his thoughts on Rupert in his *Plain Song, 1914–1916*.

To Rupert Brooke

Though we, a happy few,
Indubitably knew
That from the purple came
This poet of pure flame,

The world first saw his light
Flash on an evil night,
And heard his song from far
Above the drone of war.

Out of the primal dark
He leapt, like lyric lark,
Singing his aubade strain;
Then fell to earth again.

We garner all he gave,
And on his hero grave,
For love and honour stew,
Rosemary, myrtle, rue.

Son of the Morning, we
Had kept you thankfully;
But yours the asphodel:
Hail, singer, and farewell!

Brooke's death not only spawned hundreds of poems from professional and amateur poets, from Great Britain, the United States of America and other countries, but also inspired a torrent of prose ranging from the intellectual, to the simplistic and downright bizarre. The first edition of

Brooke's *Collected Poems*, published by John Lane Company in New York, predating the first English edition by three years, carried a eulogistical preface by George Edward Woodberry. Writing at his home in Beverly, Massachusetts, in October 1915, the frontispiece includes paragraphs like this:

> . . . Rupert Brooke was already perfected in verbal and stylistic execution. He might have grown in variety, richness and significance, in scope and in detail, no doubt; but as an artisan in metrical words and pauses, he was past apprenticeship. He was still a restless experimenter, but in such he was a master. In the brief stroke of description, which he inherited from his early attachment to the concrete; in the rush of words, especially verbs, still with the impulse of 'the bright speed' he had at the source; in his theatrical impersonation of abstractions, as in 'The Funeral of Youth', where for once the abstract and the concrete are happily fused; – in all these there are the elements, and in the last there is the perfection, of mastery.

His paeanistic outpourings conclude with the rather cloying line, 'For a new star shines in the English heavens'.

During July 1917, Mrs Brooke received yet another draft of Eddie Marsh's proposed memoir, with many pieces referring to Cathleen (still as X) removed, and some Rugby School reminiscences by an anonymous friend of Mrs Brooke's excluded. Little else had changed, though – they were still at loggerheads, Mrs Brooke claiming that '. . . in some ways it is almost absurdly inaccurate', and Marsh responding with 'Rupert is a famous poet and his life will be read critically by all sorts of people all the world over, both now and long afterwards.' Her persistence in her denunciation of Marsh's biographical paean led to him, determined to find a way round the impasse, sending a long explanatory letter which ended, 'I hope you will accept my assurance that I never meant to offend or disregard you'.

Following interventions by Dudley Ward, as a neutral party, the situation began to ease, and with even more mediation from the same quarter, agreement seemed likely. Another problem arose though, in that Mrs Brooke thought it would be cheating the public to sell the memoir and his collected poems in the same book, as so many people had already bought the poetry. Marsh did not agree, feeling the memoir to be an ideal introduction to Brooke's work. *The Collected Poems of Rupert Brooke, with a Memoir* was eventually published on 24 July 1918, the result of the Marsh/Mrs Brooke conflict resulting in a memoir of twice the original length Despite Mrs Brooke's efforts to ensure it offered a complete picture of her son, it was still somewhat idealised. W.H. Davies, however, declared it to be 'more real than anything I have ever read before . . .'. Bunny Garnett was amazed by the contents – or lack of them; 'James – who knew him better than anyone else . . . is silent – he is mentioned once as having been on a walking tour with him – Noel is of course not mentioned . . .'

In a review of the *Collected Poems of Rupert Brooke, with a Memoir*, published in *The Times Literary Supplement* on 8 August 1918, Virginia Woolf wrote:

> Mr Marsh has had to face the enormous difficulties which beset the biographers of those who have died with undeveloped powers, tragically, and in the glory of public gratitude . . . at Grantchester his feet were permanently bare; he disdained tobacco and butcher's meat; and he lived all day, and perhaps slept all night, in the open air. You might judge him extreme, and from the pinnacle of superior age assure him that the return to Nature was as sophisticated as any other pose, but you could not from the first moment of speech with him doubt that, whatever he might do, he was an originator, one of those leaders who spring up from time to time and show their power most clearly by subjugating their own generation. Under his influence the country near Cambridge was full of young men and women walking barefoot, sharing his passion for bathing and fish diet, disdaining book learning, and proclaiming that there was something deep and wonderful in the man who brought the milk and in the woman who watched the cows. One may trace some of the effects of this belief in the tone of his letters at this time; their slap-dash method, their hasty scrawled appearance upon the paper, the exclamations and abbreviations were all, in part at least, a means of exorcizing the devils of the literary and cultured. But there was too much vigour in his attitude in this respect, as in all others, to lend it the appearance of affectation. It was an amusing disguise; it was in part, like many of his attitudes, a game played for the fun of it, an experiment in living by one keenly inquisitive and incessantly fastidious; and in part it was the expression of a profound and true sympathy which had to live side by side with highly sophisticated tastes and to be reported upon by nature that was self-conscious to the highest degree. Analyse it as one may, the whole effect of Rupert Brooke in these days was a compound of vigour and of great sensitiveness. Like most sensitive people, he had his methods of self-protection; his pretence now to be this and now to be that. But, however sunburnt and slap-dash he might choose to appear at any particular moment, no one could know him even slightly without seeing that he was not only very sincere, but passionately in earnest about the things he cared for. In particular, he cared for literature and

the art of writing as seriously as it is possible to care for them. He had read everything and he had read it from the point of view of a working writer . . . It may seem strange, now that he is famous as a poet, how little it seemed to matter in those days whether he wrote poetry or not. It is proof perhaps of the exciting variety of his gifts and of the immediate impression he made of being so complete and remarkable in himself that it was sufficient to think of him merely as Rupert Brooke. It was not necessary to imagine him dedicated to any particular pursuit. If one traced a career for him many different paths seemed the proper channels for his store of vitality; but clearly he must find scope for his extraordinary gift of being on good terms with his fellow-creatures. For though it is true to say that 'he never "put himself forward" and seldom took the lead in conversation', his manner shed a friendliness wherever he happened to be that fell upon all kinds of different people, and seemed to foretell that he would find his outlet in leading varieties of men as he had led his own circle of Cambridge friends. His practical ability, which was often a support to his friends, was one of the gifts that seemed to mark him for success in active life. He was keenly aware of the state of public affairs, and if you chanced to meet him when there was talk of a strike or an industrial dispute he was evidently as well versed in the complications of social questions as in the obscurities of the poetry of Donne . . . One turns from the thought of him not with a sense of completeness and finality, but rather to wonder and to question still what would he have been, what would he have done?

Virginia thought he might one day have become a top politician, even Prime Minister, while others felt he might have taken to writing poetry full time. The latter is unlikely for, as he pointed out himself in his Fabian lecture, which was later published as *Democracy in the Arts*, there was no living to be had in writing poetry. Cathleen Nesbitt, though, felt he would have continued with the poetry. 'I think he would have become in a sense what I call a metaphysical poet . . . I think he would have been on a level with Keats, because I think he had great music in his voice . . .' Rupert himself was clearly keen to write more plays, and had talked with Denis Browne of collaborating on musicals. Cathleen thought he wrote the most beautiful prose but in terms of earning a living she confessed, 'I think he might have become a dramatist.' Maurice Browne was convinced. 'There is no doubt in my own mind that, had Brooke lived, his main work would ultimately have been dramatic. His dominant characteristic was, if I observed him aright, that "gusto" in people and life, which he shared with Keats and Synge [John Millington, the Irish playwright] and that "gusto" is the essence of drama . . . Before the war, he,

Miss Van Volkenburg, Miss Allenby [seemingly Browne's guarded alias for Cathleen Nesbitt] and I were planning a close and practical association in theatrical work in Paris, where it was our intention to establish an English theatre in the autumn of 1915.'

During 1918, Denis Browne's poem on Brooke was published posthumously.

To Rupert Brooke

I give you glory, for you are dead.
The day lightens above your head;
The night darkens about your feet;
Morning and noon and evening meet
Around and over and under you
In the world you knew, the world you knew.

Lips are kissing and limbs are clinging,
Breast to breast, in a silence singing
Of unforgotten and fadeless things:
Laughter and tears and the beat of wings
Faintly heard in a far-off heaven;
Bird calls bird; the unquiet even
Ineluctable ebb and flow
Flows and ebbs; and all things go
Moving from dream to dream; and deep
Calls deep again in a world of sleep.

There is no glory gone from the air;
Nothing is less. No, as it were
A keener and wilder radiance glows
Along the blood, and a shouting grows
Fiercer and louder, a far-flung roar
Of throats and guns: your island shore
Is swift with smoke and savage with flame;
And a myriad lovers shout your name,
Rupert! Rupert!, across the earth;
And death is dancing, and dancing birth;
And a madness of dancing blood and laughter
Rises and sings, and follows after
All the dancers who danced before,
And dance no more, and dance no more.

You will dance no more; you will love no more;
You are dead and dust on your island shore.
A little dust are the lips where
Laughter and song and kisses were.
And I give you glory, and I am glad
For the life you had and the death you had,
For the heaven you knew and the hell you knew,
And the dust and the dayspring which were you.

Had Rupert so wished, he could have written plays and poems while taking up an academic career. Late in 1910, he had been offered a lectureship in English at Newcastle, which would have led to a Chair at a university, but it clearly did not appeal to him at the time. He might even have collaborated with Denis Browne or Cleg Kelly, as librettist; indeed, various composers were to use his lyrics over the years. John Ireland of the school of English Impressionism and best known for his Second Violin Sonata, set various poetry to music, including poems by Thomas Hardy, Christina Rossetti, A.E. Housman, John Masefield and Brooke. The words of Rupert's 'Song' were used in a piece for piano and voice by Ireland in 1918, which was given the title of 'Spring Sorrow'.

Song

All suddenly the wind comes soft,
And Spring is here again;
And the hawthorn quickens with buds of green,
And my heart with buds of pain.

My heart all Winter lay so numb,
The earth so dead and frore,
That I never thought the Spring would come,
Or my heart wake any more.

But winter's broken and earth has woken,
And the small birds cry again;
And the hawthorn hedge puts forth its buds
And my heart puts forth its pain.

The setting was first recorded in 1964. Ireland also set 'The Soldier' and 'The Dead' to music, the former making its public debut in June 1917. 'The Soldier' was first recorded in 1943. In the mid 1990s the author set all five war sonnets to music and recorded them with the King's College choir. Their first public performance took place in July 1997.

The poetic tributes, it seemed, would never cease to flow. A 1919 publication, *The Muse in Arms*, contained Aubrey Herbert's 'R.B.', which erroneously gives Lemnos as Rupert's final resting place. At the time of his death there was some confusion, as the telegram informing the Admiralty of his death had been sent from Lemnos.

R.B.

It was April we left Lemnos, shining sea and snow-white camp,
Passing onward into darkness. Lemnos shone a golden lamp,
As a low harp tells of thunder, so the lovely Lemnos air
Whispered of the dawn and battle; and we left a comrade there.

He who sang of dawn and evening, English glades and light of Greece,
Changed his dreaming into sleeping, left his sword to rest in peace.
Left his visions of the springtime, Holy Grail and Golden Fleece,
Took the leave that has no ending, till the waves of Lemnos cease.

There will be enough recorders ere this fight of ours be done,
And the deeds of men made little, swiftly cheapened one by one;
Bitter loss his golden harpstrings and the treasure of his youth;
Gallant foe and friend may mourn him, for he sang the knightly truth.

Joy was his in his clear singing, clean as is the swimmer's joy;
Strong the wine he drank of battle, fierce as that they poured in Troy.
Swift the shadows steal from Athos, but his soul was morning-swift,
Greek and English he made music, caught the cloud-thoughts we let drift.

Sleep you well, you rainbow comrade, where the wind and light is strong,
Overhead and high above you, let the lark take up your song.
Something of your singing lingers, for the men like me who pass,
Till all singing ends in sighing, in the sighing of the grass.

The day planned for the unveiling of a medallion of Brooke in Rugby chapel was 28 March 1919. The relief for the plaque had been undertaken by the sculptor Havard Thomas, working to the profile of Rupert taken by the photographer Sherril Schell, with the lettering cut by Eric Gill. The wording included the words from 'The Soldier'. The Abercrombies came, Denis

Arlice Rapoto (second from right, standing) *the daughter of Brooke and Taatamata*

Browne's mother, Geoffrey Keynes, Wilfred Gibson, Walter de la Mare, and the sister of Cleg Kelly, who had also been killed. Brooke's company commander, Major-General Sir Bernard Freyburg, KCB, VC, DSO, attended and Rupert's old Commander-in-Chief, General Sir Ian Hamilton, unveiled the medallion and made a speech: 'After four and a half years of war we have come together here in Rugby School chapel. The time is a time of Armistice – an armistice which may yet lead us onwards into the paths of peace . . .' He went on to talk specifically of Brooke: 'Is it because he was a hero? There were thousands. Is it because he looked a hero? There were few. Is it because he had genius? There were others. But Rupert Brooke held all three gifts of the gods in his hand . . .' After the ceremony, Mrs Brooke received many of the guests for tea at Bilton Road, playing hostess again the following day after a concert which included an Elegy for String Orchestra and Harp in C, dedicated to Rupert, by the late Cleg Kelly.

The plaque had been paid for by subscription and the £30 over was given to the delighted W.H. Davies.

D.H. Lawrence was one of the beneficiaries of the memoir. 'Queer to receive money from the dead: as it were out of the dark sky. I have great beliefs in the dead – in Rupert dead. He fights with me I know.' Eddie Marsh offered Mrs Brooke half of the first royalty cheque, which she

An extract from 'Cleg' Kelly's Elegy For Brooke

refused. The money was eventually used to purchase Augustus John's portrait of W.H. Davies, who along with the likes of Arthur Symons and George Bernard Shaw, had sat for John during the war. The portrait, another Brooke legacy of a sort, was presented to the National Portrait Gallery by Eddie.

By 1920, Mrs Brooke had approved a more permanent covering for Rupert's grave. The loose stones were replaced by a slab of Pentelican marble.

It was transported to Skyros under the supervision of Stanley Casson, the author of *Hellenic Studies*, five years to the month after Brooke's death. Casson noted that, 'The wooden crosses still stood undisturbed and intact. The stones near the grave were as when they were first placed there.' It took three weeks to land and erect the marble slabs, as the stonemasons and local inhabitants had to cut a path to the grave, the nearest village being 15 miles away. Some of the shepherds in whose hut Casson stayed had witnessed Brooke's burial at the spot that Casson referred to as lying 'in a deserted valley at the deserted end of the island'. There was another grave down by the shoreline, where Brooke's coffin had been landed, thought by the locals to be that of a Roman woman. Casson noted that the whole area in the vicinity of the grave was full of 'pale blue anemones, orchids, rock hyacinths, russet fritillaries, wild thyme, mint and wild olives'. One of the monks of the Monastery of St George, to which the land belonged, officiated in the consecration of the new tomb.

During the summer of 1921, Hugh Dalton had a vivid dream of Brooke. 'Rupert came and talked to me . . . Rupert and I both knew that he was dead, killed in the war, but the conversation was quite matter of fact . . . Once in the course of our conversation he touched me and felt quite corporeal, but I had a shrinking feeling, which prevented me from voluntarily touching him . . .' It had been Rupert's poems that had been Dalton's literary inspiration during the war.

Noel's father Lord Olivier had a short-lived plan to publish the letters between Rupert and Margery Olivier to raise money to help her, now that she was unstable. She spent the rest of her life in a mental institution and outlived her three sisters, passing away in 1974.

It was not only Brooke's poems that continued to arouse interest, but also his image. At Marlborough College in 1923–24, the teenage John Betjeman discovered the writings of Oscar Wilde, which led him to write to Wilde's former lover and friend, Lord Alfred Douglas. Flattered by a letter from an admiring schoolboy, 'Bosie', as Douglas was known as, asked for a photograph. Thrilled to be on the receiving end of a communication from the infamous poet, the young Betjeman rushed down to the local photographer's to have himself taken, '. . . sideways-on and looking, I hoped, rather like the portrait of Rupert Brooke in that Sidgwick and Jackson edition – of Rupert Brooke with an open shirt . . .' by the time the future Poet Laureate went up to Oxford in 1926, Brooke's *1914 and Other Poems* had sold in the region of 300,000 copies. Forty-four years later, just prior to the Labour Prime Minister Harold Wilson being ousted from No. 10 Downing Street, John Betjeman would write to his great friend Mary Wilson, the Prime Minster's wife: 'I have been slowly reading all R.L. Stevenson's poems. It is amazing how much Rupert Brooke owes to him.'

Wilfred Gibson wrote another poem about Brooke in 1927, which *The Observer* published that April, and it was included in an anthology containing the year's best poetry.

Skyros
(Rupert Brooke: April 23, 1915)

Skyros – he spoke the name
With eager, boyish zest
And little guessed
His heart should come to rest
For evermore on that far island crest.

Skyros – I heard the name,
Nor ever thought 'twould be
Aught else to me,
Nor how unrestingly
My heart should haunt that far Aegean Sea.

Skyros – to me by day
An isle of marble white
Transfused by bright
Raptures of singing light
A beacon-fire of living song by night!

During the 1920s, a move was afoot to raise money to erect a statue on Skyros, carved by a great sculptor, in Rupert's memory. It would be called 'Youth'. It was initiated by a Belgian poet, and French writers Gide and Valery were supportive, as was a 'not entirely convinced' Eddie Marsh. Again Mrs Brooke was concerned that it was going ahead without her knowledge, but she ended her letter of inquisition to Eddie, 'with apologies and many thanks for all you have done for my boy'. Three months later in October 1930, she was taken ill. Mrs Brooke's niece and her daughter Winifred motored up from Essex, arriving just before the end. Winifred was the last person to see her alive. 'The nurse took us up to see her, but she was barely conscious. Later I slipped back on my own, and was sitting on the bed, when she opened her eyes and said quite clearly: "All my children have been to see me today." I don't think she spoke again.' Despite her apparent softening towards Marsh before she died, the terms of her will transferred the position of literary executor from Marsh to four other trustees, although he would be allowed to keep Brooke's manuscripts for his lifetime, the archive going to King's on his death. The four trustees were Jack Sheppard, Dudley Ward, Geoffrey Keynes and Walter de la Mare. The quartet felt that Marsh still had a major role to play, but he handed Brooke's manuscripts straight to King's and four years later left all future editions to them.

During the first week of April 1931, the monument to the memory of Rupert Brooke was erected on Skyros with the Abercrombies in attendance. Lascelles's wife Catherine remembered:

> . . . we went with an Anglo/French/Dutch company of admirers, who had subscribed to the erection of a statue to Rupert, on the topmost peak of the island. Lascelles had been asked to give the English oration at the ceremony in the afternoon. When we'd landed from the ship in the morning, we had wandered away from the rest of the people and came upon the tomb on a hillside, with a few olive trees and these shepherds sitting round a fire, heating a huge cauldron of sheep's milk. They gave us some to drink in two handled vessels that hadn't changed their shape since the days of Homer. One of them sprang to his feet and began to declaim a long poem, which we gathered was to Rupert's memory, and the undying friendship of the English and the Greeks . . . At their evident request, my husband spoke some Milton. As we could not understand a word of our different languages, it did not matter, we were praising immortal poetry, and Rupert.

A commemorative book detailing and documenting the event appeared four years later, but was published in Greek only.

Lascelles Abercrombie's earlier tribute to Rupert featured in his collection of poems published in 1930.

R.B.

Beautiful life! As air delights to find
The white heat of a fire and to be flame,
The eager world throng'd into his glowing mind
And flame of burning beauty there became.
All things were turned to fire in him, and cast
The light of their transfiguring round his ways.
His secret gleamed upon us; where he past
He shone; he brought with him a golden place.
It was the purest fire of life that shone,
This angel brightness visiting our mould.

Life knew no way to make life lovelier, none;
But then came Death: 'I know the way.
Behold!'

Writing between the wars, Wilfred Gibson remembered with affection the time when so many literary greats had come together at his home the Old Nailshop, in Dymock, in his poem 'The Golden Room':

The Golden Room

Do you remember that still summer evening
When, in the cosy cream-washed living-room
Of the Old Nailshop, we all talked and laughed –
Our neighbours from the Gallows, Catherine
And Lascelles Abercrombie; Rupert Brooke;
Elinor and Robert Frost, living a while
At Little Iddens, who'd brought over with them
Helen and Edward Thomas? In the lamplight
We talked and laughed; but, for the most part, listened
While Robert Frost kept on and on and on,
In his slow New England fashion, for our delight,
Holding us with shrewd turns and racy quips,
And the rare twinkle of his grave blue eyes?

We sat there in the lamplight, while the day
Died from rose-latticed casements, and the plovers
Called over the low meadows, till the owls
Answered them from the elms, we sat and talked –
Now, a quick flash from Abercrombie; now,
A murmured dry half-heard aside from Thomas;
Now, a clear laughing word from Brooke; and then
Again Frost's rich and ripe philosophy
That had the body and tang of good draught-cider,
And poured as clear a stream

            'T'was in July
On nineteen-fourteen that we talked:
Then August brought the war, and scattered us.

Now, on the crest of an Aegean isle,
Brooke sleeps, and dreams of England: Thomas lies

'Neath Vimy Ridge, where he, among his fellows,
Died, just as life had touched his lips to a song.

And nigh as ruthlessly has life divided
Us who survive; for Abercrombie toils
In a Black Northern town, beneath the glower
Of hanging smoke; and in America
Frost farms once more; and, far from the Old Nailshop,
We sojourn by the Western Sea.

                    And yet,
Was it for nothing that the little room,
All golden in the lamplight, thrilled with golden
Laughter from the hearts of friends that summer night?
Darkness has fallen on it; and the shadow
May never more be lifted from the hearts
That went through those black years of war, and live

And still, wherever men and women gather
For talk and laughter on a summer night,
Shall not that lamp rekindle; and the room
Glow once again alive with light and laughter;
And, like a singing star in time's abyss,
Burn golden-hearted through oblivion?

Ka Cox survived Mrs Brooke by three and a half years. During the war, she
had worked hard with Serbian refugees in Corsica, before marrying naval
officer and painter Will Arnold-Forster in 1918, moving to Cornwall in 1928
where she bore him a son, and dying at her home, Eagles Nest, Zennor, in
1934. Hook Heath Cottage, at Woking, where she and Brooke had often
conducted their doomed relationship, had, at the time, featured a mullion
window on which many of the Bloomsbury group (the circle of friends who
began to meet about 1905 at the Bloomsbury home of Virginia Woolf), Ka,
Brooke and their circle had etched their signatures. The extraordinary piece
of history was sadly destroyed during the 1970s, but one of the neighbouring
houses, which belonged until 1914 to the Duke of Sutherland, still has a
window with the names of Margaret, one of Ka's sisters, and her father Henry
Fisher-Cox and Christmas 1902 scratched clearly on the glass.

Early in 1936, almost 21 years after Rupert's death, an unusual chain of
events was sparked off by Dudley Ward. Then 50 years old, he was a CBE
and had been an eminent member of the Treasury for many years.
Unquestionably Rupert's closest confidant in matters that required the

utmost discretion Ward was, it seems, entrusted with the poet's darkest secret. Whether Rupert knew of the birth of a child to his beloved Taatamata – Mamua – or not is a matter of conjecture, as any correspondence relating to his knowledge of the matter has been either mislaid or destroyed. Late in 1935, the solid Ward, not given to flights of fancy, began to make serious enquiries as to a child who would have been born to Taatamata, towards the end of 1915. He had a few leads to go on, although a letter confirming the existence of Brooke's child came into Ward's hands at some point. Why it took him 21 years to raise the question is uncertain; maybe other non-documented enquiries had proved fruitless. His quest led him to write a letter to Viscount Hastings, who had owned a property on Moorea, an island to the north-west of Tahiti. He asked him if any of his friends out in the South Seas could throw any light on the situation. Hastings thought that his friend Norman Hall, who had recently directed Mutiny on the Bounty, starring Charles Laughton and Clark Gable, may be able to help, as he had a wide circle of friends there. Hastings wrote to Hall on the last day of January 1936:

> I hope all goes well with you in Tahiti. The other day I met a Mr Dudley Ward, who had asked to meet me, as he had heard that I lived in Tahiti. He had been a great friend of Rupert Brooke and was up at Cambridge with him. He told me that when Rupert Brooke was in Tahiti he lived with a Tahitian girl called Taata Mata (the name is familiar to me, but I cannot remember the context, or whether I met her, or from whom I heard about her). Apparently she was the only woman that Rupert Brooke ever really cared about, and after he left Tahiti he was in doubt as to whether she might have been going to have a child by him or not. He had a strong desire to reproduce himself in the form of having a son.
>
> When he went out to France he had a premonition that he might be killed and made Dudley Ward promise, that in the event of his death, Dudley Ward would let the girl know about it.
>
> It was only after Rupert Brooke died that his poetry became famous and the press took him up as the hero-poet of the time, which disturbed the Brooke family, particularly his mother.
>
> And for this reason Dudley Ward never fulfilled his promise, meaning to go out some day to the Islands himself; and in the meantime afraid that if he put about enquiries, that the press would get hold of the story to the further discomfiture of R.B.'s mother, and with that added possibility of starting claims by the Tahitian girl for money, or of a son being produced as Rupert Brooke's, which might not really be his.
>
> However his conscience seems to have been worrying him, and he

asked me if I could do anything about it. I said I would try and I wondered if you would be so kind as to help.

Whether the Taata Mata who lived with Rupert Brooke is still traceable, I don't know, but if by any chance she is still alive, I wondered if you would give the message to her, & if you could find out whether there is a Rupert Brooke child still living.

A certain discretion is advisable, as you will see . . .

Norman Hall responded on 16 March 1936:

Dear Hastings:–

Your letter has just (yesterday) reached me, having come by tramp steamer, the *Haraki*, which has brought about half of our monthly mail . . . About the Tahitian girl, Taata Mata: she is the Taata Mata who now lives on Moorea, near Maharepa. She is still a quite handsome woman and must have been a very attractive girl when Brooke knew her. I am certain that she is the one in question, for I used to hear Pare (Johnnie Gooding) of the Annex speak of Rupert Brooke when he stopped at the old Tiare Hotel. Johnnie was quite a youngster then but remembered Brooke well. He said they were all enchanted by him, particularly his mother, Lovaina, who was then the proprietress of the Tiare. Taata Mata was then a sort of protege of Lovaina's and it was at the hotel, so Pare told me, that Brooke met her . . . Taata Mata is permanently settled on Moorea and rarely comes to Tahiti in these days. Therefore, as I am leaving for California by next week's northbound steamer, I'm afraid that I shan't have an opportunity to see her before I go. If I should see her, you can count on my discretion and tact, and I shall, of course, speak of the matter to no one but herself . . . I greatly regret that I can't settle the matter beyond all dispute by seeing Taata Mata. I have known her ever since I came to the island and I'm sure I could learn the truth in a ten minutes' chat with her. But it is impossible for me to go to Moorea this week and, as I have said, I am leaving for S.F. a week from tomorrow. However, I will make enquiries of her as soon as I return, which may not be until about next November. Meanwhile, if you wish Taata Mata to be seen before this time, I suggest you write to Nordhoff about this. He would use the same discretion as myself but I don't feel at liberty to ask him to see her, since you wrote to me in confidence . . . With my sincere regards for Lady Hastings and yourself.

Sincerely yours,

sgd. Norman Hall.

The plaque in Rugby School chapel

It is not known whether Norman Hall ever asked Taatamata, or indeed if he did, whether she preferred to leave well alone. The Tahitians were adept at closing ranks from outsiders, but the silence could have come at any point along the line, either from a reticent Taatamata, Norman Hall or Viscount Hastings. Indeed if Dudley himself had been told of a child, he would undoubtedly have kept it under wraps. Besides, who was there to benefit from knowing? Ward was not the type of person to spread salacious gossip for the sake of it.

Norman Hall died in 1951, but Hall's daughter Nancy was able to confirm that her mother had always known that Arlice Rapoto, a close friend of the family, was the daughter of Brooke and Taatamata. A photograph taken in about 1950 shows an uncanny resemblance to Rupert. Arlice had a ten-year relationship with Serge Czerefkow, the estranged husband of the Grand Couteriere, Madame Gres. Nancy's mother told her, in confidence, who Arlice's father was, but it wasn't generally brought up in conversation, her friends clearly respecting her wishes for privacy, and perhaps not wanting to point up her illegitimacy. Arlice died some five or six years ago; sadly the Tahitian records of births and deaths are fairly non-existent and she apparently was childless, or so it is claimed . . .

With war looming at the end of the 1930s many turned to the poetry of the '14–'18 conflict for inspiration and strength. Brooke was the idol of Rugby schoolboy John Gillespie Magee who not only won the school poetry prize (as Brooke had done 34 years earlier) but was inspired to write a poem about him.

Sonnet to Rupert Brooke

We laid him in a cool and shadowed grove
One evening, in the dreamy scent of time,
Where leaves were green, and whispered high above
A grave as humble as it was sublime;
There, dreaming in the fading deeps of light –
The hands that thrilled to touch a woman's hair;
Brown eyes, that loved the Day, and looked on Night,
A soul that found at last its answered prayer . . .
There daylight, as a dust, slips through the trees,
And drifting, gilds the fern about his grave –
where even now, perhaps, the evening breeze
Steals slyly past the tomb of him who gave
New sight to blinded eyes; who sometimes wept –
A short time dearly loved; and after, – slept.

Magee's poem 'High Flight' was to achieve lasting fame after he was killed in December 1941 when his Spitfire was in collision with an Airspeed Oxford 1,400 feet over Lincolnshire.

During the Second World War, two of Brooke's sonnets were printed on illegal, bicycle-powered presses in German-occupied Holland. Dutch printers were forbidden to publish the work of British writers or poets during the conflict, but that did not stop them from producing limited editions of Shakespeare, Yeats, Auden, Emily Brontë, Rossetti and Brooke. The scarcity of paper was a serious problem, but the Dutch published secretly, flaunting their contempt for the Gestapo.

The spirit of Rupert Brooke was still very much alive during the Second World War. Cornish poet Charles Causley, who, like Brooke, also served in the Royal Navy, wrote these four verses at Grantchester:

At Grantchester (from Jonny Alleluia)

Bank Holiday. A sky of guns. The river
Slopping black silver on the level stair.
A war-memorial that aims for ever
Its stopped, stone barrel on the enormous air.

A hoisted church, its cone of silence stilling
The conversations of the crow, the kite.
A coasting chimney-stack, advancing, filling
With smoking blossom the lean orchard light.

The verse, I am assured, has long ceased ticking
Though the immortal clock strikes ten to three,
The fencing wasp fights for its usual picking
And tongues of honey hang from every tree.

The swilling sea with its unvarying thunder
Searches the secret face of famous stone.
On the thrown wind blown words like hurt birds wander
That from the maimed, the murdered mouth have flown.

As late as 1947, the question of Rupert's sexuality was brought up. Maurice Browne wrote to Eddie Marsh about a rumour in the States that Brooke was not only homosexual but had, in fact, died of syphilis. Marsh passed the letter on to Geoffrey Keynes, who could answer as both a long-time friend and eminent surgeon. Eddie himself scribbled a note that underlined '. . . during all the years when I've known him I never saw the slightest reason for thinking that he had a "homosexual streak".' He admitted that he had not known him as a schoolboy, but if anything had occurred, as indeed it had, he had since outgrown his adolescent feelings. Even if there had been more to tell, Marsh, a trained civil servant, would have been even more proficient in closing ranks than the Tahitians. Actress Tallulah Bankhead claimed that she had seen love letters from Brooke to other men, but as she had been born in 1903, and therefore could not realistically claim to see them until the 1920s, at least, they would surely have manifested themselves over the years. Nevertheless some people still believe that he had homosexual inclinations. Wellington Cenotaph in New Zealand, which bears a line from 'The Dead', 'These laid the world away; poured out the red sweet wine of youth', is included as part of the official lesbian/gay historical walk around Wellington. Walkers are informed that some of Brooke's poems are self-hating love lyrics to men.

Catherine Abercrombie vividly recalled Brooke as late as the 1950s:

> I have often been asked if Rupert was as good looking and glamorous as was said. Certainly that, but with more beauty of expression and a radiance of youth, helped by his tawny colouring and his eager friendly ways. I remember him so well, when he came to say goodbye before going off on the disastrous Gallipoli expedition. There was a huge sloping field of poppies coming down to the edge of our garden. I can see him now, standing gazing absorbedly at them and saying to me: 'I shall always remember that, always.' He hadn't really got over the Antwerp failure, when such a lot of men came back ill with dysentery, and he wasn't really well enough to start off again. But he was so keen to throw himself into the thick of things and tried to tease my husband into joining him. Rupert went off in high spirits, but very pulled down in health, and open to any infection . . .

In 1993, the young bugler Malachi William Davey, who had sounded the Last Post at Brooke's graveside on Skyros, died. He was the last of those present.

Brooke, like many young men in the Great War, was willing to lay down his life for his country and to fight against the nations that threatened the peace and stability of the world. In the words of Lieut. H. Reginald Freston in 'The Gift':

If his dust is one day lying in an unfamiliar land
(England he went for you),
O England, sometimes think of him, of thousands only one,
In the dawning, on the noonday, or the setting of the sun,
As once he thought of you.

The statue of Brooke erected in Rugby in 1987, his centenary year

281

BIBLIOGRAPHY

Abercrombie, Lascelles *Poems* (Oxford, 1930)
Adcock, A. St John *For Rememberance* (Hodder and Stoughton, 1918)
Asquith, Lady Cynthia *Diaries 1915–18* (Hutchinson, 1968)
Babington Smith, C. *John Masefield* (Oxford, 1978)
Belloc, Hilaire *The Four Men* (Nelson, 1912)
Benson, A.C. *Men and Memories* (John Murray), 1924)
Betjeman, John *Letters 1951–1984* (Methuen, 1995)
Brooke, Rupert *Collected Poems* (Sidgwick and Jackson, 1918)
        Democracy and the Arts (Hart-Davis, 1946)
        Letters from America (Scribners, 1916)
        Letters to His Publisher 1911–1914 (Octagon, 1975)
Browne, Maurice *Recollections of Rupert Brooke* (Alexander Greene, 1927)
Casson, Stanley *Rupert Brooke and Skyros* (Elkin Matthews, 1921)
Cheason, Denis *The Cambridgeshire Rupert Brooke* (Plaistow, 1980)
Eliot, Sir Charles *Turkey in Europe* (Edward Arnold, 1908)
Eckert, Robert P. *Edward Thomas* (Dent, 1937)
Garnett, David *The Golden Echo* (Chatto and Windus, 1953)
Gibson, W.W. *Friends* (Elkin Matthews, 1916)
Graves, Robert *Goodbye to all That* (Cape, 1929)
Handley-Taylor, G. *John Masefield – A Bibliography* (Cranbook and Owen, 1960)
Harfield, Alan *Blandford and the Military* (Dorset Publishing, 1984)
Harris, Pippa (ed) *Song of Love* (Crown, 1991)
Hassall, Christopher *Edward Marsh* (Longmans, 1959)
        Rupert Brooke (Faber and Faber, 1964)
Hastings, Michael *The Handsomest Young Man in England* (Michael Joseph, 1967)
Henley, W.G. *Poems* (D. Nutt, 1912)
Henderson, James L. *Irregularly Bold* (Andre Deutsch, 1978)
Hillier, Bevis *John Betjeman* (John Murray, 1988)
Holroyd, M. *Lytton Strachey* (Heinemann, 1968)
Keynes, G. *Bibliography of the Works of Rupert Brooke* (Hart-Davis, 1954)
        Letters of Rupert Brooke (Faber and Faber, 1968)
Mackail and Wyndham *Life and Letters of George Wyndham* (Hutchinson, 1914)
Marsh, Edward *Rupert Brooke – A Memoir* (John Lane, 1918)
Meredith, George *Poems* (Constable, 1910)
Muggeridge, Kitty and Adam, Ruth *Beatrice Webb* (Secker and Warburg, 1967)
Olivier, Sydney *Letters and Selected Writing* (Allen and Unwin, 1948)
Pimlott, Ben *Hugh Dalton* (HarperCollins, 1995)
Potter, R.M.G. *Rupert Brooke Fragments* (Hartford, 1925)
Rice, F.A. *The Granta 1889–1914* (Constable, 1924)
Rupert Brooke's Death and Burial (Imperial War Museum, 1992)
Speaight, Robert *Hilaire Belloc* (Hollis and Carter)
Spender, Stephen *Journals 1939–1983* (Faber and Faber, 1985)
Willmor, E.N. *Old Grantchester* (Birds Farm, 1976)

The following periodicals and newspapers have also been consulted: *New Numbers, The Times, The Times Literary Supplement, Granta, Meteor*

TEXT AND ILLUSTRATION CREDITS

The author and publishers are grateful to the following for permission to use copyright material in the book: Charles Causley and David Higham Associates for permission to reproduce *At Grantchester* from *The Collected Poems of Charles Causley* (Macmillan); David Higham Associates for permission to reproduce an extract from *Beatrice Webb – A Life* by Kitty Muggeridge and Ruth Adam (Secker and Warburg); Constable Publishers for permission to reproduce extracts from *The Granta* 1889–1914 edited by F.A. Rice; George T. Sassoon for permission to reproduce extracts from the works of Siegfried Sassoon; Curtis Brown Ltd for permission to reproduce *The Times* obituary of 26 April 1915 copyright Winston S. Churchill; A.P. Watt Ltd on behalf of The Executors of the Estate of David Garnett for permission to reproduce extracts from *The Golden Echo* (Chatto and Windus); Pippa Harris for permission to reproduce from the letters of Noel Olivier; Mark Ramage for permission to reproduce from the writings of Cathleen Nesbitt; Michael Gibson for permission to reproduce from the work of Wilfred Gibson; Jeff Cooper for permission to reproduce from the writings of Catherine Abercrombie and Lascelles Abercrombie; Rugby School for permission to reproduce *Sonnet to Rupert Brooke* by John Gillespie Magee; *The Times Literary Supplement* for permission to quote from a review of 8 August 1918; Faber and Faber Ltd and the Trustees of the Estate of Rupert Brooke for permission to quote from *Letters of Rupert Brooke*.

For permission to reproduce illustrations the author is grateful to the Provost and Scholars of King's College, Cambridge; the Librarian, Temple Reading Room, Rugby School; the National Library of Australia (illustration, page 269) reference MS 3095.

Every effort has been made to contact copyright owners but in some instances this has not been possible and it is hoped that any omissions will be excused.

Note: page references to illustrations are *italicised*.